Contents

OLIVE AND TOMATO BALLS

Time To Prepare: ten minutes

Time to Cook: thirty-five minutes

Yield: Servings 5

Ingredients:
- .25 cup Coconut oil
- .25 tsp. Salt
- .5 cup Cream cheese
- 2 cloves Garlic, crushed
- 2 tbsp. Basil, chopped
- 2 tbsp. Oregano, chopped
- 2 tbsp. Thyme, chopped
- 4 Kalamata olives, pitted
- 4 pcs. Sun-dried tomatoes, drained
- 5 tbsp. Parmesan cheese, grated
- Black pepper (as you wish)

Directions:
1. Cut the coconut oil, put in it to a small mixing container with the cream cheese, and allow them to tenderize for approximately 30 minutes. Mash together and mix thoroughly to blend.
2. Put in in the Kalamata olives and sun-dried tomatoes and mix thoroughly before you put in in the herbs and seasonings. Mix meticulously before placing the mixing container in your fridge to allow the results to solidify.
3. Once it has solidified, make the mixture into a total of 5 balls using an ice cream scoop. Roll each of the finished balls into the parmesan cheese before plating.
4. Stored the extra's in your refrigerator in an air-tight container for maximum 7 days.

Nutritional Info: , Calories: 212 kcal **,** Protein: 4.77 g **,** Fat: 20.75 g **,** Carbohydrates: 3.13 g

OVEN CRISP SWEET POTATO

Time To Prepare: ten minutes

Time to Cook: twenty minutes

Yield: Servings 2

Ingredients:
- 1 moderate-sized sweet potato, raw
- 1 teaspoon coconut oil
- 1 teaspoon sugar

Directions:
1. Preheat your oven to 160C.

2. Using a mandolin slicer or a peeler, slice the sweet potato into thin chips or strips. Rinse and pat dry.
3. Sprinkle the coconut oil over the potatoes. Toss until all chips are coated.
4. Position in an oven baking sheet. Bake for about ten minutes. Check the crispiness. If it is not that crunchy enough, bake for an extra five or 1o minutes or until the chips attain the crispiness desired.
5. Take out the crunchy sweet potatoes. Drizzle with sugar before you serve.

Nutritional Info: , Calories: 123 kcal , Protein: 4.23 g , Fat: 5.39 g , Carbohydrates: 14.63 g

PALEO GINGER SPICED MIXED NUTS

Time To Prepare: five minutes

Time to Cook: forty minutes

Yield: Servings 8

Ingredients:
- ½ tsp. Fine sea salt
- ½ tsp. Vietnamese cinnamon
- 1 tsp. Grated fresh ginger
- 2 cups Mix nuts; Cashew, goji berries, raw almonds, pumpkin seeds, etc.
- 2 Large Egg,
- Coconut oil spray
- Egg whites

Directions:
1. Prepare the oven by preheating to 250°F.
2. Whisk egg whites in a container until it gets fluffy. Pour in sea salt, grated ginger, and Vietnamese cinnamon. Whisk until it's one big mix.
3. Pour in the mixed nuts and stir to combine.
4. Coat the parchment-lined baking sheet with coconut oil spray and spread the nut mixture all across the baking sheet.
5. Allow it to bake for approximately twenty minutes, rotate the sheet then bake for another twenty minutes.
6. Take off the baking sheet from the oven and leave to cool.
7. Once it's fully cool and hard, break them into bits with clean hands.
8. Serve or store.

Nutritional Info: , Calories: 212 kcal , Protein: 6.92 g , Fat: 17.3 g , Carbohydrates: 10.05 g

PARTY-TIME CHICKEN NUGGETS

Time To Prepare: ten minutes

Time to Cook: twenty-five minutes

Yield: Servings 6

Ingredients:
- ½ cup tapioca flour
- ½ tsp. of garlic powder
- ½ tsp. of onion powder
- ½ tsp. of paprika
- 1½ cups of blanched almond flour
- 2 (6-ounce) grass-fed skinless, boneless chicken breasts
- 2 big organic eggs
- Freshly ground black pepper, to taste
- Salt, to taste

Directions:
1. Set the oven to 400F then grease a big baking sheet.
2. With a rolling pin, roll the chicken breasts to a uniform thickness.
3. Cut each breast into bite-sized pieces.
4. In a shallow dish, crack the eggs and beat thoroughly.
5. In another shallow dish, combine flours and spices.
6. Immerse the chicken nuggets in beaten eggs.
7. Then roll in flour mixture completely.
8. Position the nuggets onto the readied baking sheet in a single layer.
9. Bake for approximately 10-twelve minutes, turning once after five minutes.

Nutritional Info: , Calories: 312 , Fat: 17.8g , Carbohydrates: 15.4g , Protein: 23.6g , Fiber: 3.2g

PEANUT BUTTER AND HONEY OAT BARS

Time To Prepare: ten minutes

Time to Cook: twenty-five minutes

Yield: Servings 18

Ingredients:
- ¼ cup honey
- ¼ cup honey roasted peanuts, chopped
- ¼ teaspoon cinnamon powder
- ¼ teaspoon vanilla extract
- 1 cup oats
- 2 teaspoons coconut oil
- 3 tablespoons peanut butter

Directions:
1. Coat a small baking pan using a parchment paper such that the parchment paper is hanging over the sides of the baking pan.

2. Put in honey, oil, and peanut butter into a microwave-safe container. Microwave on High for around 20 -half a minute or until the peanut butter melts completely. If it takes longer than half a minute, stir and cook in increments of 10 seconds, stirring every time.
3. Remove from the microwave and put in the remaining ingredients. Mix thoroughly and pour into the readied baking pan. Spread the mixture and press using a spatula.
4. Bake in a preheated oven 300° F for approximately twenty minutes or until the top is light brown.
5. Take out of the oven and press once once more.
6. Cool for a while and slice.
7. Cool thoroughly before you serve.
8. Move leftover bars into an airtight container. Place in your fridge until use.

Nutritional Info: , Calories: 44 kcal , Protein: 1.47 g , Fat: 1.69 g , Carbohydrates: 8.06 g

PROTEIN-PACKED CROQUETTES

Time To Prepare: ten minutes

Time to Cook: five minutes

Yield: Servings 12

Ingredients:
- ¼ cup of chopped fresh cilantro leaves
- ¼ cup plus 1 tbsp. of olive oil, divided
- ¼ tsp. of ground turmeric
- ½ cup of thawed frozen peas
- ½ tsp. of paprika
- 1 cup of cooked quinoa
- 2 big peeled and mashed boiled potatoes
- 2 minced garlic cloves
- 2 tsp. of ground cumin
- Freshly ground black pepper, to taste
- Salt, to taste

Directions:
1. In a frying pan, heat 1 tbsp. of oil on moderate heat.
2. Put in peas and garlic and sauté for approximately one minute.
3. Move the peas mixture into a big container.
4. Put rest of the ingredients then mix till well blended.
5. Make equal sized oblong shaped patties from the mixture.
6. In a huge frying pan, warm remaining oil on moderate to high heat.
7. Put in croquettes in batches and fry for approximately 4 minutes per side.

Nutritional Info: , Calories: 152 , Fat: 6.9g , Carbohydrates: 20.1g , Protein: 3.5g , Fiber: 2.9g

ROASTED BEETS

Time To Prepare: ten minutes

Time to Cook: 35-45 minutes

Yield: Servings 6

Ingredients:
- 1 tablespoon of coconut oil, melted
- 1 teaspoon of salt
- 2 and a ½ pounds of beets, peeled and diced

Directions:
1. Preheat your oven to 400°F.
2. Spread the beets onto a baking sheet and sprinkle with melted coconut oil.
3. Put in salt and mix thoroughly.
4. Roast the beets in your oven for 35-45 minutes, until the beets are tender.

Nutritional Info: , Total Carbohydrates: 7g , Fiber: 2g , Net Carbohydrates: , Protein: 1g , Total Fat: 4g , Calories: 59

ROASTED GARLIC CHICKPEAS

Time To Prepare: five minutes

Time to Cook: twenty minutes

Yield: Servings 2

Ingredients:
- 1 Teaspoon Garlic Powder
- 1 Teaspoon Sea Salt
- 2 Tablespoons Olive Oil
- 4 Cups Cooked Chickpeas, Rinsed, Drained & Dried
- Black Pepper to Taste

Directions:
1. Begin by heating the oven to 400.
2. Spread your chickpeas on a baking sheet, coating them with your olive oil.
3. Bake of 20 minutes, ensuring to stir them at the ten-minute mark.
4. Put your hot chickpeas in a container, seasoning before securing them in an airtight container. They'll keep at room temperature for maximum two days.

Nutritional Info: , Calories: 150 , Protein: 6 Grams , Fat: 5 Grams , Carbohydrates: 21 Grams

SALMON & AVOCADO TOAST

Time To Prepare: ten minutes

Time to Cook: five minutes

Yield: Servings 1

Ingredients:
- ¼ tsp red pepper
- ½ avocado
- 1 tsp lemon juice
- 2 slices of gluten-free bread
- oz. pink salmon (wild)
- salt and pepper - to taste

Directions:
1. Cut the avocado.
2. Toast the bread to your taste.
3. Combine the salmon and lemon juice.
4. When the toast is ready, lay avocado slices onto it.
5. Cover with salmon.
6. Put in some red pepper, salt, and pepper to your taste.
7. Feel free to put the other ingredients you prefer (tomatoes, onions)
8. Enjoy your salmon snack!

Nutritional Info: , Calories: 481 kcal , Protein: 28.08 g , Fat: 27.52 g , Carbohydrates: 33 g

SALT & VINEGAR KALE CRISPS

Time To Prepare: five minutes

Time to Cook: 20-twenty-five minutes

Yield: Servings 2

Ingredients:
- 1 Teaspoon Sea Salt, Fine
- 2 Tablespoon Apple Cider Vinegar
- 2 Tablespoons Olive Oil
- 4 Cups Kale, Torn into 2 Inch Pieces

Directions:
1. Begin by heating the oven to 350. Get out a container, and mix all of your ingredients.
2. Put your kale on a baking sheet, baking for twenty to twenty-five minutes. Toss midway through this time.
3. Put at room temperature in an airtight container. They'll keep for two days.

Nutritional Info: , Calories: 135 , Protein: 1 Gram , Fat: 14 Grams , Carbohydrates: 3 Grams

SOFT FLOURLESS COOKIES

Time To Prepare: ten minutes

Time to Cook: twenty-five minutes

Yield: Servings 4

Ingredients:
- ¼ teaspoon of organic vanilla extract
- ¾ cup of shredded unsweetened coconut
- 1 peeled big banana
- Pinch of ground cinnamon

Directions:
1. Set the oven to 350F. Coat a cookie sheet with a big greased parchment paper.
2. In a big food processor, put all ingredients and pulse till well blended.
3. Ladle the mixture onto the prepared cookie sheet. Use your hands to flatten the cookies slightly.
4. Bake for minimum twenty-five minutes or till golden brown.

Nutritional Info: , Calories: 84 , Fat: 5.1g , Carbohydrates: 10.1g , Protein: 0.9g , Fiber: 2.3g

SPICED NUTS

Time To Prepare: ten minutes

Time to Cook: 10-fifteen minutes

Yield: Servings 2

Ingredients:
- ¼ Cup Pumpkin Puree
- ¼ Cup Sunflower Seeds
- ¼ Teaspoon Garlic Powder
- ¼ Teaspoon Red Pepper Flakes
- ½ Cup Walnuts
- ½ Teaspoon Ground Cumin
- 1 Cup Almonds
- 1 Teaspoon Ground Turmeric

Directions:
1. Begin by heating the oven to 350.
2. Mix all ingredients together, and then get out a baking sheet. Spread your nuts over your baking sheet, cooking for ten to fifteen minutes.
3. Allow it to cool well before you store it.

Nutritional Info: , Calories: 180 , Protein: 6 Grams , Fat: 16 Grams , Carbohydrates: 7 Grams

SPICY BEAN DIP

Time To Prepare: ten minutes

Time to Cook: 0 minutes

Yield: Servings 3

Ingredients:
- ¼ Teaspoon Ground Cumin

- ¼ Teaspoon Sea Salt
- 1 Tablespoon Apple Cider Vinegar
- 1 Teaspoon Lime Juice, Fresh
- 14 Ounce Can Black Beans, Drained & Rinsed
- 14 Ounce Can Kidney Beans, Drained & Rinsed
- 2 Cherry Tomatoes
- 2 Cloves Garlic
- 2 Tablespoons Water
- 2 Teaspoon Honey, Raw
- Black Pepper to Taste
- Pinch Cayenne Pepper

Directions:
1. Mix all of your ingredients in a food processor, and blend until it's smooth.
2. Cover, and place in your fridge before you serve.

Nutritional Info: , Calories: 166 , Protein: 9.4 Grams , Fat: 0.6 Grams , Carbohydrates: 34.2 Grams

SPICY ROASTED CHICKPEAS

Time To Prepare: ten minutes

Time to Cook: forty minutes

Yield: Servings 6

Ingredients:
- ¼ teaspoon of cayenne pepper
- 1 teaspoon of paprika
- 1 teaspoon of turmeric
- 2 (fifteen ounce) cans of chickpeas, drained and washed
- 2 teaspoons of coconut oil, melted

Directions:
1. Set the oven to 425°F.
2. Coat a baking sheet using a paper towels, then put the chickpeas on them and use more paper towels to take off the surplus water in the chickpeas. Remove all of the paper towels.
3. Place the oil and spices to the chickpeas and mix thoroughly.
4. Roast your chickpeas for forty minutes, stirring every ten minutes.
5. Once the chickpeas are done, take it off from the oven and let fully cool.

Nutritional Info: , Total Carbohydrates: 19g , Fiber: 6g , Net Carbohydrates: , Protein: 7g , Total Fat: 4g , Calories: 138

SWEET POTATO MUFFINS

Time To Prepare: fifteen minutes

Time to Cook: 20-twenty-five minutes

Yield: Servings 12

Ingredients:
- ¼ Cup Almond Butter
- ¼ Teaspoon Sea Salt
- ½ Teaspoon Baking Soda
- 1 ½ Cups Rolled Oats
- 1 Cup Almond Milk
- 1 Cup Sweet Potato, Cooked & Pureed
- 1 Egg
- 1 Teaspoon Baking Powder
- 1 Teaspoon Ground Cinnamon
- 1 Teaspoon Vanilla Extract, Pure
- 1/3 Cup Coconut Sugar
- 2 Tablespoons Olive Oil

Directions:
1. Begin by heating the oven to 375.
2. Coat your muffin tin with liners, and get out a food processor.
3. Pulse your oats until it forms a course flour. Move it to a small container before setting it to the side.
4. Put in all of your ingredients apart from for the oat flour, blending until the desired smoothness is achieved.
5. Slowly put in in your oat flour, pulsing until it's well blended.
6. Cut between your cupcake liners, and bake for about twenty minutes. Let them cool for minimum five minutes before you serve.

Nutritional Info: , Calories: 143 , Protein: 4 Grams , Fat: 7 Grams , Carbohydrates: 12 Grams

SWEET SUNUP SEEDS

Time To Prepare: five minutes

Time to Cook: 60 minutes

Yield: Servings 8

Ingredients:
- ¼-cup pure maple syrup
- ¼-cup sunflower oil
- ¼-sesame seeds
- ⅓ -cup honey
- ½-cup flaxseed
- 1-cup dried cranberries
- 1-cup raw pumpkin seeds
- 1-tsp vanilla extract

- 3-tsp cinnamon
- 4-cups rolled oats

Directions:
1. Preheat your oven to 350°F. Prepare two units of baking sheets by lining them using parchment paper.
2. In a large-sized mixing container, mix the rolled oats, pumpkin seeds, flaxseed, sesame seeds, and cinnamon. Mix gently until meticulously blended.
3. Pour all the liquid ingredients into the mixture and stir until mixed well.
4. On the baking sheets, spread the mixture uniformly. Place the sheets in your oven. Cook for minimum an hour. While baking, stir the mixture every quarter of an hour to achieve uniform color on its surfaces.
5. Take away the sheets from the oven. Allow cooling completely. Put in the cup of dried cranberries, and mix thoroughly.
6. Store the granola in an airtight container to maintain its freshness and crunchiness.

Nutritional Info: , Calories: 189 , Fat: 6.3g , Protein: 9.4g , Sodium: 5mg , Total Carbohydrates: 27.6g , Fiber: 4g , Net Carbohydrates: 23.6g

TANGY TURMERIC FLAVORED FLORETS

Time To Prepare: ten minutes

Time to Cook: 55 minutes

Yield: Servings 1

Ingredients:
- 1-head cauliflower, chopped into florets
- 1-Tbsp olive oil
- 1-Tbsp turmeric
- A dash of salt
- A pinch of cumin

Directions:
1. Set the oven to 400°F.
2. Combine all ingredients in a baking pan. Mix thoroughly until meticulously blended.
3. Cover the pan using foil. Roast for forty minutes. Take away the foil cover and roast additionally for fifteen minutes.

Nutritional Info: , Calories: 90 , Fat: 3g , Protein: 4.5g , Sodium: 87mg , Total Carbohydrates: 16.2g , Fiber: 5g , Net Carbohydrates: 11.2g

TOASTED PUMPKIN SEEDS

Time To Prepare: five minutes

Time to Cook: thirty minutes

Yield: Servings 2-4

Ingredients:
- ½ teaspoon extra virgin olive oil
- 1 teaspoon salt
- 1 to 2 cups pumpkin seeds
- Sea salt
- Water

Directions:
1. Put seeds in a deep cooking pan and cover with water. Put in salt.
2. Bring it to its boiling point and boil for about ten minutes.
3. Simmer uncovered for ten more minutes. This makes the seeds very crunchy when baked. Drain the seeds and pat dry using a paper towel.
4. Coat a baking sheet using parchment paper and spread out the seeds in a single layer.
5. Sprinkle with salt, then bake in an oven at 325F for minimum ten minutes, stirring midway through.
6. Cool, then store in an airtight container.

Nutritional Info: , Calories: 192 kcal , Protein: 10.41 g , Fat: 16.23 g , Carbohydrates: 4.34 g

TOFU PUDDING

Time To Prepare: ten minutes

Time to Cook: 0 minutes

Yield: Servings 4

Ingredients:
- 1 cup strawberries
- 1 teaspoon honey
- 1 teaspoon pumpkin pie spice
- 1 teaspoon vanilla
- 12 ounces silken tofu, softened and well-drained
- 2 scoops of Protein powder
- 3/4 cup blueberries
- 4 almonds
- Fresh mint leaves

Directions:
1. Combine the tofu and Protein powder in a blender until thoroughly combined.
2. Put in the blueberries, strawberries, honey, pumpkin pie spice, and vanilla. Blend until the desired smoothness is achieved.
3. Cover and put on the refrigerator to chill for minimum 2 hours.
4. Ladle into four dessert bowls and top with an almond and a mint leaf before you serve.

Nutritional Info: , Calories: 371 kcal , Protein: 23.31 g , Fat: 21.1 g , Carbohydrates: 27.17 g

TURMERIC CHICKPEA CAKES

Time To Prepare: twenty minutes

Time to Cook: thirty minutes

Yield: Servings 8

Ingredients:
- ½ cup fresh parsley, minced
- 1 teaspoon cayenne pepper, to taste (not necessary)
- 1 teaspoon salt or to taste
- 2 cans (15oz.) chickpeas, washed, drained
- 2 small onions, minced
- 2 teaspoons turmeric powder
- 4 cloves garlic, minced
- 4 tablespoons cornstarch
- 8-10 tablespoons chickpea flour
- Avocado dipping sauce to serve
- Freshly ground pepper to taste
- Grapeseed oil to fry

Directions:
1. Put a frying pan on moderate heat. Put in a little oil. When the oil is heated, put onion and garlic and sauté until translucent. Remove the heat and cool to room temperature.
2. Put in chickpeas into the food processor container and pulse until very finely chopped.
3. Put in the onion mixture, salt, pepper, cayenne pepper, and turmeric powder and pulse again until well blended.
4. Move into a container. Put in parsley and mix thoroughly.
5. Make small balls of the mixture (of approximately 1 inch diameter) and mould into patties. Put chickpea flour on a plate.
6. Put a nonstick pan on moderate heat. Put in a little oil and swirl the pan so that the oil spreads.
7. Immerse the patties in the chickpea flour and place a few on the pan. Cook in batches.
8. Cook until the underside is golden brown. Flip then cook the other side till it's golden brown.
9. Repeat steps 6-8 to fry the rest of the patties.
10. Serve with avocado dipping sauce.

Nutritional Info: , Calories: 154 kcal , Protein: 7.32 g , Fat: 2.85 g , Carbohydrates: 25.43 g

TURMERIC COCONUT FLOUR MUFFINS

Time To Prepare: five minutes

Time to Cook: twenty-five minutes

Yield: Servings 8

Ingredients:
- ½ cup Unsweetened coconut milk
- ½ tsp. Baking soda
- ½ tsp. Ginger powder
- ¾ cup & 2 tbsp. Coconut flour
- 1 tsp. Vanilla extract
- 1/3 cup Maple syrup
- 2 tsp. Turmeric
- 6 big Whole eggs
- Pepper and salt

Directions:
1. Preheat your oven to 350ºF.
2. Coat 8 muffin tins with 8 muffin liners.
3. Whisk eggs, maple syrup, milk, and vanilla extract in a mixing container until the egg begins to make bubbles.
4. In a different container, combine the coconut flour, turmeric powder, pepper, baking soda, ginger powder, and salt.
5. Place the dry mixture into the wet mixture then stir until it's all mixed and thick.
6. Ladle out the batter into prepared muffin tins.
7. Leave to bake for about twenty-five minutes or until it looked golden.
8. Allow the muffins cool for a couple of minutes before transferring them to a rack.

Nutritional Info: , Calories: 143 kcal , Protein: 6.18 g , Fat: 8 g , Carbohydrates: 11.8 g

TURMERIC GUMMIES

Time To Prepare: five minutes

Time to Cook: 4 hours and ten minutes

Yield: Servings 4

Ingredients:
- ¼ tsp. Ground pepper
- 1 tsp. Ground turmeric
- 3 ½ cups Water
- 6 tbsp. Maple syrup
- 8 tbsp. Unflavored gelatin powder

Directions:
1. Combine the ground turmeric, maple syrup, and water in a pot set on moderate heat. Stir continuously for five minutes before removing from heat and pouring in the gelatin powder. Stir using a wooden spoon to dissolve the gelatin.
2. Put back the pan on the heat and stir for another two minutes.
3. Remove the heat and take the mixture to a deep container that you will seal using plastic wrapimmediately after.
4. Place in your fridge the mixture for approximately 4 hours.

5. It must be firm now, cut it into little squares, and serve or store.

Nutritional Info: , Calories: 123 kcal **,** Protein: 2.15 g **,** Fat: 1.56 g **,** Carbohydrates: 25.67

ALMOND MASCARPONE DUMPLINGS

Time To Prepare: ten minutes

Time to Cook: ten minutes

Yield: Servings 6

Ingredients:
- ¼ cup ground almonds
- ¼ cup honey
- 1 cup all-purpose unbleached flour
- 1 cup whole-wheat flour
- 1 tablespoon butter
- 1 teaspoon extra-virgin olive oil
- 2 teaspoons apple juice
- 3 ounces mascarpone cheese
- 4 egg whites

Directions:
1. Strain together both types of flour in a big container. Stir in the almonds.
2. In a different container, whisk together the egg whites, cheese, oil, and juice on moderate speed using an electric mixer.
3. Place the flour, and egg white mixture with a dough hook on moderate speed or using your hands until a dough forms.
4. Boil 1 gallon water in a medium-size saucepot. Take a scoop of dough and use a second spoon to push it into the boiling water. Cook up to the dumpling floats to the top, minimum 5 to ten minutes. You can cook several dumplings at once — just take care not to crowd the pot.
5. Take off using a slotted spoon and drain using paper towels.
6. Warm a medium-size sauté pan on moderate to high heat.
7. Put in the butter, then put the dumplings in the pan and cook until light brown.
8. Set on serving plates and sprinkle with honey.

Nutritional Info: Calories: 254 **,** Fat: 6.4 g **,** Protein: 7 g **,** Sodium: 20 mg **,** Fiber: 3.5 g **,** Carbohydrates: 44 g

ALMOND PANCAKES WITH COCONUT FLAKES

Time To Prepare: 5 minutes

Time to Cook: ten minutes

Yield: Servings 6

Ingredients:
- ¼ cup coconut flakes, sweetened
- ¼ cup of water
- ¼ tsp. coconut oil
- ½ cup unsweetened applesauce
- 1 cup almond flour, finely milled
- 1 overripe banana, mashed
- 2 eggs, yolks, and whites separated
- 2 Tbsp. blanched almond flakes
- Dash of cinnamon powder
- Garnish
- Pinch of sea salt
- Pure maple syrup, use sparingly

Directions:
1. Whisk egg whites until tender peaks form.
2. Except for egg whites and coconut oil, mix rest of the ingredients in a different container. Mix until batter comes together.
3. Lightly fold in egg whites. Ensure that you do not over mix, or the pancake will become dense and chewy.
4. Pour oil into a nonstick frying pan set on moderate heat.
5. Wait for the oil to heat up before dropping in roughly ½ cup of batter. Cook until each side are set, and bubbles form in the middle. Turn on the other side then cook for an extra two minutes.
6. Move flapjacks to a plate. Repeat step until all batter is cooked. Pour in more oil into the frying pan only if required. This recipe should yield between four to 6 moderate-sized pancakes.
7. Stack pancakes. Pour the desired amount of pure maple syrup on top. Decorate each stack with cinnamon-flavored almond-coconut flakes just before you serve.
8. For the decorate, set the oven to 350°F for minimum ten minutes before use. Coat a baking sheet using parchment paper. Set aside.
9. Mix almond and coconut flakes together in a container. Spread mixture uniformly on a readied baking sheet.
10. Bake for 7 to ten minutes until flakes turn golden brown. Stir almond and coconut flakes once midway through roasting to stop over-browning.
11. Take away the baking sheet from the oven. Cool almond and coconut flakes for minimum ten minutes before drizzling in cinnamon powder and salt. Toss to blend. Set aside.

Nutritional Info: Calories: 62 kcal , Protein: 2.24 g , Fat: 4.01 g , Carbohydrates: 4.46 g

ALMOND SCONES

Time To Prepare: ten minutes

Time to Cook: twenty minutes

Yield: Servings 6

Ingredients:
- 1 cup almonds
- ¼ cup arrowroot flour
- 1 tablespoon coconut flour
- 1 teaspoon ground turmeric
- Salt, to taste
- Freshly ground black pepper, to taste
- 1 egg
- ¼ cup essential olive oil
- 3 tablespoons raw honey
- 1 teaspoon vanilla flavoring
- 1 1/3 cups almond flour

Directions:
1. In a mixer, put almonds then pulse till chopped roughly
2. Move the chopped almonds in a big container.
3. Put flours and spices and mix thoroughly.
4. In another container, put the rest of the ingredients and beat till well blended.
5. Place the flour mixture into the egg mixture then mix till well blended.
6. Position a plastic wrap over the cutting board.
7. Put the dough over the cutting board.
8. Use both your hands to pat into 1-inch thick circle.
9. Chop the circle in 6 wedges.
10. Set the scones onto a cookie sheet in a single layer.
11. Bake for minimum fifteen-20 minutes.

Nutritional Info: Calories: 304 , Fat: 3g , Carbohydrates: 22g , Fiber: 6g , Protein: 20g

ANTI-INFLAMMATORY BREAKFAST FRITTATA

Time To Prepare: ten minutes

Time to Cook: forty minutes

Yield: Servings 4

Ingredients:
- ¼ cup water
- ½ tsp. cracked black pepper
- ½ tsp. ground turmeric
- 1 onion, chopped
- 1 tbsp. minced garlic
- 125g firm tofu
- 4 big eggs
- 450g baby spinach
- 450g button mushrooms

- 6 egg whites
- Kosher salt to taste

Directions:
1. Set the oven to 350F.
2. Sauté the mushrooms in a little bit of extra virgin olive oil in a big non-stick ovenproof pan on moderate heat. Put in the onions once the mushrooms start turning golden and cook for about three minutes until the onions become tender.
3. Mix in the garlic then cook for minimum half a minute until aromatic before you put in the spinach. Pour in water, cover, and cook until the spinach becomes wilted for approximately 2 minutes.
4. Take off the lid and carry on cooking up to the water evaporates. Now, mix the eggs, egg whites, tofu, pepper, turmeric, and salt in a container. When all the liquid has vaporized, pour in the egg mixture, allow to cook for approximately 2 minutes until the edges start setting, then move to the oven and bake for approximately twenty-five minutes or until cooked.
5. Remove from the oven then allow it to sit for minimum five minutes before cutting it into four equivalent portions and serving.
6. Enjoy!

Nutritional Info: Calories: 521 kcal , Protein: 29.13 g , Fat: 10.45 g , Carbohydrates: 94.94 g

APPLE BREAD

Time To Prepare: twenty-five minutes

Time to Cook: 1 hour and ten minutes

Yield: Servings 8

Ingredients:
- ¼ tsp. baking powder
- 1 cup peeled, chopped apples
- 1 packet yeast
- 1 tbsp. cinnamon mixed with 1 tablespoon sugar
- 1 tsp. Salt
- 1¾ cups all-purpose flour
- 1¾ cups whole-wheat flour
- 11/3 cups warm water
- 3 tbsp. sugar
- 3 tbsp. tender butter

Directions:
1. Mix yeast, ½ teaspoon sugar, and 1/3 cup water in a container. Allow to sit for five minutes.
2. In a mixing container, put together remaining water, butter, remaining sugar, salt, and baking powder then mix.
3. Mix in the all-purpose flour, then the yeast mixture using an electric mixer. Place the whole-wheat flour. Knead the dough hook for minimum ten minutes.
4. Place the dough into an oiled container.

5. Cover then rises in a warm place for minimum a couple of hours until doubled in bulk.
6. Punch down dough, then form into a rectangle.
7. Spread the apples on the dough and dust with the cinnamon sugar.
8. Roll into a cylinder and put in an oiled loaf pan. Cover and allow it to rise in a warm for 90 minutes until doubled in size.
9. Preheat your oven to 350°F. Uncover bread and bake for about fifty minutes.

Nutritional Info: Calories: 258 , Fat: 5 g , Protein: 7 g , Sodium: 294 mg , Fiber: 4.5 g , Carbohydrates: 48 g

APPLE BRUSCHETTA WITH ALMONDS AND BLACKBERRIES

Time To Prepare: twenty minutes

Time to Cook: thirty minutes

Yield: Servings 5

Ingredients:
- ¼ cup blackberries, thawed, lightly mashed
- ½ tsp. fresh lemon juice
- 1 apple, cut into ¼-inch thick half-moons
- 1/8 cup almond slivers, toasted
- Sea salt

Directions:
1. Sprinkle lemon juice on apple slices. Place these on a tray coated with parchment paper.
2. Spread a small number of mashed berries on top of each slice. Top these off with the desired amount of almond slivers.
3. Drizzle sea salt on "bruschetta" just before you serve.

Nutritional Info: Calories: 56 kcal , Protein: 1.53 g , Fat: 1.43 g , Carbohydrates: 9.87 g

APPLE OATMEAL

Time To Prepare: ten minutes

Time to Cook: five minutes

Yield: Servings 2

Ingredients:
- ¼ cup fresh apple juice
- 1 chopped apple, (unpeeled or peeled)
- 1 cup of any non-fat milk, coconut milk or almond milk (not necessary)
- 1 cup water
- 1 teaspoon ground cinnamon
- 2/3 cups rolled oats

Directions:
1. Put the water, juice, and the apple in a deep pot. Bring to boil on moderate heat.
2. Put in the oats and cinnamon. Bring to another boil. Reduce the heat temperature and allow it to simmer for about three minutes or until it is thick.
3. Split the serving into two and serve with milk.

Nutritional Info: Calories: 277 kcal , Protein: 12.69 g , Fat: 7.69 g , Carbohydrates: 52.71 g

APPLE, GINGER, AND RHUBARB MUFFINS

Time To Prepare: fifteen minutes

Time to Cook: twenty-five minutes

Yield: Servings 4

Ingredients:
- ¼ cup brown rice flour
- ¼ cup extra virgin olive oil
- ½ cup buckwheat flour
- ½ cup thoroughly ground almonds
- ½ tsp. ground cinnamon
- ½ tsp. ground ginger
- 1 big egg
- 1 cup finely chopped rhubarb
- 1 small apple, peeled and finely diced
- 1 tbsp. linseed meal
- 1 tsp. pure vanilla extract
- 1/3 cup almond/ rice milk
- 1/8 cup unrefined raw sugar
- 2 tbsp. arrowroot flour
- 2 tbsp. crystallized ginger, finely chopped
- 2 tsp. gluten-free baking powder
- A pinch of fine sea salt

Directions:
1. Set the oven to 350Fgrease an eight-cup muffin tin and line with paper cases.
2. Mix the almond four, linseed meal, ginger and sugar in a mixing container. Sieve this mixture over the other flours, spices and baking powder and use a whisk to blend well.
3. Mix in the apple and rhubarb in the flour mixture until uniformly coated.
4. In a different container, whisk the milk, vanilla, and egg then pour it into the dry mixture. Stir until just blended – do not overwork the batter as this can yield very tough muffins.
5. Scoop the mixture into the position muffin tin and top with a few slices of rhubarb. Bake for minimum twenty-five minutes, till they start turning golden or when an inserted toothpick emerges clean.

6. Remove from the oven and allow it to sit for minimum five minutes before transferring the muffins to a wire rack for further cooling.
7. Serve warm with a glass of squeezed juice.
8. Enjoy!

Nutritional Info: Calories: 325 kcal , Protein: 6.32 g , Fat: 9.82 g , Carbohydrates: 55.71 g

BAKE APPLE TURNOVER

Time To Prepare: thirty minutes

Time to Cook: twenty-five minutes

Yield: Servings 4

Ingredients:
- ½ cup palm sugar, crumbled using your hands to loosen granules
- ½ tsp. cinnamon powder
- 1 egg white, whisked in
- 1 frozen puff pastry, thawed
- 1 Tbsp. almond flour
- 2 Tbsp. water
- 4 apples, peeled, cored, diced into bite-sized pieces
- All-purpose flour, for rolling out the dough
- For the egg wash
- For the turnovers

Directions:
1. To make the filling: mix almond flour, cinnamon powder, and palm sugar until these resemble coarse meal. Toss in diced apples until thoroughly coated. Set aside.
2. On a mildly floured surface, roll the puff pastry until ¼ inch thin. Cut into 8 pieces of 4" x 4" squares.
3. Split prepared apples into 8 equivalent portions. Ladle on individual puff pastry squares. Fold in half diagonally. Push edges to secure.
4. Put each filled pastry on a baking tray coated with parchment paper. Make sure there is ample space between pastries.
5. Freeze for minimum twenty minutes, or till ready to bake.
6. Preheat your oven to 400°F or 205°C for at ten minutes.
7. Brush frozen pastries with egg wash. Bring in a hot oven, and cook for twelve to fifteen minutes, or until these turn golden brown all over.
8. Take off the baking tray in your oven instantly. Cool slightly for easier handling.
9. Put 1 apple turnover on a plate. Serve warm.

Nutritional Info: Calories: 203 kcal , Protein: 5.29 g , Fat: 4.4 g , Carbohydrates: 38.25 g

BAKED FRENCH TOAST CASSEROLE

Time To Prepare: twenty minutes

Time to Cook: forty-five minutes

Yield: Servings 12

Ingredients:
- ½ lb. blueberries
- ½ lb. raspberries
- ¾ cup strawberries
- 1 cup of egg white liquid
- 1 lb. French bread
- 1 teaspoon of vanilla extract
- 1/3 cup maple syrup
- 1½ cups of rice milk,
- 6 eggs

Directions:
1. Cut the bread into little cubes. Keep them in a greased casserole dish.
2. Put in all the berries. Only leave a few for the topping.
3. Mix together the egg whites, eggs, rice milk, and maple syrup in a container.
4. Mix well.
5. Place the egg mixture on the top of the bread. Push the bread down. All pieces must be soaked well.
6. Put in berries on the top. Fill up the holes, if any.
7. Place in your fridge covered for a couple of hours at least.
8. Take out the casserole half an hour before you bake.
9. Set the oven to 350 degrees F.
10. Now, bake your casserole uncovered for half an hour
11. Bake for another fifteen minutes covered with a foil.
12. Let it rest for 15 minutes.
13. Serve it warm with maple syrup.

Nutritional Info: Calories 200 , Carbohydrates: 31g , Cholesterol: 93mg , Total Fat: 4g , Protein: 10g , Fiber: 2g , Sodium: 288mg , Sugar: 10g

BANANA CASHEW TOAST

Time To Prepare: ten minutes

Time to Cook: 0 minutes

Yield: Servings 3

Ingredients:
- 1 cup roasted cashews (unsalted)
- 2 ripe moderate-sized bananas
- 2 tsp. flax meals
- 2 tsp. honey
- 4 pieces oat bread
- Dash of salt

- Pinch of cinnamon

Directions:
1. Peel and slice the bananas into ½-inch pieces. Toast the bread. Use a food processor to puree the salt and cashews until they are smooth. Use the puree as a spread on the toasts. On top of the spread, position a layer of bananas.
2. Put in flax meals and a dash of cinnamon on top of the bananas. Top the toast with honey.

Nutritional Info: Calories: 634 kcal , Protein: 13.42 g , Fat: 47.6 g , Carbohydrates: 48.02 g

BANANA PANCAKES

Time To Prepare: five minutes

Time to Cook: fifteen minutes

Yield: Servings 2

Ingredients:
- ½ Teaspoon Sea Salt
- 1 Banana, Ripe
- 1 Cup Rolled Oats
- 1 Egg White
- 1 Tablespoon Coconut Oil, Divided
- 1 Teaspoon Vanilla Extract, Pure
- 2 Eggs
- 2 Teaspoons Ground Cinnamon

Directions:
1. Prepare your food processor, grinding your oats until they make a coarse flour.
2. Put in your cinnamon, egg whites, eggs, banana, vanilla, and salt. Blend until it becomes a smooth batter, and then heat a small frying pan on moderate heat. Heat a half a tablespoon of coconut oil, and then pour your batter in. Cook for a couple of minutes per side, and carry on till all of your batter has been used.

Nutritional Info: Calories: 306 , Protein: fifteen Grams , Fat: fifteen Grams , Carbohydrates: 17 Grams

BANANA-OATMEAL VEGAN PANCAKES

Time To Prepare: five minutes

Time to Cook: five minutes

Yield: Servings 12

Ingredients:
- ½ c. organic whole wheat flour
- ½ tsp. sea salt

- 1¼ c. old fashioned oats
- 1½ c. soymilk
- 2 ripe bananas
- 2 tsp. Baking powder

Directions:
1. To begin, heat griddle or frying pan on moderate heat.
2. After this, place all ingredients, apart from for banana, into a blender and process until the desired smoothness is achieved. Put in the bananas to blender and blend until the desired smoothness is achieved.
3. Lightly grease griddle with olive or coconut oil, then pour ¼ c. of batter onto griddle and cook for minimum two to three minutes, then flip and cook for approximately 2 minutes or maximum the pancake is golden brown and thoroughly cooked.
4. Repeat process with remaining batter.

Nutritional Info: Calories: 59 kcal , Protein: 3.49 g , Fat: 1.48 g , Carbohydrates: 11.52 g

BARLEY BREAKFAST BOWL WITH LEMON YOGURT SAUCE

Time To Prepare: ten minutes

Time to Cook: 0 minutes

Yield: Servings 2

Ingredients:
- ¼ c. cut almonds, toasted
- ¼ c. fresh mint or parsley, chopped
- ¼ tsp. fresh ground black pepper
- ¼ tsp. kosher salt
- ½ tsp. Sea salt
- 1 c. Greek plain yogurt
- 1 c. mung bean sprouts (or preferred variety)
- 1 small avocado – peeled/pitted, and flesh diced or cut
- 1 tsp. Fresh lemon juice
- 1 tsp. lemon zest, finely grated
- 1/3 c. Cotija cheese or queso fresco - crumbled
- 1½ c. cooked barley, keep warm
- Fresh ground black pepper, to taste
- Lemon Yogurt Sauce
- Sea salt, to taste

Directions:
1. First, prepare the Lemon Yogurt Sauce: Mix the plain yogurt, lemon zest and juice, fresh mint or parsley, and salt & pepper in a container and stir to combine well. Cover and place in your fridge until ready to serve.

2. After this, prepare the barley container: In a small mixing container, mix the barley, bean sprouts, cheese, almonds, and salt. Stir to mix thoroughly.
3. Split barley mixture into 2 serving bowls. Top each barley container with 2 tbsp. lemon yogurt sauce and avocado. Place a pinch of salt and pepper to taste, serve, and enjoy!

Nutritional Info: Calories: 432 kcal , Protein: 13.6 g , Fat: 23.37 g , Carbohydrates: 47.62 g

BEEF BREAKFAST CASSEROLE

Time To Prepare: ten minutes

Time to Cook: thirty minutes

Yield: Servings 5

Ingredients:
- ¼ cup cut black olives
- ½ cup Pico de Gallo
- 1 cup baby spinach
- 1 pound of ground beef, cooked
- 10 eggs
- Freshly ground black pepper

Directions:
1. Preheat your oven to 350 degrees Fahrenheit. Prepare a 9" glass pie plate with non-stick spray.
2. Whisk the eggs until frothy. Sprinkle with salt and pepper.
3. Layer the cooked ground beef, Pico de Gallo, and spinach in the pie plate.
4. Slowly pour the eggs over the top.
5. Top with black olives.
6. Bake for minimum 30 minutes, until firm in the center.
7. Cut into 5 pieces before you serve.

Nutritional Info: Calories: 479 kcal , Protein: 43.54 g , Fat: 30.59 g , Carbohydrates: 4.65 g

BLUEBERRY & CASHEW WAFFLES

Time To Prepare: fifteen minutes

Time to Cook: 4-5 minutes

Yield: Servings 5

Ingredients:
- ¼ cup coconut oil, melted
- ½ cup unsweetened almond milk
- ½ teaspoon organic vanilla flavor
- 1 cup fresh blueberries
- 1 cup raw cashews
- 1 tsp baking soda

- 3 organic eggs
- 3 tablespoons coconut flour
- 3 tablespoons organic honey
- Salt, to taste

Directions:
1. Preheat the waffle iron after which grease it.
2. In a mixer, put in cashews and pulse till flour-like consistency forms.
3. Move the cashew flour in a big container.
4. Put in almond flour, baking soda and salt and mix thoroughly.
5. In another container, put the rest of the ingredients and beat till well blended.
6. Place the egg mixture into the flour mixture then mix till well blended.
7. Fold in blueberries.
8. In preheated waffle iron, put in the required amount of mixture.
9. Cook for about five minutes.
10. Repeat with the rest of the mixture.

Nutritional Info: Calories: 432 , Fat: 32 , Carbohydrates: 32g , Protein: 13g

BLUEBERRY-BRAN BREAKFAST SUNDAE

Time To Prepare: ten minutes

Time to Cook: 0 minutes

Yield: Servings 2

Ingredients:
- 1/4 c. fresh blueberries
- 2 c. bran flakes
- 2 c. vanilla or lemon-flavored low-fat yogurt (if possible Greek yogurt) or flavor of choice.
- 2 tbsp. chopped pecans (or nuts of choice)
- 2 tbsp. cut almonds (or nuts of choice)
- 2 tbsp. dried cranberries (or dried or fresh fruit of choice)

Directions:
1. In a container, place 1 c. yogurt, and one c. bran flakes.
2. Top with 1/8 c. fresh blueberries, followed by 1 tbsp. Each of cut almonds, chopped pecans, and dried cranberries.
3. Repeat using the rest of the ingredients to make a second serving. Serve instantly.

Nutritional Info: Calories: 420 kcal , Protein: 21.12 g , Fat: 13.58 g , Carbohydrates: 59.8 g

BREAKFAST ARROZCALDO

Time To Prepare: twenty minutes

Time to Cook: thirty minutes

Yield: Servings 5

Ingredients:
- ¼ cup raisins
- ½ cup frozen peas, thawed
- 1 garlic clove, minced
- 1 white onion, minced
- 1½ cups brown rice, cooked
- 6 eggs, white only
- For the filling
- oil, for greasing

Directions:
1. To make the filling, spray a small amount of oil into a frying pan set on moderate heat. Put in in onion and garlic. Stir-fry until former is limp and transparent.
2. Stir-fry while breaking up clumps, approximately 2 minutes. Put in in rest of the ingredients. Stir-fry for one more minute.
3. Turn down the heat, and let filling cook for ten to fifteen minutes, or until juices are greatly reduced. Stir frequently. Turn off heat. Split into 6 equivalent portions.
4. For the eggs, spray a small amount of oil into a smaller frying pan set on moderate heat. Cook eggs. Discard yolk. Move to holding the plate.
5. To serve, place 1 portion of rice on a plate, 1 portion of filling, and 1 egg white. Serve warm.

Nutritional Info: Calories: 53 kcal , Protein: 6.28 g , Fat: 1.35 g , Carbohydrates: 3.59 g

BREAKFAST PITAS

Time To Prepare: 4 minutes

Time to Cook: six minutes

Yield: Servings 4

Ingredients:
- 1 c. raw spinach (cook if you prefer)
- 1 tsp. garlic powder
- 1 tsp. onion powder
- 2 c. bell peppers, chopped (any color)
- 2 tsp. extra virgin olive oil
- 4 whole-wheat pita pockets
- 8 egg whites

Directions:
1. Place the olive oil to a big sauté pan and place on moderate heat. When the oil is hot in shiny, throw in the bell pepper and sauté for approximately 3 minutes or until soft. Put in in the spinach now (if you wish it cooked) and sauté for approximately 1 to three minutes or just up to the sides begins to wilt.
2. Put the egg whites into a small container, whisk well. Put in in spices; whisk well. Pour the egg mixture into the sauté pan and scramble everything together.

3. Turn off the heat and stuff ½ to 1 c. mixture into a pita pocket before you serve.

Nutritional Info: Calories: 153 kcal , Protein: 12.4 g , Fat: 3.41 g , Carbohydrates: 19.32 g

BREAKFAST SAUSAGE AND MUSHROOM CASSEROLE

Time To Prepare: twenty minutes

Time to Cook: forty-five minutes

Yield: Servings 4

Ingredients:
- 1 ½ tsp. of sea salt, divided
- 1 medium onion, finely diced
- 1 red bell pepper, roasted
- 2 Tablespoons of organic ghee
- 3/4 tsp. of ground black pepper, divided
- 450g of Italian sausage, cooked and crumbled
- 6 free-range eggs
- 600g of sweet potatoes
- 8 ounces of white mushrooms, cut
- Three-fourth cup of coconut milk

Directions:
1. Peel and shred the sweet potatoes.
2. Take a container, fill it with ice-cold water, and soak the sweet potatoes in it. Set aside.
3. Peel the roasted bell pepper, remove its seeds and finely dice it.
4. Set the oven 375°F.
5. Get a casserole baking dish and grease it with the organic ghee.
6. Place a frying pan using moderate heat and cook the mushrooms in it. Cook until the mushrooms are crunchy and brown.
7. Take the mushrooms out and mix them with the crumbled sausage.
8. Now sauté the onions in the same frying pan. Cook up to the onions are tender and golden. This should take approximately four – five minutes.
9. Take the onions out and mix them in the sausage-mushroom mixture.
10. Put in the diced bell pepper to the same mixture.
11. Mix thoroughly and set aside for a while.
12. Now drain the soaked shredded potatoes, put them on a paper towel, and pat dry.
13. Bring the sweet potatoes in a container and put in about a teaspoon of salt and half a teaspoon of ground black pepper to it. Mix thoroughly and save for later.
14. Now take a big container and crack the eggs in it.
15. Break the eggs and then mix in the coconut milk.
16. Mix in the rest of the black pepper and salt.
17. Take the greased casserole dish and spread the seasoned sweet potatoes uniformly in the base of the dish.

18. After this, spread the sausage mixture uniformly in the dish.
19. To finish, spread the egg mixture.
20. Now cover the casserole dish using a piece of aluminium foil.
21. Bake for 20 - thirty minutes. To check if the casserole is baked properly, insert a tester in the center of the casserole, and it should come out clean.
22. Uncover the casserole dish and bake it again, uncovered for 5 - ten minutes, until the casserole is a little golden on the top.
23. Let it cool for approximately ten minutes.
24. Enjoy!

Nutritional Info: Calories: 598 kcal , Protein: 28.65 g , Fat: 36.75 g , Carbohydrates: 48.01 g

CARROT BREAD

Time To Prepare: ten minutes

Time to Cook: 1 hour

Yield: Servings 8

Ingredients:
- ¼ cup sultanas
- ½-inch piece of fresh ginger, peeled and grated
- 1 tablespoon apple cider vinegar
- 1 tablespoon cumin seeds
- 1 teaspoon organic baking powder
- 2 cups almond meal
- 2 tablespoons macadamia nut oil
- 3 cups carrot, peeled and grated
- 3 organic eggs
- Salt, to taste

Directions:
1. Set the oven to 35 F, then line a loaf pan using parchment paper.
2. In a big container, put together the almond meal, baking powder, cumin seeds, and salt and mix.
3. In another container, put in eggs, nut oil, and vinegar and beat till well blended.
4. Place the egg mixture into the flour mixture and mix till well blended.
5. Fold in rest of the ingredients.
6. Put the mixture into prepared loaf pan equally.
7. Bake for approximately 1 hour.

Nutritional Info: Calories: 215 , Total Fat: 17.1g , Total Carbohydrates: 10.8g , Fiber: 4.1g Sugars: 3.9g , Protein: 7.6g

CARROT CAKE OVERNIGHT OATS

Time To Prepare: five minutes + overnight

Time to Cook: 0 minutes

Yield: Servings 1

Ingredients:
- ½ cup Raisins
- 1 cup Coconut or almond milk
- 1 Large Carrot, peel, and shred
- 1 tbsp. Chia seeds
- 1 tsp. Cinnamon, ground
- 1 tsp. Vanilla
- 2 tbsp. Cream cheese, low fat, at room temperature
- 2 tbsp. Honey

Directions:
1. Mix together all of the listed ingredients and store them in a safe fridge container overnight.
2. Eat cold in the morning. If you choose to warm this, just microwave for a minute and stir thoroughly before eating.

Nutritional Info: Calories 340 , 32 grams sugar , 8 grams Protein , 4 grams Fat , 9 grams fiber , 70 grams carbs

CAULIFLOWER AND CHORIZO

Time To Prepare: 55 minutes

Time to Cook: forty minutes

Yield: Servings 4

Ingredients:
- ½ teaspoon garlic powder
- 1 cauliflower head; florets separated
- 1 pound chorizo; chopped.
- 1 yellow onion; chopped.
- 12 ounces canned green chilies; chopped.
- 2 tablespoons green onions; chopped.
- 4 eggs; whisked
- Salt and black pepper to the taste.

Directions:
1. Heat a pan on moderate heat; put the chorizo and onion; stir and brown for a few minutes
2. Put in green chilies, stir, cook for a few minutes and take off the heat.
3. In your food processor, mix cauliflower with some salt and pepper and blend.
4. Move this to a container, put in eggs, salt, pepper, and garlic powder and whisk everything.
5. Put in chorizo mix as well, whisk again and move everything to a greased baking dish.
6. Bake using your oven at 375F then bake at least forty minutes.
7. Leave casserole to cool down for a few minutes, drizzle green onions on top, slice and serve

Nutritional Info: Calories: 350 , Fat: 12 , Fiber: 4 , Carbohydrates: 6 , Protein: 20

CHEDDAR AND CHIVE SOUFFLES

Time To Prepare: ten minutes

Time to Cook: twenty-five minutes

Yield: Servings 8

Ingredients:
- ¼ cup chopped chives
- ¼ tsp cayenne pepper
- ½ cup almond flour
- ½ cup baking powder
- ½ tsp cracked black pepper
- ½ tsp xanthan gum
- ¾ cup heavy cream
- 1 tsp ground mustard
- 1 tsp salt
- 2 cups shredded cheddar cheese
- 6 organic eggs, separated

Directions:
1. Switch on the oven, then set its temperature to 350°F and allow it to preheat.
2. Take a medium container, put in flour in it, put in rest of the ingredients, apart from for baking powder and eggs, and whisk until blended.
3. Separate egg yolks and egg whites between two bowls, put in egg yolks in the flour mixture and whisk until blended.
4. Put in baking powder into the egg whites and beat using an electric mixer until stiff peaks form and then stir egg whites into the flour mixture until thoroughly combined.
5. Split the batter uniformly between eight ramekins and then bake for about twenty-five minutes until done.
6. Serve straight away or store in your fridge until ready to eat.

Nutritional Info: Calories 288 , Total Fat: 21g , Carbs: 3g , Protein: 14g

CHEESY FLAX AND HEMP SEEDS MUFFINS

Time To Prepare: five minutes

Time to Cook: thirty minutes

Yield: Servings 2

Ingredients:
- ¼ cup almond meal
- ¼ cup cottage cheese, low-fat
- ¼ cup grated parmesan cheese

- ¼ cup raw hemp seeds
- ¼ cup scallion, cut thinly
- ¼ tsp baking powder
- 1 tbsp. olive oil
- 1/8 cup flax seeds meal
- 1/8 cup nutritional yeast flakes
- 3 organic eggs, beaten
- Salt, to taste

Directions:
1. Switch on the oven, then set it 360°F and allow it to preheat.
2. In the meantime, take two ramekins, grease them with oil, and set aside until required.
3. Take a medium container, put in flax seeds, hemp seeds, and almond meal, and then mix in salt and baking powder until combined.
4. Crack eggs in a different container, put in yeast, cottage cheese, and parmesan, stir thoroughly until blended, and then stir this mixture into the almond meal mixture until blended.
5. Fold in scallions, then spread the mixture between prepared ramekins and bake for thirty minutes until muffins are firm and the top is nicely golden brown.
6. When finished, take out the muffins from the ramekins and allow them to cool to room temperature on a wire rack.
7. For meal prepping, wrap each muffin using a paper towel and place in your fridge for maximum thirty-four days.
8. When ready to eat, reheat muffins in the microwave until hot and then serve.

Nutritional Info: Calories 179 , Total Fat: 10.9g , Carbs: 6.9g , Protein: 15.4g , Sugar: 2.3g , Sodium: 311mg

CHERRY CHIA OATS

Time To Prepare: ten minutes

Time to Cook: twenty minutes

Yield: Servings 2

Ingredients:
- ¼ Cup Whole Milk Yogurt, Plain
- ¼ Teaspoon Vanilla Extract, Pure
- 1 ¼ Cup Almond Milk
- 1 Cup Quick Cook Oats
- 2 Tablespoons Almond Butter
- 2 Tablespoons Chia Seeds
- 8 Cherries, Fresh, Pitted & Halved

Directions:
1. Combine all the ingredients until they're blended well.
2. Seal in two jars and place in your fridge for twenty-five minutes before you serve.

Nutritional Info: Calories: 564 , Protein: 22 Grams , Fat: 32 Grams , Carbohydrates: 27 Grams

CHICKEN MUFFINS

Time To Prepare: 1 hour ten minutes

Time to Cook: thirty minutes

Yield: Servings 3

Ingredients:
- ½ teaspoon garlic powder
- 2 tablespoons green onions; chopped.
- 3 tablespoons hot sauce mixed with 3 tablespoons melted coconut oil
- 3/4 pound chicken breast; boneless
- 6 eggs
- Salt and black pepper to the taste.

Directions:
1. Season chicken breast with pepper, salt, and garlic powder, place on a lined baking sheet, and bake in your oven at 425F for minimum twenty-five minutes.
2. Move chicken breast to a container, shred using a fork, and mix with half of the hot sauce and melted coconut oil.
3. Toss to coat and leave aside.
4. In a container, mix eggs with salt, pepper, green onions, and the remaining hot sauce mixed with oil and whisk very well.
5. Split this mix into a muffin tray, top each with shredded chicken, introduce in your oven at 350F then bake for minimum 30 minutes.
6. Serve your muffins hot.

Nutritional Info: Calories: 140 , Fat: 8 , Fiber: 1 , Carbohydrates: 2 , Protein: 13

CHOCO-BANANA OATS

Time To Prepare: five minutes

Time to Cook: 8 minutes

Yield: Servings 2

Ingredients:
- ¼ tsp. almond extract
- ¼ tsp. Vanilla
- ¾ cup water
- 1/3 cup toasted walnuts, chopped
- 1/8 tsp. cinnamon
- 1/8 tsp. salt
- 2 cups almond milk
- 2 cups oats

- 2 ripe bananas, cut
- 2 tbsp. agave nectar
- 2 tbsp. cocoa powder, unsweetened
- 2 tbsp. vegan chocolate chips, semisweet

Directions:
1. In a big deep cooking pan, pour the almond milk, water, bananas, vanilla, and almond extract. Put in the salt, stir, and heat over high temperature.
2. Combine the oats in the pan together with the unsweetened cocoa powder, 1 tbsp. agave nectar and reduce the temperature to moderate. Cook for 7-8 minutes, or until the oats are cooked to your preference. Stir regularly.
3. Scoop the cooked oats into serving bowls and decorate with the chopped walnuts, chocolate chips, and sprinkle with the remaining agave nectar.

Nutritional Info: Calories: 522 kcal , Protein: 30.17 g , Fat: 27.01 g , Carbohydrates: 79.09 g

CILANTRO PANCAKES

Time To Prepare: ten minutes

Time to Cook: 6-8 minutes

Yield: Servings 6

Ingredients:
- ¼ teaspoon ground turmeric
- ½ cup almond flour
- ½ cup fresh cilantro, chopped
- ½ cup tapioca flour
- ½ of red onion, chopped
- ½ teaspoon chili powder
- 1 (½-inch) fresh ginger piece, grated finely
- 1 cup full-Fat coconut milk
- 1 Serrano pepper, minced
- Freshly ground black pepper, to taste
- Oil, as required
- Salt, to taste

Directions:
1. In a big container, put together the flours and spices then mix.
2. Place the coconut milk and mix till well blended.
3. Fold within the onion, ginger, Serrano pepper, and cilantro.
4. Lightly, grease a sizable nonstick frying pan with oil and warmth on medium-low heat.
5. Put in about ¼ cup of mixture and tilt the pan to spread it uniformly inside the frying pan.
6. Cook for about four minutes from either side.
7. Repeat with all the rest of the mixture.
8. Serve together with your desired topping.

Nutritional Info: Calories: 331 , Fat: 10g , Carbohydrates: 37g , Fiber: 6g , Protein: 28g

CINNAMON PANCAKES WITH COCONUT

Time To Prepare: five minutes

Time to Cook: eighteen minutes

Yield: Servings 2

Ingredients:
- ¼ cup shredded coconut and more for decorationing
- ½ tbsp. erythritol
- ½ tbsp. olive oil
- 1 tbsp. almond flour
- 1 tsp cinnamon
- 1/8 tsp salt
- 2 organic eggs
- 2oz cream cheese
- 4 tbsp. stevia

Directions:
1. Crack eggs in a container, beat until fluffy and then beat in flour and cream cheese until the desired smoothness is achieved.
2. Put in rest of the ingredients and then stir until well blended.
3. Take a frying pan, place it on moderate heat, grease it with oil, then pour in half of the batter and cook for three to four minutes per side until the pancake has cooked and nicely golden brown.
4. Move pancake to a plate and cook another pancake similarly by using the rest of the batter.
5. Drizzle coconut on top of cooked pancakes before you serve.

Nutritional Info: Calories 575 , Total Fat: 51g , Carbs: 3.5g , Protein: 19g

CINNAMON-APPLE GRANOLA WITH GREEK YOGURT

Time To Prepare: five minutes

Time to Cook: ten minutes

Yield: Servings 2

Ingredients:
- ½ apple, peeled and diced
- ½ c. raw almonds, chopped (or raw nuts of choice)
- ½ c. raw walnuts, chopped (or raw nuts of choice)
- 1 cup Greek plain or vanilla yogurt (or flavor of choice)
- 1 tbsp. almond flour

- 1 tsp. ground cinnamon
- 1/16 tsp. vanilla extract
- 1/8 c. applesauce, unsweetened preferred
- 2 tbsp. vanilla Protein powder
- 2 tsp. almond butter
- 2 tsp. honey
- dash of sea salt

Directions:
1. In a mixing container, mix the chopped almonds, chopped walnuts (or preferred raw nuts), diced apple, vanilla Protein powder, almond flour, lucuma (opt), and cinnamon and salt in a container. Mix thoroughly.
2. In a second container, mix the apple sauce, almond butter, honey, and vanilla extract. Mix thoroughly. Pour the container with the nuts into the container with the wet ingredients and blend together meticulously. Make sure all dry ingredients get coated.
3. Put the granola mixture onto a parchment paperlined baking sheet and bake until the desired crunch is obtained roughly 8 to ten minutes. Take off from oven and allow to cool or eat hot. Put ½ cup each Greek yogurt into two bowls. Split the granola and drizzle over the yogurt in each container. Serve instantly.

Nutritional Info: Calories: 312 kcal , Protein: 11.72 g , Fat: 22.37 g , Carbohydrates: 19.92 g

COCONUT & BANANA COOKIES

Time To Prepare: fifteen minutes

Time to Cook: twenty-five minutes

Yield: Servings 7

Ingredients:
- ½ tsp. ground cinnamon
- ½ tsp. ground turmeric
- 2 cups unsweetened coconut, shredded
- 3 medium bananas, peeled
- Freshly ground black pepper
- Pinch of salt, to taste

Directions:
1. Set the oven to 350°F. Coat a cookie sheet a mildly greased parchment paper.
2. In a mixer, put all together ingredients and pulse till a dough-like mixture forms.
3. Make small balls through the mixture and set onto a prepared cookie sheet in a single layer.
4. Using your fingers, press along the balls to form the cookies.
5. Bake for minimum fifteen-twenty minutes or till golden brown.

Nutritional Info: Calories: 370 , Fat: 4g , Carbohydrates: 28g , Fiber: 11g , Protein: 33g

COCO-TAPIOCA BOWL

Time To Prepare: ten minutes

Time to Cook: twenty minutes

Yield: Servings 2

Ingredients:
- ¼ cup maple syrup
- ¼ cup tapioca pearls, small sized
- ½ cup unsweetened coconut flakes, toasted
- 1 ½ tsp. lemon juice
- 1 can light coconut milk
- 2 cups water

Directions:
1. Put the tapioca in a deep cooking pan and pour over the 2 cups of water. Allow it to stand for minimum 30 minutes.
2. Pour in the coconut milk and syrup and heat the deep cooking pan over moderate temperature. Bring to its boiling point while stirring continuously.
3. Put in the lemon juice and stir and then decorate with coconut flakes.

Nutritional Info: Calories: 309 kcal , Protein: 3.93 g , Fat: 9.02 g , Carbohydrates: 54.55 g

CORNMEAL GRITS

Time To Prepare: five minutes

Time to Cook: fifteen minutes

Yield: Servings 4

Ingredients:
- 1 cup polenta meal
- 1 teaspoon salt
- 2 tablespoons butter
- 4 cups water

Directions:
1. Put water and salt in a deep cooking pan then place it to its boiling point.
2. Slowly put in polenta and continuously stir on moderate to low heat until it has become thick, approximately fifteen minutes. Mix in butter.
3. Serve instantly for tender grits or pour into a greased loaf pan and allow to cool.
4. Once cool, grits can be cut and fried or grilled.

Nutritional Info: Calories: 177 , Fat: 6 g , Protein: 3 g , Sodium: 641 mg , Fiber: 2.5 g , Carbohydrates: 27 g

CRANBERRY AND RAISINS GRANOLA

Time To Prepare: fifteen minutes

Time to Cook: twenty minutes

Yield: Servings 4

Ingredients:
- 4 cups old-fashioned rolled oats
- 1 cup dried cranberries
- 1 cup golden raisins
- 2 tablespoons olive oil
- ½ cup almonds, slivered
- 2 tablespoons warm water
- 1 teaspoon vanilla extract
- 1 teaspoon cinnamon
- 6 tablespoons maple syrup
- 1/3 cup of honey
- 1/4 cup sesame seeds
- 1/4 teaspoon of salt
- 1/8 teaspoon nutmeg

Directions:
1. In a container, combine the sesame seeds, nutmeg, almonds, oats, salt, and cinnamon.
2. In another container, combine the oil, water, vanilla, honey, and syrup. Slowly pour the mixture into the oats mixture. Toss to blend. Spread the mixture into a greased jelly-roll pan. Bake using your oven at 300°F for minimum 55 minutes. Stir and break the clumps every ten minutes.
3. Once you get it from the oven, stir the cranberries and raisins. Allow cooling. This will last for a week when stored in an airtight container and up to a month when stored in your refrigerator.

Nutritional Info: Calories: 698 kcal , Protein: 21.34 g , Fat: 20.99 g , Carbohydrates: 148.59 g

CREAM CHEESE SALMON TOAST

Time To Prepare: fifteen minutes

Time to Cook: five minutes

Yield: Servings 2

Ingredients:
- ½ cup Arugula or spinach, chopped
- ½ tsp. Basil flakes
- 1 tbsp. Red onion, chopped fine
- 2 oz. Smoked salmon
- 2 tbsp. Cream cheese, low-fat

- Whole grain or rye toast, two slices

Directions:
1. Toast the wheat bread.
2. Mix cream cheese and basil and spread this mixture on the toast.
3. Put in salmon, arugula, and onion.

Nutritional Info: Calories 291 , 15.2 grams Fat (8.5 saturated) , 17.8 grams Carbohydrates , 3 grams of sugar

CREPES WITH COCONUT CREAM & STRAWBERRY SAUCE

Time To Prepare: fifteen minutes

Time to Cook: 8 minutes

Yield: Servings 4

Ingredients:

For Sauce:
- 1 (13½-ounce) can chilled coconut milk
- 1 tablespoon honey
- 1 tablespoon organic honey
- 1 teaspoon organic vanilla flavoring
- 1½ teaspoons tapioca starch
- 12-ounces frozen strawberries, thawed and liquid reserved
- For the Coconut cream:

For Crepes:
- ¼ cup almond milk
- 2 organic eggs
- 2 tablespoons coconut flour
- 2 tablespoons tapioca starch
- Avocado oil, as required
- Pinch of salt

Directions:
1. For sauce inside a container, combine some reserved strawberry liquid and tapioca starch.
2. Put in rest of the ingredients and mix thoroughly.
3. Move a combination inside a pan on moderate to high heat.
4. Bring to its boiling point, stirring constantly.
5. Cook for minimum 2-3 minutes, till the sauce, becomes thick.
6. Turn off the heat and aside, covered till serving.
7. For coconut cream, cautiously, scoop your cream from your surface of a can of coconut milk.
8. In a mixer, put in coconut cream, vanilla flavoring, and honey and pulse for around 6-8 minutes or till fluffy.

9. For crepes in a blender, put in all ingredients and pulse till well blended and smooth.
10. Lightly, grease a substantial nonstick frying pan with avocado oil as well as heat on medium-low heat.
11. Put in a modest amount of mixture and tilt the pan to spread it uniformly inside the frying pan.
12. Cook roughly 1-2 minutes.
13. Cautiously change the side and cook for roughly 1-1½ minutes more.
14. Repeat with the rest of the mixture.
15. Split the coconut cream onto each crepe uniformly and fold into four equivalent portions.
16. Put strawberry sauce ahead before you serve.

Nutritional Info: Calories: 364 , Fat: 9g , Carbohydrates: 26g , Fiber: 7g , Protein: 15g

EDAMAME OMELET

Time To Prepare: five minutes

Time to Cook: five minutes

Yield: Servings 2

Ingredients:
- ½ cup shelled edamame
- ½ cup shredded regular or soy Cheddar cheese
- 1 bunch scallions, cut into 1-inch pieces
- 1 tbsp. low-sodium soy sauce, or to taste
- 1 tsp. minced garlic
- 3 big eggs or ¾ cup egg substitute
- 3 tbsp. olive oil, divided
- Snips of fresh cilantro, for decoration

Directions:
1. Warm 2 tablespoons oil in a small frying pan on moderate heat and sauté the garlic and scallion for approximately 2 minutes. Put in the edamame and soy sauce and sauté one minute more. Remove from the frying pan and save for later.
2. Warm the other 1 tablespoon oil in the same frying pan.
3. Whisk the eggs until combined and pour into the hot oil. Spread the shredded cheese on top. Lift up the omelet's edges, tipping the frying pan back and forth to cook the uncooked eggs.
4. Once the top looks firm, drizzle the scallion mixture over one half of the omelet and fold the other half over the top.
5. Lift the omelet out of the frying pan. Split it in half, drizzle with the cilantro, before you serve.

Nutritional Info: Calories: 416 , Fat: 31 g , Protein: 27 g , Sodium: 640 g , Fiber: 3 g , Carbohydrates: 7.5 g

EGG MUFFINS WITH FETA AND QUINOA

Time To Prepare: fifteen minutes

Time to Cook: thirty minutes

Yield: Servings 6-12

Ingredients:
- ¼ cup Black olives, chopped
- ¼ cup Onion, chopped
- ¼ tsp. Salt
- 1 cup Feta cheese
- 1 cup Quinoa, cooked
- 1 cup Tomatoes, chopped
- 1 tbsp. Oregano, fresh chop
- 2 cups baby spinach, chopped
- 2 tsp. Olive oil
- 8 Eggs

Directions:
1. Heat oven to 350. Spray oil a muffin pan with twelve cups. Cook spinach, oregano, olives, onion, and tomatoes for 5 minutes in the olive oil on moderate heat. Beat eggs. Put in the cooked mix of veggies to the eggs with the cheese and salt.
2. Ladle mix into muffin cups. Bake thirty minutes. These will remain fresh in your refrigerator for two days. To eat, just wrap in a paper towel and warm in the microwave for thirty seconds.

Nutritional Info: Calorie 113 , 5 grams carbs , 6 grams Protein , 7 grams Fat , 1-gram sugar ,

FANTASTIC SPAGHETTI SQUASH WITH CHEESE AND BASIL PESTO

Time To Prepare: ten minutes

Time to Cook: thirty-five minutes

Yield: Servings 2

Ingredients:
- ¼ cup ricotta cheese, unsweetened
- ½ tbsp. olive oil
- 1 cup cooked spaghetti squash, drained
- 1/8 cup basil pesto
- 2oz fresh mozzarella cheese, cubed
- Freshly cracked black pepper, to taste

- Salt, to taste

Directions:
1. Switch on the oven, then set its temperature to 375 °F and allow it to preheat.
2. In the meantime, take a medium container, put in spaghetti squash in it and then sprinkle with salt and black pepper.
3. Take a casserole dish, grease it with oil, put in squash mixture in it, top it with ricotta cheese and mozzarella cheese and bake for about ten minutes until cooked.
4. When finished, remove the casserole dish from the oven, sprinkle pesto on top and serve instantly.

Nutritional Info: Calories 169 , Total Fat: 11.3g , Carbs: 6.2g , Protein: 11.9g , Sugar: 0.1g , Sodium: 217mg

FENNEL SEEDS COOKIES

Time To Prepare: ten minutes

Time to Cook: twenty minutes

Yield: Servings 5

Ingredients:
- ¼ cup coconut oil, softened
- ¼ teaspoon whole fennel seeds
- ½ teaspoon fresh ginger, grated finely
- 1 teaspoon vanilla extract
- 1/3 cup coconut flour
- 2 tablespoons raw honey
- Pinch freshly ground black pepper
- Pinch of ground cinnamon
- Pinch of salt

Directions:
1. Set the oven to 360°F. Coat a cookie sheet that has a parchment paper.
2. In a substantial container, put in all together the ingredients and mix till a uniform dough form.
3. Form a small balls in the mixture make onto a prepared cookie sheet inside a single layer.
4. Using your fingers, softly push along the balls to form the cookies.
5. Bake for minimum 9 minutes or till golden brown.

Nutritional Info: Calories: 353 , Fat: 5g , Carbohydrates: 19g , Fiber: 3g , Protein: 25g

FLAXSEED PORRIDGE WITH CINNAMON

Time To Prepare: ten minutes

Time to Cook: five minutes

Yield: Servings 4

Ingredients:
- ½ cup shredded coconut
- 1 cup heavy cream
- 1 tbsp. unsalted butter
- 1 tsp cinnamon
- 1½ tsp stevia
- 2 cups of water
- 2 tbsp. flaxseed meal
- 2 tbsp. flaxseed oatmeal

Directions:
1. Take a medium pot, place it using low heat, put in all the ingredients in it, stir until combined and bring the mixture to boil.
2. When the mixture has boiled, remove the pot from heat, stir it well and split it uniformly between four bowls.
3. Let porridge rest for about ten minutes until slightly become thick and then serve.

Nutritional Info: Calories 171 , Total Fat: 16g , Carbs: 6g , Protein: 2g

FRUITY MUFFINS

Time To Prepare: ten minutes

Time to Cook: 2-3 minutes

Yield: Servings 8

Ingredients:
- ¼ cup brown rice flour
- ¼ cup extra-virgin olive oil
- ¼ cup raw sugar
- ½ cup almond meal
- ½ cup buckwheat flour
- ½ teaspoon ground ginger
- 1 big organic egg
- 1 cup rhubarb, cut finely
- 1 small apple, peeled, cored and chopped finely
- 1 tablespoon linseed meal
- 1 teaspoon organic vanilla extract
- 12 teaspoon ground cinnamon
- 2 tablespoons arrowroot flour
- 2 tablespoons crystallized ginger, chopped finely
- 2 tablespoons organic baking powder
- 7 tablespoons almond milk
- Pinch of salt

Directions:

1. Set the oven to 350F. Grease 8 cups of a big muffin tin.
2. In a big container, combine almond meal, linseed meal, sugar, and crystalized ginger.
3. In another container, put together flours, baking powder, spices, and salt, and mix.
4. Sift the flour mixture into the container of almond meal mixture and mix thoroughly.
5. In a third container, put in egg, milk, oil, and vanilla and beat till well blended.
6. Put in egg mixture into the flour mixture and mix till well blended.
7. Fold in apple and rhubarb.
8. Put the mixture into prepared muffin cups equally.
9. Bake for approximately 20-twenty-five minutes or till a toothpick inserted in the middle comes out clean.

Nutritional Info: Calories: 227 , Total Fat: 4.2g , Total Carbohydrates: 26.9g , Fiber: 4.9g
Sugars: 10.4g , Protein: 4.1g

GINGERBREAD OATMEAL BREAKFAST

Time To Prepare: ten minutes

Time to Cook: 0 minutes

Yield: Servings 4

Ingredients:

- ¼ tsp ground allspice
- ¼ tsp ground cardamom
- ¼ tsp ground coriander
- ¼ tsp ground ginger
- 1 ½ tbsp. ground cinnamon
- 1 cup steel-cut oats
- 1 tsp ground cloves
- 1/8 tsp nutmeg
- 4 cups drinking water
- Fresh mixed berries
- Organic Maple syrup, to taste

Directions:

1. Cook the oats based on the package instructions. When it comes to its boiling point, decrease the heat and simmer.
2. Mix in all the spices and carry on cooking until cooked to desired doneness.
3. Serve in four serving bowls and sprinkle with maple syrup and top with fresh berries.
4. Enjoy!

Nutritional Info: Calories: 87 kcal , Protein: 5.82 g , Fat: 3.26 g , Carbohydrates: 18.22 g

GRAPEFRUIT-POMEGRANATE SALAD

Time To Prepare: ten minutes

Time to Cook: 0 minutes

Yield: Servings 6

Ingredients:
- ¼ cup Basic Vegetable Stock
- 1 pomegranate
- 2 ruby red grapefruits
- 3 ounces Parmesan cheese
- 6 cups mesclun leaves

Directions:
1. Peel the grapefruit using a knife, take off all the pith. (the white layer under the skin).
2. Cut out every section with the knife, make sure that no pith remains. Shave Parmesan using a vegetable peeler to make curls.
3. Peel the pomegranate using a paring knife; take off the berries/seeds.
4. Toss the mesclun greens in the stock.
5. To serve, mound the greens on plates and position the grapefruit sections, cheese, and pomegranate on top.

Nutritional Info: Calories: 84 , Fat: 2 g , Protein: 4 g , Sodium: 102 mg , Fiber: 2 g , Carbohydrates: 14 g

GREEK YOGURT WITH CHERRY-ALMOND SYRUP PARFAIT

Time To Prepare: twenty-five minutes

Time to Cook: five minutes

Yield: Servings 2

Ingredients:
- 1 c. fresh black or red cherries, pitted
- 1 tsp. fresh-squeezed lemon juice
- 2 c. Greek plain yogurt, stir to loosen
- 2 tbsp. almond syrup
- 2 tbsp. coconut palm sugar
- 2 tbsp. cut almonds, to decorate
- 4 tbsp. granola of choice, to decorate (opt.)

Directions:
1. Put a deep cooking pan on moderate to high heat and mix cherries, almond syrup, sugar, lemon juice, and 1 tbsp. of water. Stir to blend, then place it to simmer, continuously stirring

until sugar is dissolved. Continue to simmer for further five minutes, until liquid begins to turn into a syrupy mixture, but the cherries are still holding firm. Put the mixture to a container and allow to cool for five minutes at room temperature, then bring it in your fridge to chill until it is completely cold.

2. Put 1 cup of Greek yogurt into 2 serving bowls and spoon ½ of the cherries and their syrupy juices over the yogurt. Decorate using cut almonds or granola, if you wish. Serve instantly.

Nutritional Info: Calories: 185 kcal , Protein: 4.75 g , Fat: 4.88 g , Carbohydrates: 33.07 g

HAM AND VEGGIE FRITTATA MUFFINS

Time To Prepare: ten minutes

Time to Cook: twenty-five minutes

Yield: Servings 12

Ingredients:
- ¼ cup coconut milk (canned)
- ½ yellow onion, finely diced
- 1 cup cherry tomatoes, halved
- 2 tablespoons coconut flour
- 4 tablespoons coconut oil
- 5 ounces thinly cut ham
- 8 big eggs
- 8 oz. frozen spinach, thawed and drained
- 8 oz. mushrooms, thinly cut
- Sea salt and pepper to taste

Directions:
1. Preheat your oven to 375 degrees Fahrenheit.
2. In a moderate-sized frying pan, warm the coconut oil on moderate heat. Put in the onion and cook until tender.
3. Put in the mushrooms, spinach, and cherry tomatoes. Sprinkle with salt and pepper. Cook until the mushrooms have become tender. About five minutes. Turn off the heat and save for later.
4. In a huge container, beat the eggs with the coconut milk and coconut flour. Mix in the cooled the veggie mixture.
5. Coat each cavity of a 12 cavity muffin tin with the thinly cut ham. Pour the egg mixture into each one and bake for about twenty minutes.
6. Take out of the oven and let cool for approximately five minutes before transferring to a wire rack.

Nutritional Info: Calories: 125 kcal , Protein: 5.96 g , Fat: 9.84 g , Carbohydrates: 4.48 g

HASH BROWNS

Time To Prepare: fifteen minutes

Time to Cook: fifteen minutes

Yield: Servings 4

Ingredients:
- 1 pound Russet potatoes, peeled, processed using a grater
- 3 Tbsp. olive oil
- Pinch of black pepper, to taste
- Pinch of sea salt

Directions:
1. Coat a microwave safe-dish using paper towels. Spread shredded potatoes on top. Microwave veggies on the maximum heat setting for a couple of minutes. Turn off the heat.
2. Pour 1 tablespoon of oil into a non-stick frying pan set on moderate heat.
3. Cooking in batches, place a generous pinch of potatoes into the hot oil. Push down using the back of a spatula.
4. Cook for about three minutes every side, or until brown and crunchy. Drain over paper towels. Repeat step for remaining potatoes. Put in more oil as required.
5. Sprinkle with salt and pepper and serve.

Nutritional Info: Calories: 200 kcal , Protein: 4.03 g , Fat: 11.73 g , Carbohydrates: 20.49 g

HONEY PANCAKES

Time To Prepare: ten minutes

Time to Cook: five minutes

Yield: Servings 2

Ingredients:
- ¼ tsp baking soda
- ½ cup almond flour
- ½ tablespoon ground cinnamon
- ½ tablespoon ground ginger
- ½ tablespoon ground nutmeg
- ½ teaspoon ground cloves
- ½ teaspoon organic vanilla extract
- ¾ cup organic egg whites
- 1 tablespoon ground flaxseeds
- 2 tablespoons coconut flour
- 2 tablespoons organic honey
- Coconut oil, as required
- Pinch of salt

Directions:

1. In a big container, combine flours, flax seeds, baking soda, spices, and salt.
2. In another container, put in honey, egg whites and vanilla and beat till well blended.
3. Place the egg mixture into the flour mixture then mix till well blended.
4. Lightly, grease a big nonstick frying pan with oil and heat on medium-low heat.
5. Put in about ¼ cup of mixture and tilt the pan to spread it uniformly inside the frying pan.
6. Cook for approximately 3-4 minutes.
7. Cautiously, customize the side and cook roughly one minute more.
8. Repeat with the rest of the mixture.
9. Serve together with your desired topping.

Nutritional Info: Calories: 291 , Fat: 8g , Carbohydrates: 26g , Fiber: 4g , Protein: 23g

HUEVOS RANCHEROS

Time To Prepare: five minutes

Time to Cook: five minutes

Yield: Servings 2

Ingredients:

- (2) 8-inch whole wheat tortillas
- 1-ounce slice of cheddar cheese
- 2 hard-boiled eggs, cut
- 2 slices of Canadian bacon or ham
- 2 tbsp. salsa

Directions:

1. Prepare the hardboiled eggs.
2. Put one tortilla on a plate, top with a slice of Canadian bacon or ham, the cut egg, and a slice of cheddar cheese. Roll the tortilla up. Repeat with the rest of the ingredients to prepare the second burrito.
3. Serve instantly with 1 tbsp. Salsa.

Nutritional Info: Calories: 741 kcal , Protein: 36.12 g , Fat: 30.75 g , Carbohydrates: 79.37 g

KALE TURMERIC SCRAMBLE

Time To Prepare: five minutes

Time to Cook: ten minutes

Yield: Servings 1

Ingredients:

- ¼ tsp. Black pepper
- ½ cup Kale, shredded
- ½ cup Sprouts
- 1 tbsp. Garlic, minced

- 1 tbsp. Turmeric, ground
- 2 Eggs
- 2 tbsp. Olive oil

Directions:
1. Beat the eggs and put in in the turmeric, black pepper, and garlic. Sauté the kale into the olive oil on moderate heat for 5 minutes, and then pour this egg mixture into the pan with the kale.
2. Carry on cooking, frequently stirring, until the eggs are cooked to your preference. Top with raw sprouts before you serve.

Nutritional Info: Calories 137 , 8.4 grams Fat , 7.9 grams carbs , 4.8 grams fiber , 1.8grams sugar , 13.2 grams protein

LEEK & SPINACH FRITTATA

Time To Prepare: ten minutes

Time to Cook: fifteen minutes

Yield: Servings 4

Ingredients:
- ½ Teaspoon Bail, Dried
- ½ Teaspoon Garlic Powder
- 1 Cup Baby Spinach, Fresh & Packed
- 1 Cup Cremini Mushrooms, Sliced
- 2 Leeks, Chopped Fine
- 2 Tablespoons Avocado Oil
- 8 Eggs
- Sea Salt & Black Pepper to Taste

Directions:
1. Set the oven to 400°F then get an ovenproof frying pan. Put it on moderate to high heat, sautéing your leeks in your avocado oil until tender. It should take roughly five minutes
2. Get out a container, and whisk the eggs with your garlic, basil, and salt. Put in them to the frying pan with your leeks, cooking for 5 minutes. You'll need to stir regularly.
3. Mix in your mushrooms and spinach, seasoning with pepper.
4. Put the frying pan in your oven then bake for about ten minutes. Serve warm.

Nutritional Info: Calories: 276 , Protein: 19 Grams , Fat: 17 Grams , Carbohydrates: fifteen Grams

MANGO GRANOLA

Time To Prepare: ten minutes

Time to Cook: thirty minutes

Yield: Servings 4

Ingredients:
- ½ cup almonds, roughly chopped
- ½ cup dates, roughly chopped
- ½ cup nuts
- 1 cup dried mango, chopped
- 2 cups rolled oats
- 2 tbsp. coconut oil
- 2 tbsp. water
- 2 tsp. cinnamon
- 2/3 cup agave nectar
- 3 tbsp. sesame seeds

Directions:
1. Set oven at 320F
2. In a big container, put the oats, almonds, nuts, sesame seeds, dates, and cinnamon then mix thoroughly.
3. In the meantime, heat a deep cooking pan on moderate heat, pour in the agave syrup, coconut oil, and water.
4. Stir and allow it to cook for minimum 3 minutes or until the coconut oil has melted.
5. Slowly pour the syrup mixture into the container with the oats and nuts and stir thoroughly, make sure that all the ingredients are coated with the syrup.
6. Move the granola on a baking sheet coated with parchment paper and place in your oven to bake for about twenty minutes.
7. After twenty minutes, take off the tray from the oven and lay the chopped dried mango on top. Put back in your oven then bake again for another five minutes.
8. Allow the granola cool completely before you serve or placing it in an airtight container for storage. The shelf life of the granola will last up to 2-3 weeks.

Nutritional Info: Calories: 434 kcal , Protein: 13.16 g , Fat: 28.3 g , Carbohydrates: 55.19 g

MAPLE OATMEAL

Time To Prepare: five minutes

Time to Cook: twenty minutes

Yield: Servings 4

Ingredients:
- ¼ cup Coconut flakes, unsweetened
- ½ cup Milk, almond or coconut
- ½ cup Pecans, chopped
- ½ cup Walnuts, chopped
- 1 tsp. Cinnamon
- 1 tsp. Maple flavoring
- 3 tbsp. Sunflower seeds
- 4 tbsp. Chia seeds

Directions:

1. Pulse the sunflower seeds, walnuts, and pecans in a food processor to crumble. Or you can just put the nuts in a sturdy plastic bag, wrap the bag using a towel, lay it on a sturdy surface, and beat the towel with a hammer until the nuts are crumbled.
2. Combine the crushed nuts with the remaining ingredients and pour them into a big pot. Simmer this mixture using low heat for thirty minutes. Stir frequently, so the mix does not cling to the bottom. Serve decorated with fresh fruit or a drizzle of cinnamon if you wish.

Nutritional Info: Calories 374 , 3.2 grams carbs , 9.25 grams Protein , 34.59 grams fat

MAPLE TOAST AND EGGS

Time To Prepare: 20 Minutes

Time to Cook: 20 Minutes

Yield: Servings 6

Ingredients:
- ¼ cup butter
- ½ cup maple syrup
- 12 bacon strips, diced
- 12 big eggs
- 12 slices white bread
- Salt and pepper to taste

Directions:

1. Fry the bacon on a frying pan on moderate heat until the , Fat: has rendered. Take the bacon out and place it using paper towels to drain surplus Fat.
2. Warm the maple syrup and butter until melted in a deep cooking pan. Set aside.
3. Trim the edges of the bread and flatten the slices with a rolling pin. Brush one side with the syrup mixture and press the slices into greased muffin cups.
4. Split the bacon into the muffin cups.
5. Break one egg into each cup.
6. Drizzle with salt and pepper to taste
7. Cover using foil, then bake in your oven at 4000F for about twenty minutes or until the eggs have set.

Nutritional Info: Calories: 671 , Fat: 46g , Carbohydrates: 44g , Protein: 21g

MEDITERRANEAN FRITTATA

Time To Prepare: five minutes

Time to Cook: twenty minutes

Yield: Servings 6

Ingredients:
- ¼ cup Black olives, chopped

- ¼ cup Feta cheese, crumbled
- ¼ cup Green olives, chopped
- ¼ cup Milk, almond or coconut
- ¼ cup Tomatoes, diced
- ¼ tsp. Black pepper
- 1 tsp. Oregano
- 1 tsp. Sea salt
- 6 Eggs
- Oil, spray or olive

Directions:
1. Heat oven to 400. Oil one eight by eight-inch baking dish.
2. Beat the milk into the eggs, and then put in other ingredients.
3. Pour all of this mixture into the baking dish and bake for 20 minutes.

Nutritional Info: Calories 107 , 2 grams sugar , 7g Fat , 3g carbs , 7 grams protein

MINI BREAKFAST PIZZA

Time To Prepare: 5 Minutes

Time to Cook: 10 Minutes

Yield: Servings 4

Ingredients:
- 4 eggs, beaten
- 2 English muffins, split and toasted
- ½ cup shredded Italian cheese
- Dried oregano leaves
- Cooking spray
- Salt and pepper to taste
- 1/3 cup commercial pizza sauce

Directions:
1. Preheat your oven to 4000F.
2. Coat a frying pan with cooking spray then heat on medium flame.
3. Flavour the eggs with salt and pepper to taste and pour into the frying pan. As the eggs start to set, pull the eggs across the pan with an inverted turner. Carry on cooking and folding the egg. Set aside.
4. Spread pizza sauce uniformly on English muffin halves and top with eggs and cheese.
5. Put on a baking sheet then bake for five minutes.
6. Decorate using oregano last.

Nutritional Info: Calories: 282 , Fat: 13g , Carbohydrates: 25g , Protein: 17g

MUSHROOM CRÊPES

Time To Prepare: 1 hour thirty minutes

Time to Cook: thirty minutes

Yield: Servings 6

Ingredients:
- 2 eggs
- ½ cup all-purpose flour
- For the filling
- 3 tablespoons all-purpose flour
- 2 cups of cremini mushrooms, cut
- ½ cup Parmesan cheese, grated
- ¾ cup milk
- 3 garlic cloves, minced
- 2 tablespoons of parsley (chopped)
- 6 slices of deli-cut cooked lean ham
- Freshly ground pepper
- 1/4 teaspoon salt
- 1/4 teaspoon of salt
- 3/4 cup milk
- 3/4 cup chicken broth
- 1/8 teaspoon cayenne
- 1/8 teaspoon nutmeg

Directions:
1. Put and mix the salt and flour in a container. In another container, whisk the eggs and milk. Slowly mix the two mixtures until the desired smoothness is achieved. Leave for fifteen minutes.
2. Spray a frying pan using non-stick cooking spray and put on moderate heat. Mix the batter a little. Put in 1/4 of the batter into the frying pan. Tilt the frying pan to make a thin and even crêpe. Cook for a couple of minutes or until the bottom is golden and the top is set. Flip and cook for twenty seconds. Move to a plate.
3. Repeat the steps with the rest of the batter. Loosely cover the cooked crêpes using plastic wrap.
4. For the filling. Combine all ingredients for filling in a deep cooking pan on moderate heat – flour, milk, cayenne, nutmeg, and pepper. Constantly whisk until thick or around seven minutes. Take off the stove. Mix in a tablespoon of parsley and cheese. Loosely cover to keep warm.
5. Spray a frying pan using non-stick cooking spray and put on moderate heat. Cook the garlic and mushrooms. Sprinkle with salt. Cook for about six minutes or until the mushrooms are tender. Put in 2 tablespoons of sherry. Cook for about 2 minutes. Take off the stove. Put in the remaining parsley and stir.
6. Place the crêpes side by side on a flat surface. Spread a tablespoon of the sauce and 2 tablespoons of the cooked mushrooms. Roll up the crêpes and move them to a greased baking dish. Put all the sauce on top. Bake using your oven at 450°F for fifteen minutes.

Nutritional Info: Calories: 232 kcal , Protein: 16.51 g , Fat: 10.8 g , Carbohydrates: 16.25 g

NUTTY OATS PUDDING

Time To Prepare: five minutes

Time to Cook: 0 minutes

Yield: Servings 3 -5

Ingredients:
- ¼ cup dry milk
- ¼ cup rolled oats
- ½ cup of water
- 1 ½ tablespoon natural peanut butter
- 1 tablespoon yogurt, fat-free
- 1 teaspoon peanuts, finely chopped

Directions:
1. Using a microwaveable-safe container, put together peanut butter and dry milk. Whisk well. Put in in water to achieve a smooth consistency. Put in in oats.
2. Cover container using plastic wrap. Create a small hole for the steam to escape.
3. Put inside the microwave oven for a minute on high powder.
4. Continue heating, this time on medium power for 90 seconds. Allow to sit for five minutes.
5. To serve, spoon an equal amount of cereals in a container top with peanuts and yogurt.

Nutritional Info: Calories: 70 kcal , Protein: 4.25 g , Fat: 3.83 g , Carbohydrates: 6.78 g

OAT PORRIDGE WITH CHERRY & COCONUT

Time To Prepare: ten minutes

Time to Cook: 0 minutes

Yield: Servings 3

Ingredients:
- 1 ½ cups regular oats
- 3 cups coconut milk
- 3 tbsp. raw cacao
- 4 tbsp. chia seed
- A pinch of stevia, optional
- Coconut shavings
- Dark chocolate shavings
- Fresh or frozen tart cherries
- Maple syrup, to taste (not necessary)

Directions:

1. Mix the oats, milk, stevia, and cacao in a moderate-sized deep cooking pan on moderate heat and bring to its boiling point. Reduce the heat, then simmer until the oats are cooked to desired doneness.
2. Split the porridge among 3 serving bowls and top with dark chocolate and coconut shavings, cherries, and a little sprinkle of maple syrup.

Nutritional Info: Calories: 343 kcal , Protein: 15.64 g , Fat: 12.78 g , Carbohydrates: 41.63 g

OATMEAL-APPLESAUCE MUFFINS

Time To Prepare: fifteen minutes

Time to Cook: twenty-five minutes

Yield: Servings 12

Ingredients:

Topping
- 1 tbsp. brown sugar
- 1 tbsp. unsalted butter, melted
- 1/4 cup rolled oats
- 1/8 tsp. cinnamon

Muffins
- ½ c. brown sugar
- ½ c. unsweetened applesauce
- ½ tsp. Baking soda
- ½ tsp. Cinnamon
- ½ tsp. Salt
- ½ tsp. sugar
- 1 c. nonfat milk
- 1 c. old fashioned rolled oats (not instant)
- 1 c. whole wheat flour
- 1 tsp. Baking powder
- 2 egg whites
- raisins or nuts (opt.)

Directions:
1. To begin, first, presoak the oats in milk for an hour,
2. Set the oven to 400°F then grease a standard 12-cup muffin pan with cooking spray or use paper liners.
3. In a mixing container, mix oat-milk mixture, applesauce, and egg whites. Blend well and save for later.
4. In a different container, put together the whole wheat flour, brown sugar, baking powder, baking soda, salt, sugar, and cinnamon then mix.
5. Slowly put wet ingredients to dry ingredients and blend until just blended, but do not over mix the batter as it will make the muffins firm. Put in raisins or nuts (opt.).

6. Prepare topping: In a small container, whisk together the oats, brown sugar, and cinnamon. Put in in melted butter and toss lightly using a fork to coat ingredients.
7. Fill each muffin cup 2/3 full of batter. Drizzle topping on the top of each batter-filled muffin cup. Tap the pan gently on the counter to even out the batter. Put muffin pan in preheated oven and cook for twenty to twenty-five minutes or until a toothpick put in the center of one of the muffins comes out clean. Remove from the oven and allow it to sit for five minutes before you serve.

Nutritional Info: Calories: 115 kcal , Protein: 5.06 g , Fat: 2.57 g , Carbohydrates: 22.33 g

OATMEAL-RAISIN SCONES

Time To Prepare: ten minutes

Time to Cook: fifteen minutes

Yield: Servings 6

Ingredients:
- ½ cup all-purpose flour
- ½ teaspoon salt
- ½ teaspoon vanilla
- 1 cup raisins
- 1 egg white
- 1½ cups rolled oats
- 11/8teaspoons baking powder
- 2 eggs or ½ cup egg substitute
- 2 tablespoons granulated sugar
- 2 tablespoons wheat germ
- 2/3 cup buttermilk
- 3 tablespoons sugar
- 6 tablespoons cold unsalted butter

Directions:
1. Preheat your oven to 400°F. Coat a baking pan w/ parchment paper or spray lightly with oil. Grind half of the oats into flour in a food processor.
2. Mix remaining oats, oat flour, all-purpose flour, wheat germ, sugar, salt, baking powder, and butter in a food processor using a metal blade. Process until mixture looks like cornmeal.
3. In a huge container, put together eggs, buttermilk, and vanilla then whisk. Mix in raisins using a spatula or wooden spoon.
4. Place the dry ingredients and fold in using a spatula. Drop scones into rounds onto the readied baking sheet.
5. Brush scones with egg white and dust with granulated sugar. Bake for fifteen minutes.

Nutritional Info: Calories: 456 , Fat: 16 g , Protein: 13 g , Sodium: 277 mg , Fiber: 6 g , Carbohydrates: 70 g

OMEGA-3-RICH COLD BANANA BREAKFAST

Time To Prepare: ten minutes

Time to Cook: 0 minutes

Yield: Servings 2

Ingredients:
- ½ cup cold milk
- 1 big cut Banana
- 2 tbsp. flaxseeds
- 2 tbsp. ground coconut
- 4 tbsp. sesame seeds
- 4 tbsp. sunflower seeds

Directions:
1. Combine the milk and honey on your breakfast container. Use your coffee grinder to grind all the seeds.
2. Put in the ground seeds to the honey and milk mixture. Put the cut bananas neatly on top. Drizzle the ground coconuts for added flavor.

Nutritional Info: Calories: 393 kcal , Protein: 14.85 g , Fat: 27.63 g , Carbohydrates: 27.37 g

OVEN-POACHED EGGS

Time To Prepare: 2minutes

Time to Cook: 11minutes

Yield: Servings 4

Ingredients:
- 2 cups of ice cubes
- 2 cups water, chilled
- 6 eggs, at room temperature
- Ice bath
- Water

Directions:
1. Set the oven to 350°F. Put 2 cups of water into a deep roasting tin, and place it into the lowest rack of the oven.
2. Put one egg into each cup of cupcake/muffin tins, together with one tablespoon of water.
3. Cautiously place muffin tins into the middle rack of the oven.
4. Bake eggs for about forty-five minutes.
5. Remove the heat instantly. Take off the muffin tins from the oven and set on a cake rack to cool before extracting eggs.
6. Pour ice bath ingredients into a big heat-resistant container.

7. Bring the eggs into an ice bath to stop the cooking process. After ten minutes, drain eggs well. Use as required.

Nutritional Info: Calories: 357 kcal , Protein: 17.14 g , Fat: 24.36 g , Carbohydrates: 16.19 g

PEACHES WITH HONEY ALMOND RICOTTA

Time To Prepare: fifteen minutes

Time to Cook: 0 minutes

Yield: Servings 4-6

Ingredients:
- ¼ cup Almond extract
- ¼ cup Peaches, cut
- ½ cup Almonds, thin slices
- 1 cup Ricotta, skim milk
- 1 tsp. Honey
- Bread, whole grain bagel or toast
- Spread
- To Serve

Directions:
1. Combine the almond extract, honey, ricotta, and almonds.
2. Spread one tablespoon of this mix on toasted bread and cover with peaches.

Nutritional Info: Calories 230 , 9 grams Protein , 8g Fat , 37g carbs , 3 g fiber , 34g sugar

PEANUT BUTTER-BANANA MUFFINS

Time To Prepare: fifteen minutes

Time to Cook: twenty-five minutes

Yield: Servings 12

Ingredients:
- ½ tsp. Baking soda
- ½ tsp. salt
- ¾ c. light brown sugar
- 1 c. low-fat buttermilk
- 1 c. mashed banana (about 3 bananas)
- 1 c. old-fashioned oats
- 1 tsp. Baking powder
- 1½ c. all-purpose flour
- 2 big eggs
- 2 tbsp. Applesauce

- 6 tbsp. creamy peanut butter

Directions:

1. Bring a small nonstick frying pan on moderate heat and spray lightly with cooking spray. Put in in the bell pepper and onion and sauté for one to two minutes, or until both are soft and the onion translucent.
2. In a small container, crack in eggs and whisk. Put in in milk; whisk until well-mixed. Pour eggs into the pan and cook, regularly stirring until eggs are scrambled to your preference.
3. To serve, spoon half the egg mixture into each tortilla, wrap, before you serve. Try serving with a side of fresh fruit for a complete meal.

Nutritional Info: Calories: 187 kcal , Protein: 8.12 g , Fat: 6.25 g , Carbohydrates: 27.82 g

POACHED SALMON EGG TOAST

Time To Prepare: ten minutes

Time to Cook: 4 minutes

Yield: Servings 2
- ¼ tsp. Black pepper
- ¼ tsp. Lemon juice
- 1 tbsp. Scallions, cut thin
- 1/8 tsp. Salt
- 2 Eggs, poached
- 2 tbs. Avocado, mashed
- 4 oz. Salmon, smoked
- Bread, two slices rye or whole-grain toasted

Directions:

1. Put in lemon juice to avocado with pepper and salt. Spread the mixed avocado over the toasted bread slices.
2. Lay smoked salmon over toast and top with a poached egg. Top with cut scallions.

Nutritional Info: Calories 389 , 17.2 grams Fat , 33.5 grams Protein , 31.5 grams carbs , 1.3 grams sugar , 9.3 grams fiber ,

PUMPKIN & BANANA WAFFLES

Time To Prepare: fifteen minutes

Time to Cook: five minutes

Yield: Servings 4

Ingredients:
- ½ cup almond flour
- ½ cup coconut flour
- ½ cup pumpkin puree
- ½ teaspoon ground cloves

- ½ teaspoon ground nutmeg
- ¾ cup almond milk
- ¾ teaspoon ground ginger
- 1 tsp baking soda
- 1½ teaspoons ground cinnamon
- 2 medium bananas, peeled and cut
- 2 tablespoons olive oil
- 5 big organic eggs
- Salt, to taste

Directions:
1. Preheat the waffle iron, and after that, grease it.
2. In a sizable container, combine flours, baking soda, and spices.
3. In a blender, put the rest of the ingredients and pulse till smooth.
4. Put in flour mixture and pulse till
5. In preheated waffle iron, put in the required quantity of mixture.
6. Cook roughly 4-5 minutes.
7. Repeat using the rest of the mixture.

Nutritional Info: Calories: 357.2 , Fat: 28.5g , Carbohydrates: 19.7g , Fiber: 4g , Protein: 14g

PUMPKIN PANCAKES

Time To Prepare: twenty-five minutes

Time to Cook: ten minutes

Yield: Servings 6

Ingredients:
- ½ cup pumpkin puree
- 1 cup coconut cream
- 1 ounce egg white Protein
- 1 tablespoon chai masala
- 1 tablespoon swerve
- 1 teaspoon baking powder
- 1 teaspoon coconut oil
- 1 teaspoon vanilla extract
- 2 ounces flax seeds; ground
- 2 ounces hazelnut flour
- 3 eggs
- 5 drops stevia

Directions:
1. In a container, mix flax seeds with hazelnut flour, egg white Protein baking powder and chai masala and stir.
2. In another container, mix coconut cream with vanilla extract, pumpkin puree, eggs, stevia, and swerve and stir thoroughly.

3. Mix the 2 mixtures and stir thoroughly.
4. Heat a pan with the oil on moderate to high heat; pour 1/6 of the batter, spread into a circle, cover, decrease the heat to low, cook for about three minutes on each side and move to a plate
5. Repeat the process using the rest of the mixture and serve pumpkin pancakes immediately.

Nutritional Info: Calories: 400 , Fat: 23 , Fiber: 4 , Carbohydrates: 5 , Protein: 21

QUINOA & BEANS BURGERS

Time To Prepare: fifteen minutes

Time to Cook: 55 minutes

Yield: Servings 12

Ingredients:
- ½ cup dry quinoa
- ½ cup fresh cilantro, chopped
- ½ teaspoon fresh ginger, grated finely
- ½ teaspoon ground turmeric
- 1 (fifteen oz.) can black beans, drained
- 1 cup cooked corn kernels
- 1 small boiled potato, peeled
- 1 small onion, chopped
- 1 teaspoon chili flakes
- 1 teaspoon flax meal
- 1 teaspoon garlic, minced
- 1 teaspoon ground cumin
- 1 teaspoon paprika
- 1½ cups water
- Freshly ground black pepper, to taste
- Salt, to taste

Directions:
1. In a pan, put in water and quinoa on high heat and provide to its boiling point.
2. Reduce the heat to moderate and simmer for around fifteen-twenty or so minutes.
3. Drain surplus water.
4. Set the oven to 375°F. Coat a sizable baking sheet that has a parchment paper.
5. In a sizable container, put in quinoa and rest of the ingredients.
6. Use a fork to mix till well blended.
7. Make equal-sized patties from the mixture.
8. Position the patties onto the readied baking sheet in the single layer.
9. Bake for around 20-twenty-five minutes.
10. Cautiously, alter the side and cook for approximately 8-ten minutes.

Nutritional Info: Calories: 400 , Fat: 9g , Carbohydrates: 27g , Fiber: 12g , Protein: 38g

QUINOA & VEGGIE CROQUETTES

Time To Prepare: fifteen minutes

Time to Cook: 9 minutes

Yield: Servings 12-fifteen

Ingredients:
- ¼ cup fresh cilantro leaves, chopped
- ¼ teaspoon ground turmeric
- ½ cup frozen peas, thawed
- 1 cup cooked quinoa
- 1 tbsp. essential olive oil
- 1 teaspoon garam masala
- 2 big boiled potatoes, peeled and mashed
- 2 minced garlic cloves
- 2 teaspoons ground cumin
- Freshly ground black pepper, to taste
- Olive oil, for frying
- Salt, to taste

Directions:
1. In a frying pan, warm oil on moderate heat.
2. Put in peas and garlic and sauté for approximately one minute.
3. Move the pea mixture into a big container.
4. Put in the remainder ingredients and mix till well blended.
5. Make equal sized oblong shaped patties from your mixture.
6. In a huge frying pan, heat oil on moderate to high heat.
7. Put in croquettes and fry for approximately 4 minutes per side.

Nutritional Info: Calories: 367 , Fat: 6g , Carbohydrates: 17g , Fiber: 5g , Protein: 22g

QUINOA AND CAULIFLOWER CONGEE

Time To Prepare: ten minutes

Time to Cook: 1 hour

Yield: Servings 8

Ingredients:
- ¼ cup loosely packed cilantro leaves, torn
- ¼ cup loosely packed spearmint leaves, torn
- ¼ cup packed basil leaves, torn
- 1 cauliflower head, minced
- 1 lime, cut into wedges

- 1 tablespoon fish sauce
- 1 tablespoon fresh ginger, grated
- 1 tablespoon olive oil
- 2 garlic cloves, grated
- 2 leeks, minced
- 2 onions, minced
- 2 red chili, minced
- 2 tablespoons brown rice
- 2 tablespoons red quinoa
- 4 eggs, soft-boiled
- 6 cups of water
- For Garnish
- Pinch of white pepper

Directions:
1. Put olive oil into a huge frying pan on moderate heat. Sauté shallots, garlic, and ginger until limp and aromatic; pour into a slow cooker set at moderate heat.
2. Except for decorationes, pour rest of the ingredients into slow cooker; stir. Place the lid on. Cook for around six hours. Turn off heat. Taste; tweak seasoning if required.
3. Ladle congee into separate bowls. Decorate using basil leaves, cilantro leaves, red chilli, and spearmint leaves. Put in 1 piece of soft-boiled egg on top of each; serve with a wedge of lime on the side. Slice egg just before eating so yolk runs into congee. Squeeze lime juice into congee just before eating.

Nutritional Info: Calories: 138 kcal , Protein: 7.23 g , Fat: 7.65 g , Carbohydrates: 10.76 g

QUINOA BREAKFAST BOWL

Time To Prepare: thirty minutes

Time to Cook: 0 minutes

Yield: Servings 6

Ingredients:
- ¼ cup Greek yogurt, plain
- ½ tsp. Salt
- 1 cup Baby spinach, chopped
- 1 cup Feta cheese
- 1 Pint Cherry tomatoes, cut in halves
- 1 tsp. Black pepper
- 1 tsp. Garlic, minced
- 1 tsp. Olive oil
- 12 Eggs
- 2 cups Quinoa, cooked

Directions:
1. Mix together the eggs, salt, pepper, garlic, onion powder, and yogurt.

2. Cook the spinach and tomatoes for 5 minutes in the olive oil on moderate heat. Pour in the egg mix and stir until eggs have set to your preferred doneness.
3. Stir in quinoa and feta until they are hot. This will store in your refrigerator for two to three days.

Nutritional Info: Calories 340 , 7.3 grams Fat , 59.4 grams carbs , 6.2 grams fiber , 21.4 grams sugar , 10.5 grams protein.

RAISIN BRAN MUFFINS

Time To Prepare: fifteen minutes

Time to Cook: thirty minutes

Yield: Servings 36

Ingredients:
- ½ cup vegetable oil
- 1 cup boiling water
- 1 cup bran flakes
- 1 cup sugar
- 1 teaspoon salt
- 1½ cups raisins
- 2 cups buttermilk
- 2 eggs, beaten
- 2½ cups All-Bran cereal
- 2½ cups all-purpose flour
- 2½ teaspoons baking soda

Directions:
1. Set the to 400°F.
2. Grease a muffin tin. Place the boiling water over 1 cup All-Bran, and allow it to sit for about ten minutes.
3. Put the baking soda, flour, and salt in a mixing container then mix, set aside.
4. Mix the oil into the bran and water mixture, then put the rest of the bran, sugar, eggs, and buttermilk.
5. Place the flour mixture to the bran mixture and mix to blend. Mix in the raisins and bran flakes then fill the muffin cups ¾ full with the batter.
6. Bake muffins for about twenty minutes.

Nutritional Info: Calories: 104 , Fat: 4 g , Protein: 2.5 g , Sodium: 187 mg , Fiber: 2 g , Carbohydrates: 17 g

SALMON BURGERS

Time To Prepare: fifteen minutes

Time to Cook: 8 minutes

Yield: Servings 3

Ingredients:
- ½ of a medium onion, chopped
- 1 (6-oz. can) skinless, boneless salmon, drained
- 1 celery rib, chopped
- 1 tablespoon dried dill, crushed
- 1 tablespoon plus 1 teaspoon coconut flour
- 1 teaspoon lemon
- 2 big eggs
- 3 tablespoons coconut oil
- Freshly ground black pepper, to taste
- Salt, to taste

Directions:
1. In a substantial container, put in salmon and which has a fork, break it into little pieces.
2. Put in rest of the ingredients excluding the for oil and mix till well blended.
3. Make 6 equal sized small patties from the mixture.
4. In a substantial frying pan, melt coconut oil on moderate to high heat.
5. Cook the patties for about four minutes per side.

Nutritional Info: Calories: 393 , Fat: 12g , Carbohydrates: 19g , Fiber: 5g , Protein: 24g

SAUTÉED VEGGIES ON HOT BAGELS

Time To Prepare: ten minutes

Time to Cook: 16 minutes

Yield: Servings 2

Ingredients:
- ½ onion, cut thin
- 1 clove of garlic, chopped
- 1 tbsp. olive oil
- 1 yellow squash, diced
- 1 zucchini, cut thin
- 2 pcs. tomatoes, cut
- 2 pcs. vegan bagels
- salt and pepper to taste
- vegan butter for spread

Directions:
1. Heat the olive oil on the medium temperature in a cast-iron frying pan.
2. Reduce the heat to moderate-low and sauté the onions for about ten minutes or until the onions start to brown.
3. Turn the heat again to moderate and then put in the diced squash and zucchini to the pan and cook for five minutes. Put in the clove of garlic and cook for one more minute.
4. Throw in the tomato slices to the pan and cook for a minute. Flavor it with pepper and salt and remove the heat.

5. Toast the bagels and cut in half.
6. Spread the bagels lightly with butter and serve with the sautéed veggies on top.

Nutritional Info: Calories: 375 kcal , Protein: 14.69 g , Fat: 11.46 g , Carbohydrates: 54.61 g

SAVORY BREAD

Time To Prepare: ten minutes

Time to Cook: 20 minutes

Yield: Servings 8-10

Ingredients:
- ½ cup plus 1tablespoon almond flour
- 1 cup raw cashew butter
- 1 tablespoon apple cider vinegar
- 1 tablespoon water
- 1 teaspoon ground turmeric
- 1 tsp. baking soda
- 2 big organic eggs
- 2 organic egg whites
- Salt, to taste

Directions:
1. Set the oven to 350F. Grease a loaf pan.
2. In a big pan, combine flour, baking soda, turmeric, and salt.
3. In another container, put in eggs, egg whites, and cashew butter and beat till smooth.
4. Slowly, put in water and beat till well blended.
5. Put in flour mixture and mix till well blended.
6. Mix in apple cider vinegar treatment.
7. Put a combination into prepared loaf pan uniformly.
8. Bake for around 20 minutes or till a toothpick inserted within the middle is released clean.

Nutritional Info: Calories: 347 , Fat: 11g , Carbohydrates: 29g , Fiber: 6g , Protein: 21g

SAVORY VEGGIE MUFFINS

Time To Prepare: fifteen minutes

Time to Cook: 18-23 minutes

Yield: Servings 5

Ingredients:
- ¼ cup concentrate powder
- ½ cup fresh parsley, chopped
- ½ tsp baking soda
- ¾ cup almond meal
- 1 bunch scallion, chopped

- 1 cup coconut butter, softened
- 1½ tablespoons nutritional yeast
- 2 medium carrots, peeled and grated
- 2 tablespoons coconut oil, melted
- 2 teaspoons apple cider vinegar
- 2 teaspoons fresh dill, chopped
- 3 tablespoons fresh lemon juice
- 4 big organic eggs
- Salt, to taste

Directions:
1. Set the oven to 350F. Grease 10 cups of your big muffin tin.
2. In a big container, combine flour, baking soda , Protein: powder, and salt.
3. In another container, put in eggs, nutritional yeast, vinegar, lemon juice, and oil and beat till well blended.
4. Put in coconut butter and beat till the mixture becomes smooth.
5. Put egg mixture into the flour mixture and mix till well blended.
6. Fold in scallion, carts, and parsley.
7. Put the amalgamation into prepared muffin cups uniformly.
8. Bake for approximately 18-23 minutes or till a toothpick inserted inside center comes out clean.

Nutritional Info: Calories: 378 , Fat: 13g , Carbohydrates: 32g , Fiber: 11g , Protein: 32g

SHIRATAKI PASTA WITH AVOCADO AND CREAM

Time To Prepare: ten minutes

Time to Cook: six minutes

Yield: Servings 2

Ingredients:
- ½ of an avocado
- ½ packet of shirataki noodles, cooked
- ½ tsp cracked black pepper
- ½ tsp dried basil
- ½ tsp salt
- 1/8 cup heavy cream

Directions:
1. Put a medium pot half full with water on moderate heat, bring it to boil, then put in noodles and cook for a couple of minutes.
2. Then drain the noodles and set aside until required.
3. Put avocado in a container, purée it using a fork,

4. Mash avocado in a container, move it to a blender, put in rest of the ingredients, and pulse until the desired smoothness is achieved.
5. Take a frying pan, place it on moderate heat and when hot, put in noodles in it, pour in the avocado mixture, stir thoroughly and cook for a couple of minutes until hot.
6. Serve straight away.

Nutritional Info: Calories 131 , Total Fat: 12.6g , Carbs: 4.9g , Protein: 1.2g , Sugar: 0.3g , Sodium: 588mg

SPICY GINGER CREPES

Time To Prepare: fifteen minutes

Time to Cook: 20 Minutes

Yield: Servings 8

Ingredients:
- ½ teaspoon red chili powder
- 1 (1-inch) fresh ginger piece, grated finely
- 1 1/3 cups chickpea flour
- 1 cup fresh cilantro leaves, chopped
- 1 cup water
- 1 green chili, seeded and chopped finely
- Cooking spray, as required
- Salt, to taste

Directions:
1. In a sizable container, combine flour, chili powder, and salt.
2. Put in ginger, cilantro, and chili and mix thoroughly.
3. Put in water and mix till a uniform mixture form.
4. Keep aside, covered for roughly ½-2 hours.
5. Lightly, grease a substantial nonstick frying pan with cooking spray and heat on moderate to high heat.
6. Put in the desired volume of the mixture and tilt the pan to spread it uniformly inside the frying pan.
7. Cook roughly 10-fifteen seconds per side.
8. Repeat while using the rest of the mixture.

Nutritional Info: Calories: 73 , Fat: 1.3 , Carbohydrates: 11g , Fiber: 2.1g, , Protein: 4.3g

SPICY MARBLE EGGS

Time To Prepare: fifteen minutes

Time to Cook: 2 hours

Yield: Servings 12

Ingredients:

- 1 dried cinnamon stick, whole
- 1 thumb-sized fresh ginger, unpeeled, crushed
- 1 tsp. dried Szechuan peppercorns
- 1 tsp. salt
- 2 dried bay leaves
- 2 oolong black tea bags
- 3 dried star anise, whole
- 3 Tbsp. brown sugar
- 3 Tbsp. light soy sauce
- 4 cups of water
- 4 Tbsp. dark soy sauce
- 6 medium-boiled eggs, unpeeled, cooled
- For the Marinade

Directions:
1. Use the back of a spoon to crack eggshells in places to create a spider web effect. Do not peel. Set aside until needed.
2. Pour marinade into big Dutch oven set using high heat. Put lid partly on. Bring water to a rolling boil, approximately five minutes. Turn off heat.
3. Close the lid. Steep ingredients for about ten minutes.
4. Use a slotted spoon to fish out and discard solids. Cool marinade completely to room proceeding.
5. Put eggs into an airtight non-reactive container just small enough to tightly fit all these in.
6. Pour in marinade. Eggs must be completely immersed in liquid. Discard leftover marinade, if any. Coat container rim with generous layers of saran wrap. Secure container lid.
7. Chill eggs for one day before you use.
8. Extract eggs and drain each piece well before you use, but keep the rest immersed in the marinade.

Nutritional Info: Calories: 75 kcal , Protein: 4.05 g , Fat: 4.36 g , Carbohydrates: 4.83 g

SPINACH MUSHROOM OMELET

Time To Prepare: three minutes

Time to Cook: fifteen minutes

Yield: Servings 2

Ingredients:
- ¼ Red onion, diced
- 1 ½ cup Spinach, fresh, chopped
- 1 Green onion, diced
- 1 oz. Feta cheese
- 2 tbsp. Olive oil,
- 3 Eggs
- 5 Mushrooms, button, cut

Directions:
1. Sauté the mushrooms, onions, and spinach for 3 minutes in one tablespoon of olive oil and set aside.
2. Beat the eggs thoroughly and cook them in the other tablespoon of olive oil for three to four minutes until edges start to brown. Drizzle all the other ingredients onto half of the omelet and fold the other half over the sautéed ingredients. Cook for a minute on each side.

Nutritional Info: Calories 337 , 25 grams Fat , 22 grams Protein , 5.4 grams carbs , 1.3 grams sugar , 1 gram fiber

SPINACH MUSHROOM OMELET

Time To Prepare: three minutes

Time to Cook: fifteen minutes

Yield: Servings 2

Ingredients:
- ¼ cup Red onion, diced
- ½ Spinach, fresh, chopped
- ½ tsp. Salt
- 1 Green onion, diced
- 1 oz. Feta cheese
- 1 tbsp. Olive oil
- 3 Egg
- 5 Mushrooms, button, cut

Directions:
1. Sauté the mushrooms, onions, and spinach for four minutes and set them aside. Beat eggs meticulously and pour into the frying pan. Cook for three to four minutes until edges start to turn brown.
2. Drizzle all other ingredients onto half of the omelet and fold the other half over. Cook the omelet for a minute on each side.

Nutritional Info: Calories 337 , 22 grams Protein , 25 grams Fat , 1.3 grams sugar , 5.4 grams carbs , 1 gram fiber

STRAWBERRIES AND CREAM TRIFLE

Time To Prepare: 10 Minutes

Time to Cook: 45 Minutes

Yield: Servings 12

Ingredients:
- 1 ½ cups condensed milk
- 1 angel food cake, cubed
- 12 ounces frozen whipped cream, thawed

- 3 pints fresh strawberries, hulled and cut
- 6 ounces packaged cream cheese, softened

Directions:
1. In a container, put together the cream cheese, sweetened condensed milk, and whip in until the desired smoothness is achieved.
2. In a trifle container, place a layer of angel food cake cubes. Put in a layer of strawberries and cream on top. Repeat the layers.
3. Bring it in your fridge to cool for minimum thirty-five minutes.

Nutritional Info: Calories: 378 , Fat: 17g , Carbohydrates: 51g , Protein: 7g

STRAWBERRY YOGURT TREAT

Time To Prepare: ten minutes

Time to Cook: 0 minutes

Yield: Servings 2

Ingredients:
- 1 cup cut strawberries
- 4 cups 0% Fat plain yogurt
- 4 tbsp. honey
- 8 tbsp. of flax meal
- 8 tbsp. walnuts (chopped)

Directions:
1. Distribute 2 cups of the yogurt into your serving bowls. Neatly layer the flax meal and the walnut in the center.
2. Put in a sprinkle of half of the honey before covering with the final layer of yogurt. Put in the honey on top of the yogurt to put in color when you serve.

Nutritional Info: Calories: 733 kcal , Protein: 38.42 g , Fat: 30.57 g , Carbohydrates: 83.44 g

STRAWBERRY-OAT-CHOCOLATE CHIP MUFFINS

Time To Prepare: ten minutes

Time to Cook: 23 minutes

Yield: Servings 12

Ingredients:
- ¼ tsp. salt
- ½ c. unsweetened vanilla almond milk
- ½ tsp. Baking powder
- ¾ tsp. Baking soda
- 1 c. rolled oats

- 1 egg
- 1 egg white
- 1 heaping cup bananas (approximately two to three big very ripe bananas)
- 1 tbsp. extra virgin olive oil
- 1 tbsp. honey or agave nectar
- 1 tsp. vanilla
- 1/3 c. mini chocolate chips
- 1/3 c. nonfat plain Greek yogurt
- 1¼ c. whole wheat pastry flour
- 12 thin slices of strawberries (about 3-4 strawberries) for decoration, if you wish
- 2/3 c. diced strawberries

Directions:

1. Set the oven to 350°F and mildly grease a standard 12-cup muffin pan or grease with paper liners. In a large-sized mixing container, mix flour, oats, baking powder, baking soda, and salt. Stir to blend. Set aside the 2 tbsp. of the mixture.
2. In a different huge mixing container, mix together the mashed banana, olive oil, honey, and vanilla. After this, beat in the egg and egg white and beat until blended. Now put in in Greek yogurt and almond milk and beat using an electric mixer on low until the desired smoothness is achieved.
3. Slowly put wet ingredients to dry ingredients and blend until just blended, but do not over mix the batter as it will make the muffins firm.
4. Fill each muffin cup 2/3 full of batter. Lightly tap the pan on the counter to even out the batter. Put a thin slice of strawberry onto each muffin, if you wish. Place the pan in your oven, then cook for eighteen to 23 minutes, up to a toothpick place in the center of the muffins, and comes out clean. Remove from the oven and allow it to sit for five to ten minutes in the pan before placing on a cooling rack.

Nutritional Info: Calories: 91 kcal , Protein: 4.02 g , Fat: 2.63 g , Carbohydrates: 16.31 g

SUN-DRIED TOMATO GARLIC BRUSCHETTA

Time To Prepare: ten minutes

Time to Cook: five minutes

Yield: Servings 6

Ingredients:
- 1 garlic clove, peeled
- 1 tsp. chives, minced
- 1 tsp. olive oil
- 2 slices sourdough bread, toasted
- 2 tsp. sun-dried tomatoes in olive oil, minced

Directions:

1. Vigorously rub garlic clove on 1 side of each of the toasted bread slices
2. Spread equivalent portions of sun-dried tomatoes on the garlic side of bread. Drizzle chives and sprinkle olive oil on top.
3. Pop both slices into oven toaster, and cook until well thoroughly heated.
4. Put bruschetta on a plate. Serve warm.

Nutritional Info: Calories: 149 kcal , Protein: 6.12 g , Fat: 2.99 g , Carbohydrates: 24.39 g

SWEET ONION AND EGG PIE

Time To Prepare: 20 Minutes

Time to Cook: 35 Minutes

Yield: Servings 10

Ingredients:
- 1 cup vaporized milk
- 1 tablespoons butter
- 11 frozen deep-dish pie crust
- 2 sweet onions, halved and cut
- 6 eggs
- Salt and pepper to taste

Directions:
1. Preheat your oven 4000F.
2. Melt the butter in a non-stick frying pan. Sauté the onions on moderate to low heat until super soft.
3. Put the onions in a container. Put in in eggs and vaporized milk. Sprinkle with salt and pepper to taste.
4. Pour the egg and onion mixture into the commercial pie crust.
5. Bake using your oven for a little more than half an hour.

Nutritional Info: Calories: 169 , Fat: 7g , Carbohydrates: 21g

SWEETENED BROWN RICE

Time To Prepare: ten minutes

Time to Cook: 45-60 minutes

Yield: Servings 8

Ingredients:
- ¼ teaspoon nutmeg
- 1 cup brown rice
- 1 tablespoon honey
- 1½ cups soy milk
- 1½ cups water
- Fresh fruit (not necessary)

Directions:
1. Put all the ingredients excluding the fresh fruit in a medium-size deep cooking pan; put the mixture to a slow simmer then cover using a tight-fitting lid.
2. Simmer for minimum 45-60 minutes, up to the rice is soft and done. Serve in bowls, topped with your favorite fresh fruit.

Nutritional Info: Calories: 155 , Fat: 1.5 g , Protein: 3.5 g , Sodium: 35 mg , Fiber: 1.5 g , Carbohydrates: 13 g

SWISS CHARD AND SPINACH WITH EGG

Time To Prepare: five minutes

Time to Cook: ten minutes

Yield: Servings 4

Ingredients:
- 1 tsp. olive oil
- 20 pieces spinach leaves
- 20 pieces Swiss chard leaves
- 4 egg whites
- 4 pieces of rice bread
- 4 tbsp. parsley (fresh)
- Sea salt, ground pepper, and dried mint

Directions:
1. Bring to its boiling point 2 cups of water in a pan just below the boiling point. Open an egg, separate the whites from the yolks. Place the whites in a small container. Lower the container towards the heated water, and gently pour the egg into the pan. Do the same with the other eggs. Poach the eggs for about four minutes. Next, gently take the eggs, one by one and move them into a plate. Do the same with the rest of the 2 eggs.
2. Cut the parsley and sauté the leaves in a pan for about six minutes. Toast the bread while doing this. When finished, make a layer of the sautéed greens and the chopped parsley on top of the toasted rice bread. Place the poached eggs above the bed of greens. Drizzle each serving with ground pepper, sea salt, and dried mint.

Nutritional Info: Calories: 49 kcal , Protein: 5.31 g , Fat: 2.73 g , Carbohydrates: 0.48 g

TOMATO AND AVOCADO OMELET

Time To Prepare: five minutes

Time to Cook: five minutes

Yield: Servings 1

Ingredients:

- ¼ avocado, diced
- 1 tablespoon cilantro, chopped
- 2 eggs
- 4 cherry tomatoes, halved
- Pinch of salt
- Squeeze of lime juice

Directions:

1. Put together the avocado, tomatoes, cilantro, lime juice, and salt in a small container, then mix thoroughly and save for later.
2. Warm a moderate-sized nonstick frying pan on moderate heat. Whisk the eggs until frothy and put in to the pan. Move the eggs around gently using a rubber spatula until they start to set.
3. Spread the avocado mixture over half of the omelet. Turn off the heat, and slide the omelet onto a plate as you fold it in half.
4. Serve instantly.

Nutritional Info: Calories: 433 kcal , Protein: 25.55 g , Fat: 32.75 g , Carbohydrates: 10.06 g

TOMATO OMELET

Time To Prepare: two minutes

Time to Cook: 8 minutes

Yield: Servings 1

Ingredients:

- ¼ cup Cheese, any type, shredded
- ½ cup Basil, fresh
- ½ cup Cherry tomatoes
- ½ tsp. Salt
- 1 tsp. Black pepper
- 2 Eggs
- 2 tbsp. Olive oil

Directions:

1. Chop the tomatoes into four equivalent portions. Fry the tomatoes for around three hours.
2. Set the tomatoes off to the side. Put in the salt and pepper to the eggs in a small container and beat together well. Pour the mix of beaten egg into the pan and use a spatula to gently work around the edges under the omelet, letting the eggs fry unmoved for 3 minutes.
3. When just the center third of the egg mix is still runny, put in on the basil, tomatoes, and cheese. Fold over half of the omelet onto the other half. Cook two more minutes before you serve.

Nutritional Info: Calories 342 , 8 grams carbs , 20 grams Protein , 25.3 grams fat

TUNA & SWEET POTATO CROQUETTES

Time To Prepare: fifteen minutes

Time to Cook: twelve minutes

Yield: Servings 8

Ingredients:
- ¼ cup almond flour
- ¼ cup tapioca flour
- ¼ teaspoon garam masala
- ¼ teaspoon ground turmeric
- ¼ teaspoon red chili powder
- ½ big onion, chopped
- ½ teaspoon ground coriander
- 1 (1-inch piece fresh ginger, minced
- 1 cup sweet potato, peeled and mashed
- 1 egg
- 1 Serrano pepper, seeded and minced
- 1 tablespoon coconut oil
- 2 (5 oz.) cans tuna
- 3 garlic cloves, minced
- Freshly ground black pepper, to taste
- Olive oil, as required
- Salt, to taste

Directions:
1. In a frying pan, warm the coconut oil on moderate heat.
2. Put onion, ginger, garlic, and Serrano pepper and sauté for roughly 5-6 minutes.
3. Mix in spices and sauté roughly one minute more.
4. Move the onion mixture in a container.
5. Put in tuna and sweet potato and mix till well blended.
6. Make equal sized oblong shaped patties in the mixture.
7. Position the croquettes inside a baking sheet in a very single layer and place in your fridge for overnight.
8. In a shallow dish, beat the egg.
9. In another shallow dish, combine both flours.
10. In a big frying pan, heat the enough oil.
11. Put in croquettes in batches and shallow fry for about two to three minutes per side.

Nutritional Info: Calories: 404 , Fat: 9g , Carbohydrates: 20g , Fiber: 4g , Protein: 30g

TURKEY BURGERS

Time To Prepare: fifteen minutes

Time to Cook: 8 minutes

Yield: Servings 5

Ingredients:
- 1 ripe pear, peeled, cored and chopped roughly
- 1 teaspoon fresh ginger, grated finely
- 1 teaspoon fresh rosemary, minced
- 1 teaspoon fresh sage, minced
- 1-2 tablespoons coconut oil
- 1-pound lean ground turkey
- 2 minced garlic cloves
- Freshly ground black pepper, to taste
- Salt, to taste

Directions:
1. In a blender, put in pear and pulse till smooth.
2. Move the pear mixture in a big container with rest of the ingredients except for oil and mix till well blended.
3. Make small equal sized 10 patties from the mixture.
4. In a heavy-bottomed frying pan, heat oil on moderate heat.
5. Put in the patties and cook for about five minutes.
6. Flip the inside and cook for roughly 2-3 minutes.

Nutritional Info: Calories: 477 , Fat: 15g , Carbohydrates: 26g , Fiber: 11g , Protein: 35g

VEGAN-FRIENDLY BANANA BREAD

Time To Prepare: fifteen minutes

Time to Cook: forty minutes

Yield: Servings 4-6

Ingredients:
- 2 ripe bananas, mashed
- 3 tbsp. chia seeds
- 6 tbsp. water
- ½ cup tender vegan butter
- ½ cup maple syrup
- 2 cups flour
- 2 tsp. baking powder
- 1 tsp. cinnamon powder
- 1 tsp. allspice
- ½ tsp. salt

- 1/3 cup brewed coffee

Directions:
1. Set oven at 350F.
2. Bring the chia seeds in a small container then soak it with 6 tbsp. of water. Stir thoroughly and save for later.
3. In a mixing container, mix using a hand mixer the vegan butter and maple syrup until it turns fluffy. Put in the chia seeds together with the mashed bananas.
4. Mix thoroughly and then put in the coffee.
5. In the meantime, sift all the dry ingredients (flour, baking powder, cinnamon powder, all spice, and salt) and then progressively put in into the container with the wet ingredients.
6. Mix the ingredients well and then pour over a baking pan coated with parchment paper.
7. Put in your oven to bake for minimum 30-40 minutes, or until the toothpick comes out clean after inserting in the bread.
8. Let the bread cool before you serve.

Nutritional Info: Calories: 371 kcal , Protein: 5.59 g , Fat: 16.81 g , Carbohydrates: 49.98 g

VEGGIE BALLS

Time To Prepare: fifteen minutes

Time to Cook: twenty-five minutes

Yield: Servings 5-6

Ingredients:
- ¼ tsp. ground turmeric
- ½ teaspoon granulated garlic
- 1 cup fresh kale leaves, trimmed and chopped
- 1 medium shallot, chopped finely
- 1 tsp. ground cumin
- 2 medium sweet potatoes, cubed into ½-inch size
- 2 tablespoons coconut milk
- Freshly ground black pepper, to taste
- Ground flax seeds, as required
- Salt, to taste

Directions:
1. Set the oven to 400°F. Coat a baking sheet using parchment paper.
2. In a pan of water, position a steamer basket.
3. Bring the sweet potato in a steamer basket and steam roughly 10-fifteen minutes.
4. In a sizable container, put the sweet potato.
5. Put in coconut milk and purée well.
6. Put in rest of the ingredients except for flax seeds and mix till well blended.
7. Make approximately 1½-2-inch balls from your mixture.
8. Position the balls onto the readied baking sheet inside a single layer.
9. Drizzle with flax seeds.

10. Bake for around 20-twenty-five minutes.

Nutritional Info: Calories: 464 , Fat: 12g , Carbohydrates: 20g , Fiber: 8g , Protein: 27g

WEEKEND BREAKFAST SALAD

Time To Prepare: thirty minutes

Time to Cook: 0 minutes

Yield: Servings 4

Ingredients:
- ½ cup Cucumber, chopped
- ½ cup Dill, chopped
- 1 cup Almonds, chopped
- 1 cup Quinoa, cooked and cooled
- 1 Large Avocado, cut thin
- 1 Large Tomato, cut in wedges
- 1 Lemon
- 10 cups Arugula
- 2 tbsp. Olive oil
- 4 Eggs, hard-boiled

Directions:
1. Mix together the quinoa, cucumber, tomatoes, and arugula. Toss these ingredients lightly with olive oil, salt, and pepper. Split the salad into 4 plates and position the egg and avocado on top. Top each salad with almonds and herbs.
2. Sprinkle with juice from the lemon.

Nutritional Info: Calories 336 , 7.7 grams Fat , 12.3 grams Protein , 54.6 grams carbs , 5.5 grams sugar , 5.2 grams fiber ,

WHITE AND GREEN QUICHE

Time To Prepare: ten minutes

Time to Cook: forty minutes

Yield: Servings 3

Ingredients:
- 1 ½ cups of coconut milk
- 1 ½ teaspoon of baking powder
- 1 small sized onion, finely chopped
- 3 cloves of garlic, minced
- 3 cups of fresh spinach, chopped
- 5 white mushrooms, cut
- fifteen big free-range eggs
- Ghee, as required to grease the dish

- Ground black pepper to taste
- Sea salt to taste

Directions:
1. Set the oven to 350°F.
2. Get a baking dish then grease it with the organic ghee.
3. Break all the eggs in a huge container then whisk well.
4. Mix in coconut milk. Beat well
5. While you are whisking the eggs, start putting in the rest of the ingredients in it.
6. When all the ingredients are completely mixed, pour all of it into the readied baking dish.
7. Bake for minimum forty minutes, up to the quiche is set in the center.
8. Enjoy!

Nutritional Info: Calories: 608 kcal , Protein: 20.28 g , Fat: 53.42 g , Carbohydrates: 16.88 g

WHOLE GRAIN BLUEBERRY SCONES

Time To Prepare: ten minutes

Time to Cook: twenty-five minutes

Yield: Servings 8

Ingredients:
- ¼ cup maple syrup
- ½ teaspoon sea salt
- 1 cup blueberries
- 1 teaspoon vanilla extract
- 2 cups of whole-wheat flour
- 2 tablespoons of coconut milk
- 2½ teaspoons baking powder
- 6 tablespoons of olive oil

Directions:
1. Set the oven 400°F. Place parchment paper on your baking sheet.
2. Put in the syrup, flour, salt, and baking powder in a container. Mix well by whisking together.
3. Pour the olive oil into a container with the dry ingredients.
4. Work the oil into your flour mix.
5. Mix the vanilla extract and coconut milk into the dry ingredients container.
6. Fold in the blueberries gently. Your dough must be sticky and thick.
7. Put some flour on your hand then mold the dough into a circle.
8. Use a knife to make triangle slices.
9. Place them over the baking sheet. Maintain an 8-inch gap.
10. Bake for about twenty-five minutes. Set aside on the baking sheet for cooling when finished.

Nutritional Info: Calories 331 , Carbohydrates: 27g , Cholesterol: 0mg , Total Fat: 23g , Protein: 4g , Fiber: 4g , Sugar: 8g

YOGURT CHEESE AND FRUIT

Time To Prepare: ten minutes

Time to Cook: 0 minutes

Yield: Servings 6

Ingredients:
- ¼ cup dried cranberries or raisins
- ¼ cup honey
- ½ cup orange juice
- ½ cup water
- 1 fresh Golden Delicious apple
- 1 fresh pear
- 1 teaspoon fresh lemon juice
- 3 cups plain nonfat yogurt

Directions:
1. Prepare the yogurt cheese the day before by lining a colander or strainer with cheesecloth. Scoop the yogurt into the cheesecloth, put the strainer over a pot or container to catch the whey, and place in your fridge for minimum 8 hours before you serve.
2. In a huge mixing container, combine the juices and water. Chop the apple then pear into wedges, put the wedges in the juice mixture, allow it to sit for minimum five minutes. Strain off the liquid.
3. When the yogurt is firm, remove from fridge, slice, and place on plates. Position the fruit wedges around the yogurt. Sprinkle with honey and drizzle with cranberries or raisins just before you serve.

Nutritional Info: Calories: 177 , Fat: 1 g , Protein: 6.5 g , Sodium: 87 mg , Fiber: 2 g , Carbohydrates: 35 g

YUMMY STEAK MUFFINS

Time To Prepare: ten minutes

Time to Cook: twenty minutes

Yield: Servings 4

Ingredients:
- ¼ teaspoon of sea salt
- 1 cup of finely diced onion
- 1 cup red bell pepper, diced
- 2 Tablespoons of water
- 8 free-range eggs
- 8 ounce thin steak, cooked and finely chopped
- Dash of freshly ground black pepper

Directions:

1. Set the oven to 350°F
2. Take 8 muffin tins and line then using parchment paper liners.
3. Get a big container and crack all the eggs in it.
4. Beat well the eggs.
5. Blend in all the rest of the ingredients.
6. Ladle the batter into the position muffin tins. Fill three-fourth of each tin.
7. Place the muffin tins in the preheated oven for approximately twenty minutes, until the muffins are baked and set in the center.
8. Enjoy!

Nutritional Info: Calories: 151 kcal , Protein: 17.92 g , Fat: 7.32 g , Carbohydrates: 3.75 g

ZUCCHINI BREAD

Time To Prepare: ten minutes

Time to Cook: 60 minutes

Yield: Servings 16

Ingredients:
- ¼ teaspoon baking powder
- 1 cup canola oil
- 1 cup chopped pecans
- 1 cup raisins
- 1 tablespoon cinnamon
- 1 teaspoon baking soda
- 1 teaspoon salt
- 1½ cups 100% whole-wheat flour
- 1½ cups all-purpose flour
- 2 cups grated zucchini
- 2 cups sugar
- 3 eggs, beaten, or ¾ cup of egg substitute

Directions:
1. Preheat your oven to 350°F. Oil 2 loaf pans and save for later.
2. Put and mix the flour, salt, baking soda, baking powder, and cinnamon in a container.
3. Combine the eggs, oil, and sugar in a different container.
4. Put in the zucchini and dry ingredients alternately until fully blended into a smooth batter. Fold in the pecans and raisins and scrape the batter into the loaf pans.
5. Bake for 60 minutes, cool on a rack, and wrap when cool.

Nutritional Info: Calories: 396 , Fat: 20 , Protein: 5 g , Sodium: 237 mg , Fiber: 3 g , Carbohydrates: 52 g

ZUCCHINI PANCAKES

Time To Prepare: fifteen minutes

Time to Cook: 6-10 min

Yield: Servings 8

Ingredients:
- ¼ cup fresh cilantro, chopped
- ¼ teaspoon cumin seeds
- ¼ teaspoon ground turmeric
- ¼ tsp cayenne
- ½ cup red onion, chopped finely
- ½ cup zucchini, shredded
- 1 cup chickpea flour
- 1 green chile, seeded and chopped finely
- 1½ cups water, divided
- Salt, to taste

Directions:
1. In a big container, put in flour and ¾ cup with the water and beat till smooth.
2. Put in remaining water and beat till a thin
3. Fold inside the onion, ginger, Serrano pepper, and cilantro.
4. Lightly, grease a substantial nonstick frying pan with oil and heat on medium-low heat.
5. Put in about ¼ cup of mixture and tilt the pan to spread it uniformly in the frying pan.
6. Cook for around 4-6 minutes.
7. Cautiously, alter the side and cook for roughly 2-4 minutes.
8. Repeat while using the rest of the mixture.
9. Serve with your desired topping.

Nutritional Info: Calories: 389 , Fat: 13g , Carbohydrates: 25g , Fiber: 4g , Protein: 21g

ALMOND BLUEBERRY SMOOTHIE

Time To Prepare: ten minutes

Time to Cook: 0 minutes

Yield: Servings 1

Ingredients:
- 1 banana
- 1 cup frozen blueberries
- 1 tbsp. almond butter
- 1/2 cup almond milk
- Water, as required

Directions:
1. Put in everything to a blender jug.
2. Cover the jug firmly.
3. Blend until the desired smoothness is achieved. Serve and enjoy!

Nutritional Info: Calories: 211 , Fat: 0.2 g , Protein: 5.6 g , Carbohydrates: 3.4 g , Fiber: 2.3 g

ALMOND BUTTER SMOOTHIES

Time To Prepare: five minutes

Time to Cook: 0 minutes

Yield: Servings 1

Ingredients:
- 1 banana, if possible frozen for a creamier shake
- 1 cup of hemp milk
- 1 scoop of hemp protein
- 1 Tablespoon natural almond butter
- few ice cubes

Directions:

Blend all ingredients together and enjoy!

Nutritional Info: Calories: 533 kcal , Protein: 31.23 g , Fat: 26.31 g , Carbohydrates: 47.13 g

APPLE CINNAMON WATER

Time To Prepare: five minutes

Time to Cook: five minutes

Yield: Servings 4

Ingredients:
- 1 whole apple, diced
- 5 cinnamon sticks
- Water to cover contents

Directions:
1. Put ingredients in the steamer basket. Put in pot.
2. Put in water cover contents.
3. Secure the lid. Cook on HIGH pressure five minutes.
4. When done, depressurize swiftly.
5. Remove steamer basket. Discard cooked produce.
6. Let flavored water cool. Chill completely before you serve.

Nutritional Info: Calories: 194 , Fat: 0g , Carbohydrates: 12g , Protein: 0g

BABY KALE PINEAPPLE SMOOTHIE

Time To Prepare: five minutes

Time to Cook: 0 minutes

Yield: Servings 1

Ingredients:

- 1 cup almond milk
- 1 cup Kale
- 1 tablespoon hemp protein powder
- 1/2 cup frozen pineapple

Directions:

Put the almond milk, pineapple, and greens in the blender and blend until the desired smoothness is achieved.

Nutritional Info: Calories: 389 kcal , Protein: 20.29 g , Fat: 16.2 g , Carbohydrates: 42.29 g

BEET AND CHERRY SMOOTHIE

Time To Prepare: five minutes

Time to Cook: 0 minutes

Yield: Servings 4

Ingredients:
- ½ cup frozen cherries, pitted
- ½ teaspoon frozen banana
- 1 tablespoon almond butter
- 10-ounce almond milk, unsweetened
- 2 small beets, peeled and slice into four

Directions:
1. Put in all ingredients in a blender.
2. Blend until the desired smoothness is achieved.

Nutritional Info: Calories 470 , Carbohydrates: 24 g , Fat: 38 g , Protein: 16 g

BEET SMOOTHIE

Time To Prepare: ten minutes

Time to Cook: 0 minutes

Yield: Servings 2

Ingredients:
- 1 tbsp. almond butter
- 1/2 banana, peeled and frozen
- 1/2 cup cherries, pitted
- 10 oz. almond milk, unsweetened
- 2 beets, peeled and quartered

Directions:
1. In your blender, combine the milk with the beets, banana, cherries, and butter.
2. Pulse thoroughly, pour into glasses, before you serve. Enjoy!

Nutritional Info: Calories: 165 , Fat: 5 g , Protein: 5 g , Carbohydrates: 22 g , Fiber: 6 g

BERRY SHRUB

Time To Prepare: ten minutes

Time to Cook: twenty minutes

Yield: Servings 4

Ingredients:
- ½ a cup of chopped fresh oregano
- 1 cup of dried elderberries
- 2 cups of apple cider vinegar
- 2 cups of honey
- 2 cups of water

Directions:
1. Put in listed ingredients to the instant pot.
2. Secure the lid. Cook on HIGH pressure twenty minutes.
3. When done, depressurize naturally.
4. Pour ingredients through a sieve into a jar.
5. Let cool down. Chill.

Nutritional Info: Calories: 127 , Fat: 0g , Carbohydrates: 6g , Protein: 0g

BLACKBERRY & GINGER MILKSHAKE

Time To Prepare: five minutes

Time to Cook: 0 minutes

Yield: Servings 2

Ingredients:
- 1 thumb-sized piece of ginger, grated
- 2 cups of almond milk
- 2 cups of blackberries, washed
- 2 cups of chopped peaches

Directions:
1. Combine all ingredients to a blender or juicer and blend until the desired smoothness is achieved.
2. Serve with a scattering of fresh blackberries and enjoy!

Nutritional Info: Calories: 619 kcal , Protein: fifteen.42 g , Fat: 11.63 g , Carbohydrates: 123.04 g

BLACKBERRY ITALIAN DRINK

Time To Prepare: five minutes

Time to Cook: fifteen minutes

Yield: Servings 4

Ingredients:
- 1 bottle sparkling water
- 1 cup blackberries
- 1 lemon, cut
- 2 tbsp. honey

Directions:
1. Put in 1 cup (non-carbonated) water to the instant pot.
2. Put in blackberries to the instant pot.
3. Secure the lid. Cook on HIGH pressure ten minutes.
4. When done, depressurize naturally.
5. Mash the berries in the instant pot. Move to dish. Let cool.
6. As blackberries cook, in a separate small deep cooking pan with a heavy bottom. Put in honey. Simmer five minutes. Cool down.
7. To make the drink. Ladle 1 teaspoon honey. Pour in fruit mixture. Put in carbonated water. Stir.

Nutritional Info: Calories: 249 , Fat: 0.6g , Carbohydrates: 55g , Protein: 7.5g

BLENDED COCONUT MILK AND BANANA BREAKFAST SMOOTHIE

Time To Prepare: ten minutes

Time to Cook: 0 minutes

Yield: Servings 4

Ingredients:
- 2 cups almond milk
- 2 cups coconut milk
- 4 ripe moderate-sized bananas
- 4 tbsp. flax seeds
- 4 tsp. cinnamon

Directions:
1. Peel the banana and cut it into ½-inch pieces. Put all the ingredients in the blender and blend into a smoothie.
2. Put in a dash of cinnamon at the top of the smoothie before you serve.

Nutritional Info: Calories: 332 kcal , Protein: 12.49 g , Fat: 14.42 g , Carbohydrates: 42.46 g

BLUEBERRY AND SPINACH SHAKE

Time To Prepare: five minutes

Time to Cook: 0 minutes

Yield: Servings 2

Ingredients:
- 1 cup of low-fat Greek yogurt (not necessary)
- 1 cup of organic blueberries (or washed if non-organic)
- 1/2 cup of spinach
- ice cubes to the desired concentration

Directions:
1. Put in ingredients together in a blender until the desired smoothness is achieved and then serve in a tall glass.
2. Drizzle a few fresh berries on top if you prefer!

Nutritional Info: Calories: 233 kcal , Protein: 10.68 g , Fat: 5.38 g , Carbohydrates: 37.13 g

BLUEBERRY LIME JUICE

Time To Prepare: five minutes

Time to Cook: five minutes

Yield: Servings 4

Ingredients:
- 1 cup fresh blueberries
- Water to cover contents
- Zest and juice of 1 lime

Directions:
1. Put ingredients in a mesh steamer basket for instant pot. Put in pot.
2. Pour in water to immerse contents.
3. Secure the lid. Cook on HIGH pressure five minutes.
4. When done, depressurize swiftly.
5. Remove steamer basket. Discard cooked produce.
6. Let flavored water cool. Chill completely before you serve.

Nutritional Info: Calories: 86 , Fat: 0g , Carbohydrates: 22g , Protein: 0g

BLUEBERRY MATCHA SMOOTHIE

Time To Prepare: five minutes

Time to Cook: 0 minutes

Yield: Servings 2

Ingredients:
- ¼ Teaspoon Ground Cinnamon
- ¼ Teaspoon Ground Ginger
- 1 Banana
- 1 Tablespoon Chia Seeds
- 1 Tablespoon Matcha Powder
- 2 Cups Almond Milk
- 2 Cups Blueberries, Frozen
- 2 Tablespoons Protein Powder, Optional
- A Pinch Sea Salt

Directions:

Blend all ingredients until the desired smoothness is achieved.

Nutritional Info: Calories: 208 , Protein: 8.7 Grams , Fat: 5.7 Grams , Carbohydrates: 31 Grams

BLUEBERRY POMEGRANATE SMOOTHIE

Time To Prepare: five minutes

Time to Cook: 0 minutes

Yield: Servings 2

Ingredients:
- ¼ cup of canned coconut milk
- 1 cup of pomegranate juice, unsweetened
- 1 tbsp. of hemp seeds
- 2 cup of frozen blueberries
- 6 to 8 ice cubes

Directions:
1. Mix the smoothie ingredients in your high-speed blender.
2. Pulse the ingredients a few times to cut them up.
3. Combine the mixture on the highest speed setting for thirty to 60 seconds.
4. Pour into glasses and serve.

Nutritional Info: Calories: 282 kcal , Protein: 5.64 g , Fat: 13.8 g , Carbohydrates: 37.75 g

BLUEBERRY SMOOTHIE

Time To Prepare: ten minutes

Time to Cook: 0 minutes

Yield: Servings 1

Ingredients:

- 1 banana, peeled
- 1 tbsp. almond butter
- 1 tsp. maca powder
- 1/2 cup almond milk, unsweetened
- 1/2 cup blueberries
- 1/2 cup water
- 1/4 tsp. ground cinnamon
- 2 handfuls baby spinach

Directions:
1. In your blender, combine the spinach with the banana, blueberries, almond butter, cinnamon, maca powder, water, and milk.
2. Pulse thoroughly, pour into a glass, before you serve. Enjoy!

Nutritional Info: Calories: 341 , Fat: 12 g , Protein: 10 g , Carbohydrates: 54 g , Fiber: 12 g

BROCCOLI SMOOTHIE

Time To Prepare: five minutes

Time to Cook: 0 minutes

Yield: Servings 4

Ingredients:
- 1 ½ cups strawberries
- 1 ½ cups water
- 1 cup broccoli florets
- 1 cup chopped spinach
- 2 bananas, cut, frozen
- 2 cups frozen mango chunks
- 2 cups pineapple juice

Directions:
1. Combine all ingredients into a blender and blend until the desired smoothness is achieved.
2. Pour into 4 tall glasses before you serve.

Nutritional Info: Calories: 222 kcal , Protein: 3.51 g , Fat: 1.98 g , Carbohydrates: 51.45 g

CARROT AND ORANGE TURMERIC DRINK

Time To Prepare: five minutes

Time to Cook: 0 minutes

Yield: Servings 2

Ingredients:
- 1 cup orange juice

- 1 tbsp. lemon juice
- 1/2 inch ginger slice
- 1/4 tsp. turmeric powder
- 2 carrots, peeled, chopped
- 2 tbsp. sugar

Directions:
1. In a blender, put in orange juice, sugar, turmeric powder, carrots, and lemon juice.
2. Blend well.

Serve!

Nutritional Info: Calories: 153 kcal , Protein: 4.47 g , Fat: 3.3 g , Carbohydrates: 27.02 g

CHERRY SMOOTHIE

Time To Prepare: five minutes

Time to Cook: 0 minutes

Yield: Servings 4-6

Ingredients:
- 1 ½ cups vanilla Greek yogurt
- 2 bananas, cut
- 3 cups cherry juice
- 3 cups pitted, froze dark sweet cherries
- Fresh cherries, pitted
- Mint sprigs
- To decorate: Optional

Directions:
1. Combine all ingredients into a blender and blend until the desired smoothness is achieved.
2. Pour into 4 tall glasses.
3. Decorate using optional ingredients if using before you serve.

Nutritional Info: Calories: 114 kcal , Protein: 2.36 g , Fat: 1.88 g , Carbohydrates: 23.49 g

CHOCOLATE CHERRY SMOOTHIE

Time To Prepare: five minutes

Time to Cook: 0 minutes

Yield: Servings 2

Ingredients:
- 2 cups almond milk, unsweetened
- 2 dates, pitted, chopped or 2 teaspoons pure maple syrup
- 2 scoops protein powder or 4 tablespoons almond butter (not necessary)
- 4 cups pitted, frozen cherries

- 4 tablespoons cocoa or cacao powder
- Cacao nibs
- Granola
- Hemp hearts
- To serve: Optional

Directions:
1. Combine all ingredients into a blender and blend until the desired smoothness is achieved.
2. Pour into 2 tall glasses and serve topped with optional ingredients.

Nutritional Info: Calories: 339 kcal , Protein: 16.37 g , Fat: 21.34 g , Carbohydrates: 27.99 g

CHOCOLATE LATTE WITH REISHI

Time To Prepare: five minutes

Time to Cook: ten minutes

Yield: Servings 2

Ingredients:
- 1 teaspoon Reishi powder
- 2 tablespoons coconut butter
- 4 cups almond milk, unsweetened
- 4 teaspoons raw cacao powder
- A pinch ground cinnamon
- A pinch sea salt
- Sweetener of your choice

Directions:
1. Put in almond milk into a deep cooking pan. Put the deep cooking pan using low heat.
2. When the milk is warm and just starts to bubble, remove the heat. Move into a blender.
3. Put in the remaining ingredients and blend for 30 – 40 seconds or until the desired smoothness is achieved.
4. Pour into mugs before you serve.

Nutritional Info: Calories: 461 kcal , Protein: 19.32 g , Fat: 30.57 g , Carbohydrates: 28.08 g

COOKED ICED TEA

Time To Prepare: two minutes

Time to Cook: 4 minutes

Yield: Servings 4

Ingredients:
- 2 tbsp. honey
- 4 regular tea bags
- 6 cups water

Directions:
1. Put in ingredients to the instant pot.
2. Secure the lid. Cook on HIGH pressure 4 minutes.
3. When done, depressurize naturally.
4. Allow to cool to room temperature. Serve over ice.

Nutritional Info: Calories: 22 , Fat: 0g , Carbohydrates: 6g , Protein: 0g

CUCUMBER KIWI GREEN SMOOTHIE

Time To Prepare: five minutes

Time to Cook: 0 minutes

Yield: Servings 2

Ingredients:
- ¼ cup of canned coconut milk
- 1 cup of coconut water
- 1 cup of seedless cucumber, chopped
- 2 ripe kiwi fruit
- 2 tbsps. of fresh chopped cilantro
- 6 to 8 ice cubes
- ice cubes

Directions:
1. Mix the smoothie ingredients in your high-speed blender.
2. Pulse the ingredients a few times to cut them up.
3. Combine the mixture on the highest speed setting for thirty to 60 seconds.
4. Pour into glasses and serve.

Nutritional Info: Calories: 140 kcal , Protein: 5.1 g , Fat: 10.52 g , Carbohydrates: 7.4 g

CUCUMBER MELON SMOOTHIE

Time To Prepare: five minutes

Time to Cook: 0 minutes

Yield: Servings 2

Ingredients:
- 1 ½ cups of chopped honeydew
- 1 cup of chilled coconut water
- 1 cup of seedless cucumber, diced
- 2 tbsp. of fresh mint
- 6 to 8 ice cubes

Directions:
1. Mix the smoothie ingredients in your high-speed blender.
2. Pulse the ingredients a few times to cut them up.

3. Combine the mixture on the highest speed setting for thirty to 60 seconds.
4. Pour into glasses and serve.

Nutritional Info: Calories: 300 kcal , Protein: 5.83 g , Fat: 8.55 g , Carbohydrates: 51.21 g

DREAMY YUMMY ORANGE CREAM SMOOTHIE

Time To Prepare: five minutes

Time to Cook: 0 minutes

Yield: Servings 2

Ingredients:
- ¼ cup of fresh orange juice
- ½ cup of canned full-fat coconut milk
- 1 cup of almond milk
- 1 navel orange, peel removed
- 6 to 8 ice cubes

Directions:
1. Mix the smoothie ingredients in your high-speed blender.
2. Pulse the ingredients a few times to cut them up.
3. Combine the mixture on the highest speed setting for thirty to 60 seconds.
4. Pour into glasses and serve.

Nutritional Info: Calories: 269 kcal , Protein: 8.63 g , Fat: 21.36 g , Carbohydrates: 12.75 g

FIG SMOOTHIE

Time To Prepare: five minutes

Time to Cook: 0 minutes

Yield: Servings 2

Ingredients:
- 1 Banana
- 1 Cup Almond Milk
- 1 Cup Whole Milk Yogurt, Plain
- 1 Tablespoon Almond Butter
- 1 Teaspoon Flaxseed, Ground
- 1 Teaspoon Honey, Raw
- 3-4 Ice Cubes
- 7 Figs, Halved (Fresh or Frozen)

Directions:

Blend all together ingredients until the desired smoothness is achieved, and serve instantly.

Nutritional Info: Calories: 362 , Protein: 9 Grams , Fat: 12 Grams , Carbohydrates: 60 Grams

FLU FIGHTING TONIC

Time To Prepare: five minutes

Time to Cook: ten minutes

Yield: Servings 2

Ingredients:
- ½ teaspoon turmeric powder
- 2 tablespoons clear honey if possible manuka
- Boiling water, as required
- Juice of 2 lemons
- Lemon slices to decorate

Directions:
1. Split the lemon juice into 2 mugs. Put in ¼ teaspoon turmeric powder into each mug.
2. Put in a tablespoon of honey into each mug.
3. Pour boiling water to fill up the mugs. Stir.
4. Decorate using a slice of lemon before you serve.

Nutritional Info: Calories: 123 kcal , Protein: 3.59 g , Fat: 3.23 g , Carbohydrates: 22.78 g

FRESH CRANBERRY AND LIME JUICE

Time To Prepare: five minutes

Time to Cook: 0 minutes

Yield: Servings 2

Ingredients:
- 1/2½ cups of mixed berries (frozen are fine)
- 1/2½ cups of spinach
- 2 limes, juiced
- 4 cups of cranberries

Directions:

Mix all the ingredients with water in a juicer until pureed and serve instantly over ice.

Nutritional Info: Calories: 578 kcal , Protein: 6.83 g , Fat: 9.92 g , Carbohydrates: 119.35 g

FRESH TROPICAL JUICE

Time To Prepare: five minutes

Time to Cook: 0 minutes

Yield: Servings 2

Ingredients:
- 1 whole pineapple, peeled and slice into chunks.
- 1 cup of water
- 1/2 can of low-fat coconut milk

Directions:
1. Put in all ingredients to a juicer and blend until the desired smoothness is achieved.
2. Serve over ice.

Nutritional Info: Calories: 116 kcal , Protein: 3.72 g , Fat: 3.13 g , Carbohydrates: 19.55 g

GINGER ALE

Time To Prepare: five minutes

Time to Cook: thirty minutes

Yield: Servings 4

Ingredients:
- 1 pound fresh ginger, unpeeled, diced
- 1 quart carbonated water
- 1 tbsp. honey
- Ice for serving
- Juice and rind of 2 lemons
- Lime wedges

Directions:
1. Put ginger and lemon juice in a food processor. Pulse to smooth consistency.
2. Move puree to the instant pot. Mix in honey.
3. Put in lemon peel to the instant pot.
4. Secure the lid. Cook on HIGH pressure thirty minutes.
5. When done, depressurize naturally. Strain and chill.
6. Serve over ice.

Nutritional Info: Calories: 108 , Fat: 0g , Carbohydrates: 28g , Protein: 0g

GINGER, CARROT, AND TURMERIC SMOOTHIE

Time To Prepare: five minutes

Time to Cook: 0 minutes

Yield: Servings 2

Ingredients:
- ½ cup Mango, fresh or frozen chunks
- 1 big Carrot, peeled and chopped
- 1 cup Coconut water

- 1 Orange, peeled and separated
- 1 tbsp. Hemp seeds, raw, shelled
- 1 tsp. Ginger, ground
- 1 tsp. Turmeric, ground
- 1/8 tsp. Cayenne pepper

Directions:

Puree all of the ingredients with one-half cup of ice until the desired smoothness is achieved and drink instantly.

Nutritional Info: Calories 250 , 35 grams sugar , 4.5 grams fat , 7 grams fiber , 48 grams carbs , 6 grams protein

GOLDEN CHAI LATTE

Time To Prepare: five minutes

Time to Cook: ten minutes

Yield: Servings 2

Ingredients:
- ¼ teaspoon ground cinnamon
- ½ cup water
- ½ tablespoon maple syrup
- ½ tablespoon turmeric powder
- 1 ¼ cups cashew milk or any other non-dairy milk of your choice
- 1 teaspoon loose leaf chai tea
- 1/8 teaspoon ground nutmeg
- A pinch ground cardamom

Directions:
1. Put in water and 1-cup milk into a deep cooking pan. Put the deep cooking pan on moderate heat.
2. Put in chai leaves in a tea strainer (the type that that has a lid and you can close). Lower the strainer in the deep cooking pan. Put in spices.
3. When it just comes to a light boil, remove the heat. Allow it to cool for five minutes. Take out the tea strainer and discard the leaves.
4. Put in maple syrup and stir.
5. Pour into glasses. Sprinkle remaining cashew milk on top. Decorate using cinnamon and nutmeg before you serve.

Nutritional Info: Calories: 142 kcal , Protein: 8.59 g , Fat: 6.26 g , Carbohydrates: 13.3 g

GREEN VANILLA SMOOTHIE

Time To Prepare: ten minutes

Time to Cook: 0 minutes

Yield: Servings 1

Ingredients:
- 1 1/2 cups fresh spinach leaves
- 1 banana, cut in chunks
- 1 cup grapes
- 1 tub (6 oz.) vanilla yogurt
- 1/2 apple, cored and chopped

Directions:
1. Put in everything to a blender jug.
2. Cover the jug firmly.
3. Blend until the desired smoothness is achieved. Serve and enjoy!

Nutritional Info: Calories: 131 , Fat: 0.2 g , Protein: 2.6 g , Carbohydrates: 9.1 g , Fiber: 1.3 g

HIBISCUS TEA

Time To Prepare: five minutes

Time to Cook: ten minutes

Yield: Servings 4

Ingredients:
- 1 tbsp. honey
- 1 tsp fresh ginger, grated
- 10 cups water
- 2 cup dried hibiscus petals
- Rind from 1 pineapple

Directions:
1. Wash hibiscus leaves meticulously with cold water.
2. Take away the dust.
3. Put in water, honey, and ginger to the instant pot. Stir.
4. Mix in hibiscus petals and pineapple rind.
5. Secure the lid. Cook on HIGH pressure ten minutes.
6. When done, depressurize naturally.
7. Remove pineapple rind. Pass liquid through a fine-mesh strainer.
8. Cool thoroughly. Chill before you serve.

Nutritional Info: Calories: 114 , Fat: 0g , Carbohydrates: 28g , Protein: 0g

HOT APPLE CIDER

Time To Prepare: five minutes

Time to Cook: fifteen minutes

Yield: Servings 4

Ingredients:
- ½ cup fresh cranberries
- ½ cup honey
- ½ star of anise
- ½ tsp whole cloves
- 1 lemon, peeled, cut into segments
- 1 orange, peeled, cut into segments
- 2 cinnamon sticks
- 7 medium apples, cored, quarter
- Water to cover ingredients

Directions:
1. Put in apples, lemon, orange, and cranberries to the instant pot.
2. Put in cinnamon stick, star anise, and cloves.
3. Pour in water to immerse ingredients.
4. Secure the lid. Cook on HIGH pressure fifteen minutes.
5. Depressurize naturally.
6. Mash fruit using a masher to release juices.
7. Strain the liquid. Chill completely before you serve.

Nutritional Info: Calories: 153 , Fat: 9g , Carbohydrates: 14g , Protein: 4g

HOT PEPPERMINT VANILLA LATTE

Time To Prepare: five minutes

Time to Cook: five minutes

Yield: Servings 4

Ingredients:
- ¼ cup honey
- 1 tsp vanilla
- 2 cups coffee
- 23 drops peppermint oil
- 4 cups almond milk

Directions:
1. Put in listed ingredients to the instant pot.
2. Secure the lid. Cook on HIGH pressure five minutes.
3. When done, depressurize naturally.
4. Serve warm.

Nutritional Info: Calories: 279 , Fat: 3g , Carbohydrates: 61g , Protein: 3g

INSTANT HORCHATA

Time To Prepare: five minutes

Time to Cook: five minutes

Yield: Servings 4

Ingredients:
- 1 cinnamon stick, broken into little chunks
- 32 ounces rice milk
- 6 tbsp. honey

Directions:
1. Put in listed ingredients to the instant pot.
2. Secure the lid. Cook on HIGH pressure five minutes.
3. When done, depressurize naturally over ten minutes.
4. Cool thoroughly. Chill before you serve.

Nutritional Info: Calories: 226 , Fat: 1g , Carbohydrates: 53g , Protein: 2g

JAMAICAN HIBISCUS TEA

Time To Prepare: five minutes

Time to Cook: five minutes

Yield: Servings 4

Ingredients:
- ½ tsp ginger, minced
- 1 cup dried hibiscus flowers
- 1 tbsp. honey
- 8 cups water
- Ice as required
- Juice of 1 lime

Directions:
1. Put in hibiscus flowers, water, honey, and ginger to the instant pot.
2. Secure the lid. Cook on HIGH pressure five minutes.
3. When done, depressurize naturally.
4. Cool thoroughly. Move to glass decanter. Mix in lime Juice. Pour over ice.

Nutritional Info: Calories: 197 , Fat: 0g , Carbohydrates: 18g , Protein: 0g

KALE SMOOTHIE

Time To Prepare: ten minutes

Time to Cook: 0 minutes

Yield: Servings 2

Ingredients:
- 10 kale leaves
- 2 pears, chopped

- 5 bananas, peeled and slice into chunks
- 5 cups almond milk
- 5 tbsp. almond butter

Directions:
1. In your blender, combine the kale with the bananas, pears, almond butter, and almond milk.
2. Pulse thoroughly, split into glasses, before you serve. Enjoy!

Nutritional Info: Calories: 267 , Fat: 11 g , Protein: 7 g , Carbohydrates: fifteen g , Fiber: 7 g

KIWI STRAWBERRY SMOOTHIE

Time To Prepare: ten minutes

Time to Cook: 0 minutes

Yield: Servings 1

Ingredients:
- ¼ cup Chia seed powder
- ½ cup Strawberries, fresh or frozen, chopped
- 1 Banana, diced
- 1 cup Milk, almond or coconut
- 1 Kiwi, peeled and chopped
- 1 tsp. Basil, ground
- 1 tsp. Turmeric, ground

Directions:

Drink instantly after all the ingredients have been thoroughly combined.

Nutritional Info: Calories 250 , 9.9 grams sugar , 1 gram fat , 34 grams carbs , 4.3 grams fiber ,

LEMON GINGER ICED TEA

Time To Prepare: five minutes

Time to Cook: ten minutes

Yield: Servings 2-3

Ingredients:
- ¼ teaspoon turmeric
- 1 tablespoon fresh lemon juice or to taste (not necessary)
- 1 tablespoon maple syrup
- 2 – 3 lemon slices
- 2 inches fresh ginger, peeled, thinly cut or to taste
- 3-4 cups water
- A pinch ground cinnamon

Directions:

1. Pour water into a deep cooking pan. Put in ginger, turmeric, lemon slices, and cinnamon. Put the deep cooking pan on moderate heat.
2. Cover and simmer for eight - ten minutes.
3. Strain and pour into a jar. Place the maple syrup, and lemon juice, then stir. Chill for eight – 10 hours.
4. Stir thoroughly. Pour into glasses before you serve.

Nutritional Info: Calories: 55 kcal , Protein: 2.32 g , Fat: 2.13 g , Carbohydrates: 7.47 g

MANGO AND GINGER INFUSED WATER

Time To Prepare: five minutes

Time to Cook: five minutes

Yield: Servings 4

Ingredients:
- 1 cup fresh mango, chopped
- 2-inch piece ginger, peeled, cubed
- Water to cover ingredients

Directions:
1. Put ingredients in the mesh steamer basket.
2. Put basket in the instant pot.
3. Put in water to immerse contents.
4. Secure the lid. Cook on HIGH pressure five minutes.
5. When done, depressurize swiftly.
6. Remove steamer basket. Discard cooked produce.
7. Let flavored water cool. Chill completely and serve.

Nutritional Info: Calories: 209 , Fat: 1g , Carbohydrates: 51g , Protein: 2g

MANGO TOMATO SMOOTHIE

Time To Prepare: five minutes

Time to Cook: 0 minutes

Yield: Servings 4

Ingredients:
- 1 cup almond milk
- 2 cups chopped cilantro
- 2 cups pineapple chunks
- 2 mangoes, peeled, pitted
- 4 Campari tomatoes, chopped
- 6 cups fresh baby spinach

Directions:
1. Combine all ingredients into a blender and blend until the desired smoothness is achieved.
2. Pour into 4 tall glasses before you serve.

Nutritional Info: Calories: 395 kcal , Protein: 13.1 g , Fat: 8.19 g , Carbohydrates: 73.65 g

MIXED FRUIT & NUT MILKSHAKE

Time To Prepare: five minutes

Time to Cook: 0 minutes

Yield: Servings 2

Ingredients:
- 1 tbsp. of honey
- 1/2 cup of almond milk
- 1½ grapefruit; peeled and chopped
- 1/2½ inch piece of ginger, minced
- 12 strawberries
- 2 tbsp. of chopped almonds
- juice of 1 orange

Directions:
1. Put everything but the strawberries in a blender until the desired smoothness is achieved.
2. Put in in the strawberries and blend until pureed, serving in a tall glass.

Nutritional Info: Calories: 140 kcal , Protein: 5.89 g , Fat: 5.84 g , Carbohydrates: 17.36 g

PARSLEY GINGER GREEN JUICE

Time To Prepare: five minutes

Time to Cook: 0 minutes

Yield: Servings 2

Ingredients:
- 2 cucumbers, chopped
- 2 green apples, cored
- 2 lemons, peeled, halved
- 4 cups chopped parsley
- 4 cups chopped spinach
- 4 inches fresh ginger, peeled, cut
- 6 stalks celery, chopped

Directions:
1. Juice together all the ingredients in a juicer.
2. Pour into 2 glasses before you serve.

Nutritional Info: Calories: 239 kcal , Protein: 10.74 g , Fat: 5.08 g , Carbohydrates: 44.86 g

PEACH AND RASPBERRY LEMONADE

Time To Prepare: five minutes

Time to Cook: five minutes

Yield: Servings 4

Ingredients:
- ½ cup fresh raspberries
- 1 cup fresh peaches, chopped
- Water to cover ingredients
- Zest and juice of 1 lemon

Directions:
1. Put ingredients in mesh basket for instant pot. Put in pot.
2. Put in water to barely cover the fruit.
3. Secure the lid. Cook on HIGH pressure five minutes.
4. When done, depressurize swiftly.
5. Remove steamer basket. Discard cooked produce.
6. Let flavored water cool. Chill completely before you serve.

Nutritional Info: Calories: 77 , Fat: 0g , Carbohydrates: 19g , Protein: 0g

PEACH MAPLE SMOOTHIE

Time To Prepare: ten minutes

Time to Cook: 0 minutes

Yield: Servings 1

Ingredients:
- 1 cup fat-free yogurt
- 1 cup ice
- 2 tbsp. maple syrup
- 4 big peaches, peeled and chopped

Directions:
1. Put in everything to a blender jug.
2. Cover the jug firmly.
3. Blend until the desired smoothness is achieved. Serve and enjoy!

Nutritional Info: Calories: 125 , Fat: 0.4 g , Protein: 5.6 g , Carbohydrates: 8 g , Fiber: 2.3 g

PEACHY KEEN SMOOTHIE

Time To Prepare: five minutes

Time to Cook: 0 minutes

Yield: Servings 2

Ingredients:
- 1 ½ cups of frozen peaches
- 1 cup of almond milk
- 1 small frozen banana
- 2 tbsp. of raw hemp seeds
- 6 to 8 ice cubes
- Pinch of ground ginger

Directions:
1. Mix the smoothie ingredients in your high-speed blender.
2. Pulse the ingredients a few times to cut them up.
3. Combine the mixture on the highest speed setting for thirty to 60 seconds.
4. Pour into glasses and serve.

Nutritional Info: Calories: 388 kcal , Protein: 10.59 g , Fat: 11.93 g , Carbohydrates: 64.08 g

PINEAPPLE & GINGER JUICE

Time To Prepare: five minutes

Time to Cook: 0 minutes

Yield: Servings 2

Ingredients:
- 2 apples, cored, chopped
- 2 cucumbers, chopped
- 2 cups chopped pineapple
- 2 cups spinach
- 2 inches ginger, peeled, cut
- 2 lemons, peeled, halved
- 8 celery stalks, chopped

Directions:
1. Juice together all the ingredients in a juicer.
2. Pour into 2 glasses before you serve.

Nutritional Info: Calories: 339 kcal , Protein: 7.44 g , Fat: 4.23 g , Carbohydrates: 75.38 g

PINEAPPLE AND GREENS SMOOTHIE

Time To Prepare: five minutes

Time to Cook: 0 minutes

Yield: Servings 2

Ingredients:
- ¾ cup of almond milk

- 1 cup of chopped spinach
- 1 cup of frozen pineapple
- 1 small frozen banana
- 1 tbsp. of honey
- 2 tbsp. Of chia seeds

Directions:
1. Mix the smoothie ingredients in your high-speed blender.
2. Pulse the ingredients a few times to cut them up.
3. Combine the mixture on the highest speed setting for thirty to 60 seconds.
4. Pour into glasses and serve.

Nutritional Info: Calories: 272 kcal , Protein: 5.27 g , Fat: 4.5 g , Carbohydrates: 56.37 g

PINEAPPLE- GINGER SMOOTHIE

Time To Prepare: five minutes

Time to Cook: 0 minutes

Yield: Servings 1

Ingredients:
- ½ inch thick ginger, cut
- 1 cup coconut milk
- 1 cup pineapple slice

Directions:
1. Put all ingredients in a blender.
2. Pulse until the desired smoothness is achieved.
3. Chill before you serve.

Nutritional Info: Calories 299 , Fat: 8 g , Protein: 9 g , Carbohydrates: 51 g

PINEAPPLE SMOOTHIE

Time To Prepare: ten minutes

Time to Cook: 0 minutes

Yield: Servings 2

Ingredients:
- 1 1/2 cups pineapple chunks
- 1 cup coconut water
- 1 orange, peeled and slice into quarters
- 1 tbsp. fresh grated ginger
- 1 tsp. chia seeds
- 1 tsp. turmeric powder
- A pinch black pepper

Directions:
1. In your blender, combine the coconut water with the orange, pineapple, ginger, chia seeds, turmeric, and black pepper.
2. Pulse thoroughly, pour into a glass.

Makes for a great breakfast!

Nutritional Info: Calories: 151 , Fat: 2 g , Protein: 4 g , Carbohydrates: 12 g , Fiber: 6 g

PINK CALIFORNIA SMOOTHIE

Time To Prepare: ten minutes

Time to Cook: 0 minutes

Yield: Servings 1

Ingredients:
- 1 container (8 oz.) lemon yogurt
- 1/3 cup orange juice
- 7 big strawberries

Directions:
1. Put in everything to a blender jug.
2. Cover the jug firmly.
3. Blend until the desired smoothness is achieved. Serve and enjoy!

Nutritional Info: Calories: 144 , Fat: 0.4 g , Protein: 5.6 g , Carbohydrates: 8 g , Fiber: 2.3 g

PUMPKIN PIE SMOOTHIE

Time To Prepare: five minutes

Time to Cook: 0 minutes

Yield: Servings 2

Ingredients:
- ½ Cup Pumpkin, Canned & Unsweetened
- 1 Banana
- 1 Cup Almond Milk
- 1 Teaspoon Ground Cinnamon
- 1 Teaspoon Ground Nutmeg
- 1 Teaspoon Maple Syrup, Pure
- 1 Teaspoon Vanilla Extract Pure
- 2 Tablespoons Almond Butter, Heaping
- 2-3 Ice Cubes

Directions:

Blend all ingredients together until the desired smoothness is achieved.

Nutritional Info: Calories: 235 , Protein: 5.6 Grams , Fat: 11 Grams , Carbohydrates: 27.8 Grams

PURPLE FRUIT SMOOTHIE

Time To Prepare: ten minutes

Time to Cook: 0 minutes

Yield: Servings 1

Ingredients:
- 2 frozen bananas, cut in chunks
- 1 cup orange juice
- 1 tbsp. honey, optional
- 1 tsp. vanilla extract, optional
- 1/2 cup frozen blueberries

Directions:
1. Put in everything to a blender jug.
2. Cover the jug firmly.
3. Blend until the desired smoothness is achieved. Serve and enjoy!

Nutritional Info: Calories: 133 , Fat: 1.1 g , Protein: 3.6 g , Carbohydrates: 7.6 g , Fiber: 1.3 g

RASPBERRY BANANA SMOOTHIE

Time To Prepare: ten minutes

Time to Cook: 0 minutes

Yield: Servings 1

Ingredients:
- 1 banana
- 1 cup almond milk
- 1 cup frozen raspberries
- 1 cup raspberry yogurt
- 1 tbsp. flaxseed meal
- 1/4 cup Concord grape juice
- 1/4 cup rolled oats
- 16 whole almonds

Directions:
1. Put in everything to a blender jug.
2. Cover the jug firmly.
3. Blend until the desired smoothness is achieved and then serve. Enjoy!

Nutritional Info: Calories: 214 , Fat: 0.4 g , Protein: 5.6 g , Carbohydrates: 8 g , Fiber: 2.3 g

RASPBERRY SMOOTHIE

Time To Prepare: ten minutes

Time to Cook: 0 minutes

Yield: Servings 2

Ingredients:
- 1 avocado, pitted and peeled
- 1/2 cup raspberries
- 3/4 cup raspberry juice
- 3/4 cup orange juice

Directions:
1. In your blender, combine the avocado with the raspberry juice, orange juice, and raspberries.
2. Pulse thoroughly, split into 2 glasses, before you serve. Enjoy!

Nutritional Info: Calories: 125 , Fat: 11 g , Protein: 3 g , Carbohydrates: 9 g , Fiber: 7 g

SPICY TOMATO SMOOTHIE

Time To Prepare: five minutes

Time to Cook: 0 minutes

Yield: Servings 2

Ingredients:
- ¼ cup chopped red onion
- 1 jalapeño, cut, deseed if you wish
- 1 small bunch cilantro, chopped
- 1 small cucumber
- 2 big carrots, chopped
- 2 cloves garlic, peeled
- 6 small vine tomatoes
- Juice of 2 limes

Directions:
1. Combine all ingredients into a blender and blend until the desired smoothness is achieved.
2. Pour into 2 tall glasses before you serve.

Nutritional Info: Calories: 269 kcal , Protein: 24.87 g , Fat: 8.71 g , Carbohydrates: 26.89 g

STRAWBERRY OATMEAL SMOOTHIE

Time To Prepare: ten minutes

Time to Cook: 0 minutes

Yield: Servings 1

Ingredients:
- 1 cup soy milk
- 1 banana, broken into chunks
- 14 frozen strawberries
- 1/2 cup rolled oats
- 1/2 tsp. vanilla extract
- 1 1/2 tsp. honey

Directions:
1. Put in everything to a blender jug.
2. Cover the jug firmly.
3. Blend until the desired smoothness is achieved. Serve and enjoy!

Nutritional Info: Calories: 172 , Fat: 0.4 g , Protein: 5.6 g , Carbohydrates: 8 g , Fiber: 2 g

SWEET & SAVOURY SMOOTHIE

Time To Prepare: five minutes

Time to Cook: 0 minutes

Yield: Servings 2

Ingredients:
- 1 apple, peeled and cut
- 1 banana, peeled and cut
- 1 cup of almond or soy milk
- 1 cup of fresh pineapple, peeled and cut
- 1 tbsp. of lemon juice
- 1/2 tbsp. of ginger, grated
- 1/4 tsp of ground turmeric
- 2 cups of carrots, peeled and cut
- 2 cups of filtered water.

Directions:
1. Blend carrots and water to make a pureed carrot juice.
2. Pour into a Mason jar or sealable container, cover, and store in the refrigerator.
3. When done, put in the rest of the smoothie ingredients to a blender or juicer until the desired smoothness is achieved.
4. Put in the carrot juice in at the end, blending meticulously until the desired smoothness is achieved.
5. Serve with or without ice.

Nutritional Info: Calories: 225 kcal , Protein: 6.03 g , Fat: 5.78 g , Carbohydrates: 39.93 g

SWEET CRANBERRY JUICE

Time To Prepare: five minutes

Time to Cook: 8 minutes

Yield: Servings 4

Ingredients:
- ½ cup honey
- 1 cinnamon stick
- 1 gallon filtered water
- 4 cups fresh cranberries
- Juice of 1 lemon

Directions:
1. Put in cranberries, ½ of water, cinnamon cling to the instant pot.
2. Secure the lid. Cook on HIGH pressure 8 minutes.
3. Depressurize naturally.
4. Once cool, strain liquid. Put in remaining water.
5. Mix in honey and lemon. Cool thoroughly.
6. Chill before you serve.

Nutritional Info: Calories: 184 , Fat: 0g , Carbohydrates: 49g , Protein: 1g

TRIPLE FRUIT SMOOTHIE

Time To Prepare: ten minutes

Time to Cook: 0 minutes

Yield: Servings 1

Ingredients:
- 1 banana, peeled and chopped
- 1 container (8 oz.) peach yogurt
- 1 cup ice cubes
- 1 cup strawberries
- 1 kiwi, cut
- 1/2 cup blueberries
- 1/2 cup orange juice

Directions:
1. Put in everything to a blender jug.
2. Cover the jug firmly.
3. Blend until the desired smoothness is achieved. Serve and enjoy!

Nutritional Info: Calories: 124 , Fat: 0.4 g , Protein: 5.6 g , Carbohydrates: 8 g , Fiber: 2.3 g

TROPICAL MANGO COCONUT SMOOTHIE

Time To Prepare: five minutes

Time to Cook: 0 minutes

Yield: Servings 2

Ingredients:
- ½ cup of canned coconut milk
- ½ cup of fresh orange juice
- 1 ½ cups of frozen mango
- 1 ½ tsp of honey
- 1 medium frozen banana
- 1 tbsp. of fresh lemon juice

Directions:
1. Mix the smoothie ingredients in your high-speed blender.
2. Pulse the ingredients a few times to cut them up.
3. Combine the mixture on the highest speed setting for thirty to 60 seconds.
4. Pour into glasses and serve.

Nutritional Info: Calories: 354 kcal , Protein: 6.7 g , Fat: 18.09 g , Carbohydrates: 47.42 g

TROPICAL PINEAPPLE KIWI SMOOTHIE

Time To Prepare: five minutes

Time to Cook: 0 minutes

Yield: Servings 2

Ingredients:
- 1 ½ cup of frozen pineapple
- 1 cup of canned full-fat coconut milk
- 1 ripe kiwi; peeled and chopped
- 1 tsp of spirulina powder
- 3 tsp of lime juice
- 6 to 8 ice cubes

Directions:
1. Mix the smoothie ingredients in your high-speed blender.
2. Pulse the ingredients a few times to cut them up.
3. Combine the mixture on the highest speed setting.
4. Pour into glasses and serve.

Nutritional Info: Calories: 480 kcal , Protein: 7.38 g , Fat: 31.92 g , Carbohydrates: 48.35 g

TURMERIC AND GINGER TONIC

Time To Prepare: five minutes

Time to Cook: ten minutes

Yield: Servings 4

Ingredients:
- 1/8 teaspoon cayenne pepper
- 2 tablespoons grated, fresh ginger
- 2 tablespoons grated, fresh turmeric
- 6 cups water
- Juice of 2 lemons
- Maple syrup or honey to taste
- The rind of 2 lemons, peeled

Directions:
1. Put in water, ginger, turmeric, cayenne pepper, and lemon rind into a deep cooking pan.
2. Put the deep cooking pan on moderate to high heat. (Do not boil)
3. Once the mixture is hot, remove from heat.
4. Strain into 4 mugs. Put in honey and lemon juice and stir.
5. Serve warm.

Nutritional Info: Calories: 48 kcal **,** Protein: 2.28 g **,** Fat: 1.81 g **,** Carbohydrates: 7.03 g

TURMERIC DELIGHT

Time To Prepare: five minutes

Time to Cook: 0 minutes

Yield: Servings 2

Ingredients:
- ¼ Teaspoon Ginger
- ½ Teaspoon Cinnamon
- 1 Banana, Sliced
- 1 Tablespoon Lemon Juice, Fresh
- 1 Teaspoon Turmeric
- 2 Cups Yogurt, Plain & Whole Milk
- 2 Teaspoons Honey, Raw

Directions:

Combine all ingredients into a blender then blend until the desired smoothness is achieved.

Nutritional Info: Calories: 234 **,** Protein: 9.3 Grams **,** Fat: 8.2 Grams **,** Carbohydrates: 33.5 Grams

TURMERIC HOT CHOCOLATE

Time To Prepare: five minutes

Time to Cook: ten minutes

Yield: Servings 2

Ingredients:
- 1/8 tsp. cayenne pepper, optional
- 1/8 tsp. pepper
- 2 cups milk
- 2 tsp. ground turmeric
- 3 tbsp. cacao or cocoa powder
- 4 tsp. coconut oil
- 4 tsp. honey

Directions:
1. Put in milk, turmeric, cocoa, and coconut oil into a deep cooking pan. Put the deep cooking pan on moderate heat. Coconut oil and pepper are added because it helps to absorb the turmeric.
2. Whisk regularly until well blended.
3. When it starts to boil, remove from heat. Put in honey, cayenne pepper, and pepper and whisk well.
4. Split into 2 cups before you serve.

Nutritional Info: Calories: 339 kcal , Protein: 12.76 g , Fat: 21.19 g , Carbohydrates: 30.35 g

TURMERIC TEA

Time To Prepare: five minutes

Time to Cook: fifteen minutes

Yield: Servings 2

Ingredients:
- ½ teaspoon ground ginger
- ½ teaspoon turmeric powder
- ½ tsp ground cinnamon
- 2 cups water
- 2 lemon juices
- 2 tablespoons honey

Directions:
1. Put in water into a deep cooking pan. Put the deep cooking pan on moderate heat.
2. When it starts to boil, put in turmeric, cinnamon, and ginger and stir slowly.
3. Remove the heat. Cover and allow the mixture to steep for 12 – fifteen minutes. Put in honey and lemon juice.
4. Stir and pour into mugs.
5. Serve.

Nutritional Info: Calories: 121 kcal , Protein: 3.57 g , Fat: 3.2 g , Carbohydrates: 21.97 g

VANILLA AVOCADO SMOOTHIE

Time To Prepare: ten minutes

Time to Cook: 0 minutes

Yield: Servings 1

Ingredients:
- 1 cup almond milk
- 1 ripe avocado, halved and pitted
- 1/2 cup vanilla yogurt
- 3 tbsp. honey
- 8 ice cubes

Directions:
1. Put in everything to a blender jug.
2. Cover the jug firmly.
3. Blend until the desired smoothness is achieved. Serve and enjoy!

Nutritional Info: Calories: 143 , Fat: 1.2 g , Protein: 4.6 g , Carbohydrates: 21 g , Fiber: 2.3 g

VANILLA BLUEBERRY SMOOTHIE

Time To Prepare: five minutes

Time to Cook: 0 minutes

Yield: Servings 1

Ingredients:
- 1 cup fresh blueberries
- 1 tbsp. flaxseed oil
- 2 cups hemp milk
- 2 tbsp. hemp protein powder
- Handful of ice/ 1 cup frozen blueberries

Directions:
1. Mix milk and fresh blueberries plus ice (or frozen blueberries) in a blender.
2. Blend for a minute, move to a glass, and mix in flaxseed oil.

Nutritional Info: Calories: 1041 kcal , Protein: 35.21 g , Fat: 41.04 g , Carbohydrates: 140.4 g

VANILLA TURMERIC ORANGE JUICE

Time To Prepare: five minutes

Time to Cook: 0 minutes

Yield: Servings 2

Ingredients:
- ½ teaspoon turmeric powder
- 1 teaspoon ground cinnamon
- 2 cups unsweetened almond milk
- 2 teaspoons vanilla extract

- 6 oranges, peeled, separated into segments, deseeded
- Pepper to taste

Directions:
1. Juice the oranges. Put in the remaining ingredients.
2. Pour into 2 glasses before you serve.

Nutritional Info: Calories: 223 kcal , Protein: 11.47 g , Fat: 11.79 g , Carbohydrates: fifteen.9 g

VOLUPTUOUS VANILLA HOT DRINK

Time To Prepare: ten minutes

Time to Cook: 0 minutes

Yield: Servings 1

Ingredients:
- 1 scoop of hemp protein
- 1/2 Tbsp. ground cinnamon (or more to taste)
- 1/2 Tbsp. vanilla extract
- 3 cups unsweetened almond milk (or 1 1/2 cup full-fat coconut milk + 1 1/2 cups water)
- Stevia to taste

Directions:
1. Put the almond milk into a pitcher. Put ground cinnamon, hemp, vanilla extract in a small deep cooking pan on moderate to high heat. Heat until the pure liquid stevia is just melted and then pour the pure liquid stevia mixture into the pitcher.
2. Stir until the pure liquid stevia is well blended with the almond milk. Bring the pitcher in your refrigerator and let it cool for minimum two hours. Stir thoroughly before you serve.

Nutritional Info: Calories: 656 kcal , Protein: 42.12 g , Fat: 33.05 g , Carbohydrates: 44.45 g

WASSAIL

Time To Prepare: five minutes

Time to Cook: ten minutes

Yield: Servings 4

Ingredients:
- ½ tsp nutmeg
- 1 inch peeled ginger
- 10 cloves
- 2 vanilla beans, split or 2 Tbsp pure vanilla extract
- 4 cups orange juice
- 5 cinnamon sticks
- 8 cups apple cider
- Zest and juice of 2 lemons

Directions:

1. Pour cider and orange juice in the instant pot.
2. Put cinnamon sticks, nutmeg piece, cloves, lemon zest, vanilla beans in the steamer basket.
3. If you didn't use vanilla beans, pour in vanilla extract. Put in lemon juice.
4. Secure the lid. Cook on HIGH pressure ten minutes.
5. When done, depressurize naturally.
6. Discard contents of the steamer basket.
7. Serve hot from the pot.

Nutritional Info: Calories: 221 , Fat: 0g , Carbohydrates: 42g , Protein: 0g

WHITE HOT CHOCOLATE

Time To Prepare: five minutes

Time to Cook: six minutes

Yield: Servings 2

Ingredients:

- ¼ cup cocoa powder/butter
- 2 - 2½ Tbsp honey
- 2 tsp vanilla extract
- 3 cups coconut milk
- Pinch of sea salt

Directions:

1. Put in milk, cocoa powder/butter, honey, vanilla extract, and salt to the instant pot.
2. Secure the lid. Cook on LOW pressure six minutes.
3. Depressurize swiftly.
4. Use a hand blender to blend contents 25 seconds.
5. Serve hot.

Nutritional Info: Calories: 331 , Fat: 14g , Carbohydrates: 47g , Protein: 4g

WONDERFUL WATERMELON DRINK

Time To Prepare: five minutes

Time to Cook: 0 minutes

Yield: Servings 2

Ingredients:

- 1 cup of coconut water
- 1 cup of watermelon chunks
- 1/2 cup of tart cherries
- 2 cups of frozen mixed berries
- 2 tbsp. of chia seeds

Directions:

1. Combine all ingredients in a blender or juicer then blend until pureed.
2. Serve instantly and enjoy!

Nutritional Info: Calories: 330 kcal , Protein: 10.22 g , Fat: 9.71 g , Carbohydrates: 53.3 g

ZESTY CITRUS SMOOTHIE

Time To Prepare: five minutes

Time to Cook: 0 minutes

Yield: Servings 1

Ingredients:
- 1 cup almond milk
- 1 med orange peeled, cleaned, and cut into sections
- 1 tbsp. flaxseed oil
- 2 tsp hemp protein powder
- half cup lemon juice
- Handful of ice

Directions:
1. Mix milk, lemon juice, orange, and ice in a blender.
2. Blend for a minute, move to a glass, and mix in flaxseed oil.

Nutritional Info: Calories: 427 kcal , Protein: 17.5 g , Fat: 28.88 g , Carbohydrates: 24.96 g

BEET HUMMUS

Time To Prepare: five minutes

Time to Cook: 0 minutes

Yield: Servings 2

Ingredients:
- ¼ tsp of chili flakes
- ½ cup of olive oil
- ½ tsp of oregano
- ½ tsp of salt
- 1 ½ tsp of cumin
- 1 ¾ cup of chickpeas
- 1 clove of garlic
- 1 nub of fresh ginger
- 1 skinless roasted beet
- 1 tsp of curry
- 1 tsp of maple syrup
- 2 tbsp. of sunflower seeds
- Juice of one lemon

Directions:
1. Blend all together the ingredients in a food processor until they're smooth and decorate them with sunflower seeds.
2. Enjoy!

Nutritional Info: , Calories: 423 kcal , Protein: 13.98 g , Fat: 24.26 g , Carbohydrates: 40.13 g

BROCCOLI AND BLACK BEANS STIR FRY

Time To Prepare: ten minutes

Time to Cook: fifteen minutes

Yield: Servings 4

Ingredients:
- 1 tablespoon sesame oil
- 2 cloves garlic, thoroughly minced
- 2 cups cooked black beans
- 2 teaspoons ginger, finely chopped
- 4 cups broccoli florets
- 4 teaspoons sesame seeds
- A big pinch red chili flakes
- A pinch turmeric powder
- Lime juice to taste (not necessary)
- Salt to taste

Directions:
1. Pour enough water to immerse the bottom of the deep cooking pan by an inch. Put a strainer on the deep cooking pan. Put broccoli florets on the strainer. Steam the broccoli for about six minutes.
2. Put a big frying pan on moderate heat. Put in sesame oil. When the oil is just warm, put in sesame seeds, chili flakes, ginger, garlic, turmeric powder and salt. Sauté for about 2 minutes until aromatic.
3. Put in steamed broccoli and black beans and sauté until meticulously heated.
4. Put in lime juice and stir.
5. Serve hot.

Nutritional Info: , Calories: 196 kcal , Protein: 11.2 g , Fat: 7.25 g , Carbohydrates: 23.45 g

CARAMELIZED PEARS AND ONIONS

Time To Prepare: five minutes

Time to Cook: thirty-five minutes

Yield: Servings 4

Ingredients:
- 1 tablespoon olive oil
- 2 firm red pears, cored and quartered
- 2 red onion, cut into wedges
- Salt and pepper, to taste

Directions:
1. Preheat the oven to 425 degrees F
2. Put the pears and onion on a baking tray
3. Sprinkle with olive oil
4. Sprinkle with salt and pepper
5. Bake using your oven for a little more than half an hour
6. Serve and enjoy!

Nutritional Info: , Calories: 101 , Fat: 4g , Carbohydrates: 17g , Protein: 1g

CAULIFLOWER BROCCOLI MASH

Time To Prepare: five minutes

Time to Cook: ten minutes

Yield: Servings 6

Ingredients:
- 1 big head cauliflower, cut into chunks
- 1 small head broccoli, cut into florets
- 1 teaspoon salt
- 3 tablespoons extra virgin olive oil
- Pepper, to taste

Directions:
1. Take a pot and put in oil then heat it
2. Put in the cauliflower and broccoli
3. Sprinkle with salt and pepper to taste
4. Keep stirring to make vegetable soft
5. Put in water if required
6. When is already cooked, use a food processor or a potato masher to puree the vegetables
7. Serve and enjoy!

Nutritional Info: , Calories: 39 , Fat: 3g , Carbohydrates: 2g , Protein: 0.89g

CILANTRO AND AVOCADO PLATTER

Time To Prepare: ten minutes

Time to Cook: 0 minutes

Yield: Servings 6

Ingredients:

- ¼ cup of fresh cilantro, chopped
- ½ a lime, juiced
- 1 big ripe tomato, chopped
- 1 green bell pepper, chopped
- 1 sweet onion, chopped
- 2 avocados, peeled, pitted and diced
- Salt and pepper as required

Directions:
1. Take a moderate-sized container and put in onion, bell pepper, tomato, avocados, lime and cilantro
2. Mix thoroughly and give it a toss
3. Sprinkle with salt and pepper in accordance with your taste
4. Serve and enjoy!

Nutritional Info: , Calories: 126 , Fat: 10g , Carbohydrates: 10g , Protein: 2g

CITRUS COUSCOUS WITH HERB

Time To Prepare: five minutes

Time to Cook: fifteen minutes

Yield: Servings 2

Ingredients:
- ¼ cup of water
- ¼ orange, chopped
- ½ teaspoon butter
- 1 teaspoon Italian seasonings
- 1/3 cup couscous
- 1/3 teaspoon salt
- 4 tablespoons orange juice

Directions:
1. Pour water and orange juice in the pan.
2. Put in orange, Italian seasoning, and salt.
3. Bring the liquid to boil and take it off the heat.
4. Put in butter and couscous. Stir thoroughly and close the lid.
5. Leave the couscous rest for about ten minutes.

Nutritional Info: Calories 149 , Fat: 1.9 , Fiber: 2.1 , Carbs: 28.5 , Protein: 4.1

COOL GARBANZO AND SPINACH BEANS

Time To Prepare: 5-ten minutes

Time to Cook: 0 minute

Yield: Servings 4

Ingredients:
- ½ onion, diced
- ½ teaspoon cumin
- 1 tablespoon olive oil
- 10 ounces spinach, chopped
- 12 ounces garbanzo beans

Directions:
1. Take a frying pan and put in olive oil
2. Put it on moderate to low heat
3. Put in onions, garbanzo and cook for five minutes
4. Mix in cumin, garbanzo beans, spinach and flavor with sunflower seeds
5. Use a spoon to smash gently
6. Cook meticulously
7. Serve and enjoy!

Nutritional Info: , Calories: 90 , Fat: 4g , Carbohydrates:11g , Protein:4g

COUSCOUS SALAD

Time To Prepare: ten minutes

Time to Cook: six minutes

Yield: Servings 4

Ingredients:
- ¼ teaspoon ground black pepper
- ¾ teaspoon ground coriander
- ½ teaspoon salt
- ¼ teaspoon paprika
- ¼ teaspoon turmeric
- 1 tablespoon butter
- 2 oz. chickpeas, canned, drained
- 1 cup fresh arugula, chopped
- 2 oz. sun-dried tomatoes, chopped
- 1 oz. Feta cheese, crumbled
- 1 tablespoon canola oil
- 1/3 cup couscous
- 1/3 cup chicken stock

Directions:
1. Bring the chicken stock to boil.
2. Put in couscous, ground black pepper, ground coriander, salt, paprika, and turmeric. Put in chickpeas and butter. Mix the mixture well and close the lid.

3. Allow the couscous soak the hot chicken stock for about six minutes.
4. In the meantime, in the mixing container mix together arugula, sun-dried tomatoes, and Feta cheese.
5. Put in cooked couscous mixture and canola oil.
6. Mix up the salad well.

Nutritional Info: Calories 18 , Fat: 9 , Fiber: 3.6 , Carbs: 21.1 , Protein: 6

CREAMY POLENTA

Time To Prepare: 8 minutes

Time to Cook: forty-five minutes

Yield: Servings 4

Ingredients:
- ½ cup cream
- 1 ½ cup water
- 1 cup polenta
- 1/3 cup Parmesan, grated
- 2 cups chicken stock

Directions:
1. Put polenta in the pot.
2. Put in water, chicken stock, cream, and Parmesan. Mix up polenta well.
3. Then preheat oven to 355F.
4. Cook polenta in your oven for about forty-five minutes.
5. Mix up the cooked meal with the help of the spoon cautiously before you serve.

Nutritional Info: Calories 208 , Fat: 5.3 , Fiber: 1 , Carbs: 32.2 , Protein: 8

CRISPY CORN

Time To Prepare: 8 minutes

Time to Cook: five minutes

Yield: Servings 3

Ingredients:
- ½ teaspoon ground paprika
- ½ teaspoon salt
- ¾ teaspoon chili pepper
- 1 cup corn kernels
- 1 tablespoon coconut flour
- 1 tablespoon water
- 3 tablespoons canola oil

Directions:
1. In the mixing container, mix together corn kernels with salt and coconut flour.

2. Put in water and mix up the corn with the help of the spoon.
3. Pour canola oil in the frying pan and heat it.
4. Put in corn kernels mixture and roast it for about four minutes. Stir it occasionally.
5. When the corn kernels are crispy, move them in the plate and dry with the paper towel's help.
6. Put in chili pepper and ground paprika. Mix up well.

Nutritional Info: Calories 179 , Fat: fifteen , Fiber: 2.4 , Carbs: 11.3 , Protein: 2.1

CUCUMBER YOGURT SALAD WITH MINT

Time To Prepare: ten minutes

Time to Cook: 0 minutes

Yield: Servings 2

Ingredients:
- ¼ cup organic coconut milk
- ¼ cup organic mint leaves
- ¼ teaspoon pink Himalayan sea salt
- ½ cup chopped organic red onion
- 1 tablespoon extra virgin olive oil
- 1 tablespoon plain organic goat yogurt
- 1 teaspoon organic dill weed
- 2 chopped organic cucumbers
- 3 tablespoons fresh organic lime juice

Directions:
1. Cut the red onion, dill, cucumbers, and mint and mix them in a big container.
2. Blend them until they're smooth.
3. Top the dressing onto the cucumber salad and mix meticulously. Chill for minimum 1 hour and serve.
4. Enjoy!

Nutritional Info: , Calories: 207 kcal , Protein: 6.9 g , Fat: 13.87 g , Carbohydrates: 18.04 g

CURRY WHEATBERRY RICE

Time To Prepare: ten minutes

Time to Cook: 1 hour fifteen minutes

Yield: Servings 5

Ingredients:
- ¼ cup milk
- ½ cup of rice
- 1 cup wheat berries

- 1 tablespoon curry paste
- 1 teaspoon salt
- 4 tablespoons olive oil
- 6 cups chicken stock

Directions:
1. Put wheatberries and chicken stock in the pan.
2. Close the lid and cook the mixture for an hour over the moderate heat.
3. Then put in rice, olive oil, and salt.
4. Stir thoroughly.
5. Mix up together milk and curry paste.
6. Put in the curry liquid in the rice-wheatberry mixture and stir thoroughly.
7. Boil the meal for fifteen minutes with the closed lid.
8. When the rice is cooked, all the meal is cooked.

Nutritional Info: Calories 232 , Fat: fifteen , Fiber: 1.4 , Carbs: 23.5 , Protein: 3.9

FARRO SALAD WITH ARUGULA

Time To Prepare: ten minutes

Time to Cook: thirty-five minutes

Yield: Servings 2

Ingredients:
- ½ cup farro
- ½ teaspoon ground black pepper
- ½ teaspoon Italian seasoning
- ½ teaspoon olive oil
- 1 ½ cup chicken stock
- 1 cucumber, chopped
- 1 tablespoon lemon juice
- 1 teaspoon salt
- 2 cups arugula, chopped

Directions:
1. Mix up together farro, salt, and chicken stock and move mixture in the pan.
2. Close the lid and boil it for a little more than half an hour.
3. In the meantime, place all rest of the ingredients in the salad container.
4. Chill the farro to the room temperature and put in it in the salad container too.
5. Mix up the salad well.

Nutritional Info: Calories 92 , Fat: 2.3 , Fiber: 2 , Carbs: 15.6 , Protein: 3.9

FETA CHEESE SALAD

Time To Prepare: ten minutes

Time to Cook: 0 minutes

Yield: Servings 2

Ingredients:
- 1 tbsp. olive oil (extra virgin)
- 1 tsp balsamic vinegar
- 2 cucumbers
- 30 g feta cheese
- 4 spring onions
- 4 tomatoes
- Salt

Directions:
1. Cube the tomatoes and cucumbers.
2. Thinly slice the onions.
3. Crush the feta cheese.
4. Mix tomatoes, onions, and cucumbers.
5. Put olive oil, vinegar, and a small amount of salt.
6. Put in feta cheese.
7. Enjoy your meal!

Nutritional Info: , Calories: 221 kcal , Protein: 9.24 g , Fat: 13.84 g , Carbohydrates: 17.18 g

FRESH STRAWBERRY SALSA

Time To Prepare: ten minutes

Time to Cook: 0 minutes

Yield: Servings 6-8

Ingredients:
- ¼ cup fresh lime juice
- ½ cup fresh cilantro
- ½ cup red onion, finely chopped
- ½ teaspoon lime zest, grated
- 1-2 jalapeños, deseeded, finely chopped
- 2 kiwi fruit, peeled, chopped
- 2 pounds fresh ripe strawberries, hulled, chopped
- 2 teaspoons pure raw honey

Directions:
1. Put in lime juice, lime zest and honey into a big container and whisk well.
2. Put in remaining ingredients then mix thoroughly. Cover and set aside for a while for the flavors to set in and serve.

Nutritional Info: , Calories: 119 kcal , Protein: 9.26 g , Fat: 4.38 g , Carbohydrates: 11.73 g

GOAT CHEESE SALAD

Time To Prepare: fifteen minutes

Time to Cook: thirty minutes

Yield: Servings 4

Ingredients:
- ½ cup of walnuts
- ½ head of escarole (medium), torn
- 1 bunch of trimmed and torn arugula
- 1/3 cup extra virgin olive oil
- 2 bunches of medium beets (~1 ½ lbs.) with trimmed tops
- 2 tbsp. of red wine vinegar
- 4 oz. crumbled of goat cheese (aged cheese is preferred)
- Kosher salt + freshly ground black pepper

Directions:
1. Place the beets in water in a deep cooking pan and apply salt as seasoning. Now, boil them using high heat for approximately twenty minutes or until they're soft. Peel them off when they're cool using your fingers or use a knife.
2. To taste, whisk the vinegar with salt and pepper in a big container. Then mix in the olive oil for the dressing. Toss the beets with the dressing, so they're uniformly coated and marinate them for approximately fifteen minutes – 2 hours.
3. Set the oven to 350F. Bring the nuts on a baking sheet and toast them for approximately 8 minutes (stirring them once) until they turn golden brown. Let them cool.
4. Mix and toss the escarole and arugula with the beets and put them in four plates. Put in the walnuts and goat cheese as toppings before you serve.
5. Enjoy!

Nutritional Info: , Calories: 285 kcal , Protein: 11.85 g , Fat: 25.79 g , Carbohydrates: 2.01 g

GREEN BEANS

Time To Prepare: five minutes

Time to Cook: ten minutes

Yield: Servings 5

Ingredients:
- ½ teaspoon kosher salt
- ½ teaspoon of red pepper flakes
- 1½ lbs. green beans, trimmed
- 2 garlic cloves, minced
- 2 tablespoons of extra-virgin olive oil
- 2 tablespoons of water

Directions:
1. Heat oil in a frying pan on medium temperature.
2. Include the pepper flake. Stir to coat in the olive oil.
3. Include the green beans. Cook for seven minutes.
4. Stir frequently. The beans must be brown in some areas.
5. Put in the salt and garlic. Cook for a minute, while stirring.
6. Pour water and cover instantly.
7. Cook covered for 1 more minute.

Nutritional Info: Calories 82 , Carbohydrates: 6g , Total Fat: 6g , Protein: 1g , Fiber: 2g , Sugar: 0g , Sodium: 230mg

GREEN, RED AND YELLOW RICE

Time To Prepare: five minutes

Time to Cook: fifteen minutes

Yield: Servings 10

Ingredients:
- ¼ cup garlic, finely chopped
- 1 cup fresh cilantro, chopped
- 2 cups brown rice, washed
- 2 cups frozen corn, thawed
- 2 cups green onions, chopped
- 2 cups red bell pepper, chopped
- 2 tablespoons olive oil
- Cayenne pepper to taste
- Pepper to taste
- Salt to taste

Directions:
1. Put a big deep cooking pan on moderate heat. Put in 4 cups water and brown rice and cook in accordance with the instructions on the package. Once cooked, cover and save for later.
2. Put a big frying pan on moderate heat. Put in oil. When the oil is heated, put in garlic and sauté for approximately one minute until aromatic.
3. Put in corn, red bell pepper, green onion, salt, pepper and cayenne pepper and sauté for at least two minutes.
4. Put in rice and cilantro. Mix thoroughly and heat meticulously.
5. Serve.

Nutritional Info: , Calories: 89 kcal , Protein: 2.41 g , Fat: 4.01 g , Carbohydrates: 11.26 g

HOT PINK COCONUT SLAW

Time To Prepare: five minutes

Time to Cook: 0 minutes

Yield: Servings 3

Ingredients:
- ¼ cup fresh cilantro, chopped
- ¼ teaspoon salt
- ½ cup big coconut flakes, unsweetened or shredded coconut, unsweetened
- ½ cup radish, thinly cut or shredded carrots
- ½ small jalapeño, deseeded, discard membranes, chopped
- ½ tablespoon honey or maple syrup
- 1 cup red onion, thinly cut
- 1 tablespoon olive oil
- 2 cups purple cabbage, thinly cut
- 2 tablespoons apple cider vinegar
- 2 tablespoons lime juice

Directions:
1. Combine all ingredients into a container and toss thoroughly. Cover and set aside for about forty minutes.
2. Toss thoroughly before you serve.

Nutritional Info: , Calories: 179 kcal , Protein: 3.92 g , Fat: 10.64 g , Carbohydrates: 18.53 g

LENTIL SALAD

Time To Prepare: ten minutes

Time to Cook: 0 minutes

Yield: Servings 2

Ingredients:
- ½ cup parsley
- 1 red bell pepper
- 1 tbsp. lime juice
- 1 tbsp. olive oil
- 2 cups lentil
- 3 spring onions
- A pinch of salt
- fifteen basil leaves
- Turmeric – to your taste

Directions:
1. Cook the lentils based on the package instructions. Put in a garlic clove while cooking.
2. When cooled, remove the garlic clove and put the lentils into a big container.
3. Chop all the vegetables then put in them to the lentils.
4. Put in lime juice, a small amount of salt, and olive oil.
5. Mix thoroughly.

Nutritional Info: , Calories: 207 kcal , Protein: 11.53 g , Fat: 10.49 g , Carbohydrates: 22.37 g

MASCARPONE COUSCOUS

Time To Prepare: fifteen minutes

Time to Cook: 7.5 hours

Yield: Servings 4

Ingredients:
- ½ cup mascarpone
- 1 cup couscous
- 1 teaspoon ground paprika
- 1 teaspoon salt
- 3 ½ cup chicken stock

Directions:
1. Put chicken stock and mascarpone in the pan and bring the liquid to boil.
2. Put in salt and ground paprika. Stir gently and simmer for a minute.
3. Take off the liquid from the heat and put in couscous. Stir thoroughly and close the lid.
4. Leave couscous for about ten minutes.
5. Mix the cooked side dish well before you serve.

Nutritional Info: Calories 227 , Fat: 4.9 , Fiber: 2.4 , Carbs: 35.4 , Protein: 9.7

FRIED PINEAPPLE SLICE

Time To Prepare: ten minutes

Time to Cook: 8 minutes

Yield: Servings 8

Ingredients:
- ¼ cup of coconut oil
- ¼ cup of coconut palm sugar
- ¼ teaspoon of ground cinnamon
- 1 fresh pineapple (peeled and slice into big slices)

Directions:
1. Warm a huge cast-iron frying pan on moderate heat.
2. Put in oil and sugar and cook until the coconut oil has melted while stirring constantly.
3. Put in the pineapple slices into two batches and cook for roughly 1-2 minutes.
4. Flip the medial side and cook for approximately one minute. Carry on cooking for one more minute.
5. Repeat the steps with the rest of the slices.
6. Drizzle with cinnamon before you serve.

Nutritional Info: , Calories: 138 , Fat: 7g , Carbohydrates: 20.9g , Sugar: 15.7g , Protein: 0.6g , Sodium: 15mg

FRUIT COBBLER

Time To Prepare: ten minutes

Time to Cook: twenty minutes

Yield: Servings 8

Ingredients:
- ¼ Cup Coconut Oil, Melted
- ¼ Cup Coconut Sugar
- ½ Teaspoon Vanilla Extract, Pure
- ¾ Cup Almond Flour
- ¾ Cup Rolled Oats
- 1 Teaspoon Coconut Oil
- 1 Teaspoon Ground Cinnamon
- 2 Cups Nectarines, Fresh & Sliced
- 2 Cups Peaches, Fresh & Sliced
- 2 Tablespoons Lemon Juice, Fresh
- Dash Salt
- Filter Water for Mixing

Directions:
1. Begin by heating the oven to 425.
2. Get out a cast-iron frying pan, coating it with a teaspoon of coconut oil.
3. Mix your lemon juice, peaches, and nectarines together in the frying pan.
4. Prepare your food processor, mixing your almond flour, oats, coconut sugar, and remaining coconut oil. Put in in your cinnamon, vanilla, and salt, pulsing until the oat mixture looks like a dry dough.
5. If you need more moisture, put in filtered water a tablespoon at a time, and then break the dough into chunks, spreading it across the fruit.
6. Bake for 20 minutes before you serve warm.

Nutritional Info: , Protein: 4 Grams , Fat: 12 Grams , Carbohydrates: fifteen Grams

FRUIT SALAD

Time To Prepare: 10 Minutes

Time to Cook: 20 Minutes

Yield: Servings 2-3

Ingredients:
- ½ of 1 Watermelon, chopped into little pieces
- 1 Pineapple, cut into little pieces
- 1 Pomegranate, small
- 1 Red Papaya, cut into little pieces
- 1 tsp. Ginger, freshly grated

- 4 Strawberries, chopped
- Dash of Turmeric

Directions:
1. To start with, place all the fruits in a large-sized container.
2. Next, spoon in the turmeric and ginger over the fruits.
3. Toss thoroughly before you serve.

Nutritional Info: , Calories: 118Kcal , Protein: 1.6g , Carbohydrates: 36.6g , Fat: 0.5g

GLAZED BANANA

Time To Prepare: ten minutes

Time to Cook: five minutes

Yield: Servings 2

Ingredients:
- 1 peeled and cut under-ripened banana
- 1 tbsp. of filtered water
- 1 tbsp. of olive oil
- 1 tbsp. of raw honey
- 1/8 tsp. of ground cinnamon

Directions:
1. In a nonstick frying pan, warm oil on moderate heat.
2. Put in banana slices and cook for approximately 1-2 minutes per side.
3. In the meantime, in a small container, put in water and honey and beat thoroughly.
4. Move the banana slices on a serving plate.
5. Instantly, pour honey mixture over banana slices.
6. Keep aside to cool to room temperature. Serve with the drizzling of cinnamon.

Nutritional Info: , Calories: 145 , Fat: 7.2g , Carbohydrates: 22.2g , Protein: 0.7g , Fiber: 1.6g

GLORIOUS BLUEBERRY CRUMBLE

Time To Prepare: ten minutes

Time to Cook: thirty minutes

Yield: Servings 6

Ingredients:
- ½ cup of softened coconut oil
- ½ tsp. of ground cinnamon
- 1 cup of almond meal
- 1 cup of toasted and finely crushed almonds
- 2 tbsp. of coconut sugar
- 4 cups of fresh blueberries

Directions:

1. Set the oven to 350F then lightly, grease a pie dish.
2. In a huge container, combine all ingredients apart from blueberries.
3. Split half of the almond mixture at the bottom of the prepared pie dish.
4. Put blueberries over almond mixture uniformly.
5. Top with the rest of the almond mixture uniformly.
6. Bake for minimum 30 minutes or till the top becomes golden brown.
7. Serve warm.

Nutritional Info: , Calories: 411 , Fat: 34.3g , Carbohydrates: 24.9g , Protein: 7.4g , Fiber: 6.4g

GREEN TEA PUDDING

Time To Prepare: twenty minutes

Time to Cook: ten minutes

Yield: Servings 3

Ingredients:
- 1 Tsp. Matcha Green Tea Powder
- 1/4 Cup Brown Sugar
- 1/4 Cup Corn Starch
- 1/8-Tbsp. Cinnamon Powder
- 100g Butter
- 2 Cup Heavy Milk
- 3 Eggs
- Salt

Directions:

1. In a big pot, mix brown sugar, milk, cornstarch, and matcha powder.
2. In moderate heat, keep whisking until combined.
3. Combine the hot batter with whisked eggs slowly.
4. Cook for three to five minutes.
5. Strain the mixture and put in butter.
6. Place the mixture in a container, place in your fridge for a few hours before you serve.

Nutritional Info: , Calories: 359 kcal , Carbohydrates: 60 g , Fat: 3.0 g , Protein: 18.4 g

GRILLED PEACHES

Time To Prepare: ten minutes

Time to Cook: ten minutes

Yield: Servings 6

Ingredients:
- ¼ cup of walnuts, chopped
- ½ cup of coconut cream

- 1 teaspoon of organic vanilla extract
- 3 medium peaches (halved and pitted)
- Ground cinnamon

Directions:
1. Preheat the grill on moderate to low heat. Grease the grill grate.
2. Position the peach slices on the grill with the cut-side down.
3. Grill each side for three to five minutes or until the desired doneness is attained.
4. .In the meantime, mix coconut cream with vanilla extract in a container. Beat until the desired smoothness is achieved.
5. Ladle the whipped cream over each peach half.
6. Top with walnuts and drizzle with cinnamon. Serve instantly.

Nutritional Info: , Calories: 110 , Fat: 8g , Carbohydrates: 8.8g , Sugar: 7.8g , Protein: 2.4g , Sodium: 3mg

HOT CHOCOLATE

Time To Prepare: 5 Minutes

Time to Cook: 5 Minutes

Yield: Servings 2

Ingredients:
- ¼ tsp. Turmeric
- ½ tsp. Cinnamon
- 1 tbsp. Coconut Oil
- 1 tbsp. Honey, raw
- 2 cups Almond Milk
- 2 tbsp. Cocoa Powder, unsweetened

Directions:
1. To start with, bring the almond milk to its boiling point in a deep deep cooking pan on moderate heat.
2. Now, bring this mixture to a simmer and then mix in the cocoa powder to it.
3. Next, spoon in the turmeric powder and cinnamon to it. Mix thoroughly/
4. Next, put in honey to it and once blended well, put in the coconut oil
5. Give the drink a good stir until everything comes together.
6. Serve instantly.

Nutritional Info: , Calories: 150 Kcal , Protein: 2.1g , Carbohydrates: 15.2g , Fat: 11.1gm

LEMON SORBET

Time To Prepare: ten minutes

Time to Cook: 0 minutes

Yield: Servings 2

Ingredients:
- ½ cup of raw honey
- ½ cups of fresh lemon juice
- 2 cups of filtered water
- 2 tablespoons of fresh lemon zest, grated

Directions:
1. Put into your freezer the ice-cream maker tub for a day before making the sorbet.
2. Combine all ingredients in a pan, excluding the freshly squeezed lemon juice and cook on moderate heat.
3. Simmer for minimum 1 minute, up to the sugar dissolves while stirring constantly.
4. Take away the mixture from the heat and put in lemon juice.
5. Move the combination to an airtight container and place in your fridge for around 2hours.
6. Put it into an ice-cream maker and process according to the manufacturer's instructions.
7. Put in one tablespoon of oil when the motor is running.
8. Return the ice-cream into the airtight container and freeze for roughly 2 hours.

Nutritional Info: , Calories: 305 , Fat: 1.5g , Carbohydrates: 74.9g , Sugar: 73.8g , Protein: 1.9g , Sodium: 40mg

LEMON VEGAN CAKE

Time To Prepare: ten minutes

Time to Cook: ten minutes

Yield: Servings 3

Ingredients:
- ½ lemon extract
- 1 cup of pitted dates
- 1 lemon juice and zest
- 1½ cup agave
- 1½ cups of dairy-free yogurt
- 1½ cups pineapple, crushed
- 1½ teaspoon vanilla extract
- 2½ cups pecans ½
- 3 avocados, halved & pitted
- 3 cups of cauliflower rice, prepared
- Pinch of cinnamon

Directions:
1. Coat your baking sheet using parchment paper.
2. Pulse the pecans in a food processor.
3. Put in the agave and dates. Pulse for one minute.
4. Move this mix to the baking sheet. Wipe the container of your processor.
5. Combine the pineapple, agave, avocados, cauliflower, lemon juice, and zest in a food processor. Pulse till smooth

6. Now put in the lemon extract, cinnamon, and vanilla extract. Pulse.
7. Pour this mix into your pan, on the crust.
8. Place in your fridge for around five hours at least.
9. Take out the cake and keep it at room temperature for about twenty minutes.
10. Take out the cake's outer ring.
11. Mix together the vanilla extract, agave, and yogurt in a container.
12. Pour on your cake.

Nutritional Info: Calories 688 , Carbohydrates: 100g , Fat: 28g , Protein: 9g , Sugar: 40g

LEMONADE ICE POPS

Time To Prepare: 4 hours and ten minutes

Time to Cook: 0 minutes

Yield: Servings 4

Ingredients:
- 1 cup hot water
- 2 cups cold water
- 2 iced tea and lemonade tea bags

Directions:
1. Put hot water in a container, put in tea bags, cover, and set aside for about ten minutes to steep. Squeeze the tea bags to take off all the water and then discard them. Put in cold water, split into your ice pop maker, freeze for around six hours, before you serve.
2. Enjoy!

Nutritional Info: , Calories: 38 , Fat: 0 , Fiber: 0 , Carbohydrates: 0 , Protein: 1

MATCHA AND BLUEBERRIES PUDDING

Time To Prepare: three hours

Time to Cook: 0 minutes

Yield: Servings 2

Ingredients:
- 1 banana, cut
- 1 cup blueberries
- 1 cup matcha green tea powder
- 2 cups almond milk
- 4 tablespoons chia seeds

Directions:

1. Put chia seeds, milk and matcha powder in a container. Stir, cover, then place in your fridge for around three hours. Split into bowls, top with banana slices and blueberries before you serve.
2. Enjoy!

Nutritional Info: , Calories: 324 , Fat: 9 , Fiber: 18 , Carbohydrates: 24 , Protein: 8

MEDITERRANEAN ROLLED BAKLAVA WITH WALNUTS

Time To Prepare: twenty minutes

Time to Cook: forty minutes

Yield: Servings 12

Ingredients:
- 1 cup Cream of wheat or plain breadcrumbs
- 1 Lemon zest
- 1 medium Lemon
- 1/3 cup Milk
- 2 cups Walnuts
- 3 cups Granulated sugar
- 3 cups Water
- 3 sticks Melted Unsalted butter
- 3 tbsp. Sugar
- 8 sheets Thawed phyllo dough
- Syrup:

Directions:
1. Mix 3 cups of sugar, 3 cups of water and lemon slices in a pan and leave to boil
2. Reduce the heat, then allow it to simmer until the sugar completely dissolves. It should take fifteen minutes. You should have a nice smooth syrup now. Now allow to cool for a bit.
3. Cut the walnuts in a blender into bits using short pulses.
4. Pour the walnuts in a container together with the cream of wheat, lemon zest and 4 tablespoons of sugar.
5. Mix in milk and save for later.
6. Now, preheat the oven to 375°F.
7. Spread out the phyllo dough and fit it into a baking pan. Trim off the edges that do not fit with scissors. Cover the rest of the phyllo sheets while you work so they do not dry out.
8. Put a sheet on a clean flat surface and glaze with melted butter. Do this for all the sheets until it's finished.
9. Position the walnut mixture on one side of the sheets and roll them up like you're trying to make a sausage. Do this for all the sheets and walnuts.
10. Position the walnut rolls on an ungreased baking pan and glaze with the leftover butter.
11. Bake for approximately 45 minutes. It's ready when it looks golden.

12. Turn off the oven then pull out the baking pan. Sprinkle syrup over the baklava, ensuring the syrup gets everywhere.
13. Bring back the baking pan into the oven then let sit for five minutes.
14. Remove from the oven and allow to cool for a few hours. Cut the rolls into small amounts before you serve.

Nutritional Info: , Calories: 488 kcal **,** Protein: 4.49 g **,** Fat: 36.89 g **,** Carbohydrates: 38.21 g

MINT CHOCOLATE CHIP ICE-CREAM

Time To Prepare: five minutes

Time to Cook: 0 minutes

Yield: Servings 2

Ingredients:
- ½ cup Raw cashews or coconut cream, optional.
- 1/8 tsp. Pure peppermint extract
- 2 Frozen overripe bananas
- 3 tbsp. Chocolate chips or sugar-free chocolate chips
- Pinch Salt
- Pinch Spirulina or any natural food coloring, optional.

Directions:
1. Mint or imitation peppermint won't be a substitute for this. Use pure peppermint extract and pour in slowly.
2. Peel and chop the bananas first. Put the slices in a Ziplock bag then freeze.
3. For the ice cream, put all the ingredients in a blender and pulse. You can skip the chocolate chips and just put in them after blending.
4. Serve the moment it's ready or freeze until it's firm enough, then serve!

Nutritional Info: , Calories: 250 kcal **,** Protein: 6.13 g **,** Fat: 24.37 g **,** Carbohydrates: 7.72 g

NO-BAKE CARROT CAKE BITES

Time To Prepare: fifteen minutes

Time to Cook: 0 minutes

Yield: Servings 6

Ingredients:
- ½ teaspoon of ground ginger
- ¾ cup of shredded coconut
- 1 and a ½ cups of carrots
- 1 cup of pitted Medjool dates
- 1 cup of walnuts
- 1 tablespoon of pure maple syrup
- 1 teaspoon of cinnamon

Directions:

1. Put all together the ingredients into a high-speed blender or food processor, and blend until the mixture comes together, putting in a teaspoon of water at a time if required.
2. Take the carrot mixture and press down into a cupcake tin, and place in your fridge until firm.
3. Pop the carrot cakes out of the muffin tin, and enjoy!

Nutritional Info: , Total Carbohydrates: 32g **,** Fiber: 5g **,** Net Carbohydrates: **,** Protein: 3g **,** Total Fat: 12g **,** Calories: 231

NO-BAKE CHEESECAKE

Time To Prepare: twenty minutes

Time to Cook: 0 minutes

Yield: Servings 12

Ingredients:

For Crust:
- 1 cup of dates (pitted and chopped)
- 1 cup of raw almonds
- two to three tablespoons of unsweetened coconut, shredded

For Filling:
- ½ cup of coconut oil, melted
- ¾ cup of fresh lemon juice
- ¾ cup of raw honey
- 1 teaspoon of organic vanilla extract
- 10 drops of liquid stevia
- 2 tablespoons of fresh lemon rind, grated finely
- 3½ cups of cashews, soaked overnight
- A thinly cut lemon
- Salt

Directions:

1. Put together the dates, almonds, and coconut in a blender and pulse.
2. Move the puree a greased springform pan.
3. Smooth the outer lining of the crust using a spatula.
4. Put cashews and oil in a food processor and pulse.
5. Put in the rest of the ingredients except for lemon slices and pulse until it turns creamy and smooth.
6. Put the combination over the crust uniformly.
7. Smooth the counter of filling using the corner of a spatula.
8. Place in your fridge for one hour.
9. Take it off from the fridge and decorate with lemon slices.
10. Chop it into desired sized slices before you serve.

Nutritional Info: , Calories: 468 , Fat: 32g , Carbohydrates: 6.6g , Sugar: 44.1g , Protein: 8.4g , Sodium: 23mg

PALEO RASPBERRY CREAM PIE

Time To Prepare: twenty minutes

Time to Cook: 0 minutes

Yield: Servings 12

Ingredients:

For the crust:
- ½ cup Unsweetened shredded coconut
- 1 ½ tbsp. Maple syrup
- 1 cup Roasted or salted cashews
- 1 tsp. Vanilla extract
- Pinch Salt

Raspberry filling:
- ¼ cup & 2 tsp. Fresh lemon juice
- ¼ cup Coconut cream from the top solid part of a can of coconut milk that has been placed in the fridge overnight
- ½ cup & 1 tbsp. Maple syrup
- ¾ cup Unrefined coconut oil
- 1 ½ cup Roasted or salted cashews
- 2 tsp. Vanilla extract
- 3 cups Fresh raspberries
- Pinch Salt

Directions:
1. Prepare 12 muffin pans, line them with muffin liners, and set them aside.
2. Make the crust. Set a pan on moderate heat and the coconut and stir until it's completely toasted. Stay by the pan because coconuts tend to burn very easily.
3. Move the toasted coconuts to a container and leave to cool for five minutes or so. Honestly, this toasting step isn't particularly necessary, but I feel it adds amazing flavor to pie crust.
4. To make the crust, put all the ingredients in a blender and pulse at the lowest speed until the mix gets all clumpy. Also, do not pulse for too long, or you might end up with a paste. To know if it's ready, put a small amount of the mixture on your fingers and pinch. If it gets clumpy, you're on track, if not, put in a little water and pulse at the lowest speed for further minutes.
5. Scoop the mix into the lined tins using your fingers to pack the mix firmly inside the pan.
6. Place the pans to place in your fridge while you get to make the filling.
7. In a tiny pot set using low heat, mix in all the ingredients until the oil and coconut cream melts completely. Clean the blender using a paper towel and pour in the filling.
8. Pulse at high-speed for like 60 seconds or until it's super smooth. The only clumps we can forgive are the raspberry seeds.

9. Sprinkle a quarter of the filling over the top of each crust. There must be extra filling; you can store and use that in a different dish.
10. Put the coated muffins in your refrigerator to cool. This will take a few hours, like 6 hours, so if you do not have time for that, put it in the freezer.
11. To serve, allow them to defrost for 80 minutes or until obviously creamy.

Nutritional Info: , Calories: 565 kcal , Protein: 7.74 g , Fat: 43.72 g , Carbohydrates: 42.72 g

PEANUT BUTTER BALLS

Time To Prepare: twenty minutes

Time to Cook: thirty minutes

Yield: Servings 5

Ingredients:
- 1 Tsp. Vanilla Extract
- 2 Tbsp. Peanut Oil.
- 200g Powdered Sugar
- 250g Chocolate
- 250g Creamy Peanut Butter
- 90g Melted Butter

Direction:
1. Mix everything apart from the oil and chocolates to make a batter
2. Place in your fridge the batter for about forty-five minutes.
3. Make small balls with the batter using and put them on a parchment paper. Place in your fridge for one more hour.
4. Melt some dark chocolate. Place the peanut balls into the chocolate and place in your fridge for about twenty minutes.
5. Serve with strawberry.

Nutritional Info: , Calories: 340 kcal , Carbohydrates: 32 g , Fat: 21 g , Protein: 1.4 g.

PEANUT BUTTER COOKIES

Time To Prepare: fifteen Minutes

Time to Cook: 0 Minute

Yield: Servings 9

Ingredients:
- ½ a cup of peanut butter (creamy and unsalted)
- 1 and a ¼ teaspoon of vanilla extract
- 1 cup of pitted Medjool dates
- 1 cup of raw almonds
- Sea salt as required

Directions:

1. Take a food processor and put in almonds, peanut butter, vanilla, dates and blend the whole mixture until a dough-like texture comes (should take a few minutes)
2. If you desire, put in some more peanut butter to make the dough sticker.
3. Form balls using the dough and press down using a fork to create a criss-cross pattern
4. Drizzle salt liberally
5. Serve instantly.

Nutritional Info: , Calories: 350 Cal , Fat: 17 g , Carbohydrates: 27 g , Protein: 18 g

PINEAPPLE CAKE

Time To Prepare: fifteen minutes

Time to Cook: 50 minutes

Yield: Servings 8

Ingredients:
- ½ tsp. Baking powder
- 1 tbsp. Almond flour
- 1 tsp. Vanilla extract
- 2 slices Fresh pineapples
- 2 Whole medium eggs
- 3 tbsp. Melted coconut oil
- 5 tbsp. Raw honey
- fifteen pcs. Frozen sweet cherries

Directions:
1. Preheat your oven to 350°F.
2. Take away the skin and core of the pineapples. Set aside.
3. Sprinkle 1½ tablespoons of raw honey in a round cake tin.
4. Layer the pineapple rings and sweet cherries on the honey in a decorative fashion.
5. Bring the cake tin in your oven then bake for fifteen minutes.
6. While all that is going on, mix in the almond and baking powder.
7. In a different container, mix the eggs and leftover honey. Sprinkle in coconut oil and stir.
8. Now put in the almond mix to the egg mix and stir meticulously.
9. Take out the cake tin and sprinkle batter over the top of the partly baked pineapple rings and use a spatula to spread it uniformly.
10. Place the cake tin back in your oven and bake for an additional thirty-five minutes.
11. When it's all set, take it out of the oven and leave it to sit for about ten minutes before place it to a plate.
12. Serve with extra cherries if you prefer.

Nutritional Info: , Calories: 120 kcal , Protein: 2.3 g , Fat: 6.99 g , Carbohydrates: 12.98 g

PINEAPPLE PIE

Time To Prepare: fifteen minutes

Time to Cook: 50 minutes

Yield: Servings 8

Ingredients:
- ½-tsp baking powder
- 1-cup almond flour
- 1-tsp pure vanilla extract
- 2-pcs eggs
- 2-pcs fresh pineapple, peeled, cored, and cut into rings
- 3-Tbsps liquid coconut oil
- 5-Tbsps raw honey (divided)
- fifteen-pcs sweet cherries, fresh or frozen

Directions:
1. Preheat the oven to 350 °F.
2. Pour 1½-tablespoon of the honey in a round baking tin. Position the cherries and pineapple rings on the bed of honey in a decorative pattern. Put the pan in your oven, then bake for minimum fifteen minutes.
3. Meanwhile, mix in all the rest of the ingredients in a mixing container. Mix thoroughly until forming the mixture into dough. Set aside.
4. Take the pan out from the oven. Push down the batter over the pineapple rings, smoothing it at the top.
5. Return the pan in your oven, and bake further for a little more than half an hour.

Nutritional Info: , Calories: 213 , Fat: 7.1g , Protein: 15.9g , Sodium: 39.2mg , Total Carbohydrates: 23.7g , Fiber: 2.4g , Net Carbohydrates: 21.3g

PISTACHIOED PANNA-COTTA COCOA

Time To Prepare: eighteen minutes

Time to Cook: two minutes

Yield: Servings 6

Ingredients:
- 12-oz. dark chocolate
- 1-Tbsp coconut oil
- 3-pcs big bananas, cut into thirds
- Cocoa nibs, chopped
- Salted pistachios, chopped
- Spiced or smoked almonds, chopped

Directions:
1. Coat a baking pan using parchment paper.
2. Melt the dark chocolate with oil in your microwave. Set aside.
3. Pierce a Popsicle stick midway into one end of each banana.

4. Immerse each banana into the melted chocolate. Put dipped bananas into the baking sheet. Drizzle liberally with the cocoa nibs, almonds, and pistachios. Put the sheet in your freezer to harden and set.

Nutritional Info: , Calories: 454 , Fat: 15.1g , Protein: 22.7g , Sodium: 91mg , Total Carbohydrates: 61.6g , Fiber: 4.9g , Net Carbohydrates: 56.7g

PUMPKIN ICE CREAM

Time To Prepare: fifteen minutes

Time to Cook: 0 minutes

Yield: Servings 6

Ingredients:
- ½ cup of dates (pitted and chopped)
- ½ teaspoon of ground cinnamon
- ½ teaspoon of vanilla flavor
- 1 (fifteen-ounce) can of sugar-free pumpkin puree
- 1 ½ teaspoon of pumpkin pie spice
- 2 (14-ounce) cans of unsweetened coconut milk
- Pinch of salt

Directions:
1. Combine all ingredients in a high-speed blender and pulse.
2. Move the puree to an airtight container and freeze for roughly 1-2 hours.
3. Move the frozen puree to an ice-cream maker and process following the manufacturers.
4. Return the ice-cream to the airtight container and freeze for approximately 1-2 hours before you serve.

Nutritional Info: , Calories: 373 , Fat: 31.9g , Carbohydrates: 24.7g , Sugar: 16.2g , Protein: 4.2g , Sodium: 51mg

PURE AVOCADO PUDDING

Time To Prepare: three hours

Time to Cook: 0 minutes

Yield: Servings 4

Ingredients:
- ¼ teaspoon cinnamon
- ¾ cup cocoa powder
- 1 cup almond milk
- 1 teaspoon vanilla extract
- 2 avocados, peeled and pitted
- 2 tablespoons stevia
- Walnuts, chopped for serving

Directions:
1. Put in avocados to a blender and pulse well
2. Put in cocoa powder, almond milk, stevia, vanilla bean extract and pulse the mixture well
3. Put into serving bowls then top with walnuts
4. Chill for two to three hours and serve!

Nutritional Info: , Calories: 221 , Fat: 8g , Carbohydrates: 7g , Protein: 3g

RASPBERRY DILUTED FROZEN SORBET

Time To Prepare: 10 min

Time to Cook: 20 min

Yield: Servings 4

Ingredients:
- 1 tsp honey
- 14oz / 400g frozen raspberry
- fl oz / 50g almond milk
- Mint

Directions:
1. Place the almond milk and raspberry in a mixer till it's smooth and leave the consistency in the freezer for about twenty minutes.
2. When serving, place them in ice cream bowls and serve with mint on top.

Nutritional Info: , Calories: 47 , Carbohydrates: 11 g , Protein: 1 g , Fat: 0.4 g , Sugar: 37.2 g , Fiber: 6.0 g , Sodium: 24 mg

RASPBERRY GUMMIES

Time To Prepare: five minutes

Time to Cook: fifteen minutes

Yield: Servings 6

Ingredients:
- ¼ cup of grass-fed gelatin
- ¾ cup of cold water
- 1 cup of frozen raspberries
- 3 tablespoons of raw honey

Directions:
1. Put the water and frozen raspberries into a blender, and blend until the desired smoothness is achieved. Put into a big deep cooking pan on moderate heat.
2. Put in the honey and gelatin and whisk together. Reduce the heat, then whisk for another five minutes.

3. Pour into molds or a baking dish, and place in your fridge for minimum 1 hour until firm. If you use a baking dish, chop the gelatin into squares; if not, just pop the gelatin out of the molds.

Nutritional Info: , Total Carbohydrates: 9g , Fiber: 1g , Net Carbohydrates: , Protein: 0g , Total Fat: 0g , Calories: 37

RASPBERRY GUMMIES

Time To Prepare: five minutes

Time to Cook: fifteen minutes

Yield: Servings 6

Ingredients:
- ¼ cup of grass-fed gelatin
- ¾ cup of cold water
- 1 cup of frozen raspberries
- 3 tablespoons of raw honey

Directions:
1. Pour water into a blender followed by frozen raspberries. Puree and move them to a deep cooking pan on moderate heat.
2. Put in honey and gelatin. Whisk. Reduce the heat, then whisk constantly for five minutes.
3. Place the mixture on a baking dish or molds and place in your fridge for 60 minutes or until it firms.
4. If you used a baking dish, chop the gelatin into squares. Pop the gelatin out with the molds.

Nutritional Info: , Total Carbohydrates: 9g , Fiber: 1g , Protein: 0g , Total Fat: 0g , Calories: 37

RAW BLACK FOREST BROWNIES

Time To Prepare: 2 hours and ten minutes

Time to Cook: 0 minute

Yield: Servings 6

Ingredients:
- ¼ teaspoon salt
- ½ cup almonds, chopped
- ½ cup dates pitted
- 1 and ½ cups cherries, pitted, dried and chopped
- 1 cup raw cacao powder
- 2 cups walnuts, chopped

Directions:
1. Put all ingredients in a food processor
2. Pulse until small crumbs are formed
3. Push the brownie batter in a pan

4. Freeze for a couple of hours
5. Slice before you serve and enjoy!

Nutritional Info: , Calories: 294 , Fat: 18g , Carbohydrates: 33g , Protein: 7g

REFRESHING RASPBERRY JELLY

Time To Prepare: ten minutes+ 1 hour freezing

Time to Cook: thirty minutes

Yield: Servings 4

Ingredients:
- ¼ cup of water
- 1 tbsp. of fresh lemon juice
- 2 pound of fresh raspberries

Directions:
1. In a moderate-sized pan, put in raspberries and water on low heat and cook for approximately 8-ten minutes until done completely.
2. Put in lemon juice and cook for approximately 30 minutes, stirring once in a while.
3. Turn off the heat and put the mixture into a sieve.
4. Position a strainer over a container.
5. Through strainer, strain the mixture by pushing using the backside of a spoon.
6. Place the mixture into a blender then pulse till a jelly-like texture is formed.
7. Move into serving glass bowls and place in your fridge for minimum for approximately 1 hour.

Nutritional Info: , Calories: 119 , Fat: 1.5g , Carbohydrates: 27.2g , Protein: 2.8g , Fiber: 14.8g

ROASTED BANANAS

Time To Prepare: two minutes

Time to Cook: seven minutes

Yield: Servings 1

Ingredients:
- 1 banana, cut into diagonal pieces
- Avocado oil cooking spray

Directions:
1. Take parchment paper and line the air fryer basket with it.
2. Preheat the air fryer to 190 degrees C or 375 degrees F.
3. Keep your slices of banana in the basket. Make sure they do not touch
4. Apply avocado oil to mist the slices of banana.
5. Cook for five minutes.
6. Take out the basket. Flip the slices cautiously.

7. Cook for two more minutes. The slices of banana must be caramelized and brown. Remove them from the basket.

Nutritional Info: Calories 121 , Carbohydrates: 27g , Cholesterol: 0mg , Total Fat: 1g , Protein: 1g , Sugar: 14g , Fiber: 3g , Sodium: 1mg

RUM BUTTER COOKIES

Time To Prepare: ten minutes + chilling time

Time to Cook: five minutes

Yield: Servings 12

Ingredients:
- ½ cup coconut butter
- ½ cup confectioners' Swerve
- 1 stick butter
- 1 teaspoon rum extract
- 4 cups almond meal

Directions:
1. Melt the coconut butter and butter. Mix in the Swerve and rum extract.
2. Afterward, put in in the almond meal and mix to blend.
3. Roll the balls and put them on a parchment-lined cookie sheet.
4. Keep in your fridge until ready to serve.

Nutritional Info: 400 Calories 40g , Fat: 4.9g , Carbs: 5.4g , Protein: 2.9g

SHERBET PINEAPPLE

Time To Prepare: 20 Minutes

Time to Cook: 0 Minute

Yield: Servings 4

Ingredients:
- 1 can of 8-ounce pineapple chunks
- ¼ teaspoon of ground ginger
- ¼ teaspoon of vanilla extract
- 1 can of 11-ounce orange sections
- 2 cups of pineapple, lemon or lime sherbet
- 1/3 cup of orange marmalade

Directions:
1. Drain the pineapple, ensure you reserve the juice.
2. Take a moderate-sized container and put in pineapple juice, ginger, vanilla and marmalade to the container
3. Put in pineapple chunks, drained mandarin oranges as well
4. Toss thoroughly and coat everything

5. Free them for fifteen minutes and let them chill
6. Ladle the sherbet into 4 chilled stemmed sherbet dishes
7. Top each of them with fruit mixture

Enjoy!

Nutritional Info: , Calories: 267 Cal , Fat: 1 g , Carbohydrates: 65 g , Protein: 2 g

SPICED TEA PUDDING

Time To Prepare: ten minutes

Time to Cook: ten minutes

Yield: Servings 3

Ingredients:
- ½ cup coconut flakes
- ½ teaspoon cloves
- 1 ½ cups berries
- 1 can coconut milk
- 1 cup almond milk
- 1 tablespoon chia seeds
- 1 tablespoon ground cinnamon
- 1 tablespoon raw honey
- 1 teaspoon allspice
- 1 teaspoon cardamom
- 1 teaspoon green tea powder
- 1 teaspoon nutmeg
- 2 tablespoons pumpkin seeds
- 2 teaspoons ground ginger

Directions:
1. In your blender, puree tea powder with coconut milk, almond milk, cinnamon, coconut flakes, nutmeg, allspice, cloves, honey, cardamom, and ginger split into bowls. Heat a pan on moderate heat, put in berries until bubbling, then move to your blender and pulse well. Split the berries into the bowls with the coconut milk mix, top with chia seeds and pumpkin seeds before you serve.
2. Enjoy!

Nutritional Info: , Calories: 150 , Fat: 6 , Fiber: 5 , Carbohydrates: 14 , Protein: 8

SPICY POPPER MUG CAKE

Time To Prepare: five minutes

Time to Cook: five minutes

Yield: Servings 2

Ingredients:

- ¼ teaspoon sunflower seeds
- ½ a jalapeno pepper
- ½ teaspoon baking powder
- 1 bacon, cooked and cut
- 1 big egg
- 1 tablespoon almond butter
- 1 tablespoon cashew cheese
- 1 tablespoon flaxseed meal
- 2 tablespoons almond flour

Directions:
1. Take a frying pan then place it on moderate heat
2. Put cut bacon and cook until they have a crunchy texture
3. Take a microwave proof container and mix all of the listed ingredients(including cooked bacon), clean the sides
4. Microwave for 75 seconds making to put your microwave to high power
5. Take out the cup and slam it against a surface to take the cake out
6. Decorate using a bit of jalapeno and serve!

Nutritional Info: , Calories: 429 , Fat: 38g , Carbohydrates: 6g , Protein: 16g

STRAWBERRY GRANITA

Time To Prepare: ten minutes

Time to Cook: ten minutes

Yield: Servings 8

Ingredients:
- ¼ teaspoon balsamic vinegar
- ½ teaspoon lemon juice
- 1 cup of water
- 2 lb. strawberries, halved & hulled
- Agave to taste
- Just a small pinch of salt

Directions:
1. Wash the strawberries in water.
2. Keep in a blender. Put in water, agave, balsamic vinegar, salt, and lemon juice.
3. Pulse multiple times so that the mixture moves. Blend until smooth.
4. Pour into a baking dish. The puree must be 3/8 inch deep only.
5. Place in your fridge the dish uncovered till the edges start to freeze. The center must be slushy.
6. Stir crystals from the edges lightly into the center. Stir thoroughly to mix.
7. Chill till the granite is nearly fully frozen.
8. Scrape loose the crystals like before and mix.
9. Place in your fridge once more. Using a fork, stir 3-4 times till the granite has become light.

Nutritional Info: Calories 72 , Carbohydrates: 17g , Fat: 0g , Sugar: 14g , Fiber: 2g , Protein: 1g

STRAWBERRY ICE CREAM

Time To Prepare: 5 Minutes

Time to Cook: 5 Minutes

Yield: Servings 2-3

Ingredients:
- 1 Banana, frozen & cut
- 1 cup Strawberries, frozen
- 1 tsp. Vanilla extract
- 2 tbsp. Coconut Milk

Directions:
1. Begin by placing strawberries and banana in a high-speed blender and blend it for two to three minutes.
2. While you blend, spoon in the coconut milk, and the vanilla extract.
3. Carry on blending until the mixture is thick and smooth.
4. Serve the ice-cream instantly since it does not keep well in the freezer.

Nutritional Info: , Calories: 78 Kcal , Protein: 1g , Carbohydrates: 13.6g , Fat:2.7g

STRAWBERRY ORANGE SORBET

Time To Prepare: five minutes

Time to Cook: 0 minutes

Yield: Servings 3

Ingredients:
- 1 cup Orange juice or coconut water
- 1 pound Frozen strawberries

Direction:
1. Pour strawberries in a blender and pulse until all you have left are flakes. two minutes tops.
2. Now put in the coconut water or orange juice and pulse until you get a nice and smooth puree. Have a spatula handy because you might need to scrape some of the puree off the walls of the blender sometimes.
3. Serve the moment you're done or put in the freezer for about forty-five minutes for a sorbet feel.
4. Also, you can pour the smoothie into popsicle molds and freeze for hours or even overnight.
5. Enjoy!

Nutritional Info: , Calories: 118 kcal , Protein: 2.88 g , Fat: 2.19 g , Carbohydrates: 23.25 g

STRAWBERRY SHORTCAKE

Time To Prepare: fifteen minutes

Time to Cook: 0 minutes

Yield: Servings 4

Ingredients:
- .25 cup Semi-sweet chocolate chips
- 1 tbsp. Low-calorie margarine
- 12 hulled Strawberries
- 2.3-inch Shortcake, quartered

Directions:
1. Using waxed paper, line a cookie sheet.
2. Thread 2 shortcake pieces and 3 strawberries on 4 skewers.
3. In a small deep cooking pan, mix together the margarine and chocolate chips before placing the deep cooking pan on the stove over a burner turned to low heat. Stir until the ingredients are well mixed.
4. Sprinkle the chocolate onto the kabobs and then put them in your fridge for about four minutes to cool.

Nutritional Info: , Calories: 40 kcal , Protein: 1.85 g , Fat: 2.3 g , Carbohydrates: 3.32 g

STRAWBERRY SOUFFLÉ

Time To Prepare: fifteen minutes

Time to Cook: twelve minutes

Yield: Servings 6

Ingredients:
- 18 ounces of fresh strawberries, hulled
- 5 organic egg whites, divided
- 4 teaspoons of fresh lemon juice
- 1/3 cup of raw honey, divided

Directions:
1. Preheat your oven to 350F.
2. Place the strawberries in a blender then pulse until a puree form.
3. Strain the strawberry puree using a strainer while discarding the seeds.
4. Mix the strawberry puree to three tablespoons of honey, two egg whites, and fresh lemon juice. Pulse until a frothy and light-weight develops.
5. Beat the eggs in a separate container up to it becomes frothy.
6. Put in the remaining honey and beat until a stiff peak forms.
7. Gently- fold the egg whites into the strawberry mixture.
8. Move the mixture toto six big ramekins and place them on a baking sheet.

9. Bake for around 10-twelve minutes.
10. Take out of the oven and serve instantly.

Nutritional Info: , Calories: 100 , Fat: 0.3g , Carbohydrates: 22.3g , Sugar: 19.9g , Protein: 3.7g , Sodium: 30mg

SWEET ALMOND AND COCONUT FAT BOMBS

Time To Prepare: ten minutes + twenty minutes chill time

Time to Cook: 0 minutes

Yield: Servings 4

Ingredients:
- ¼ cup melted coconut oil
- 3 tablespoons cocoa
- 9 and ½ tablespoons almond butter
- 9 tablespoons melted almond butter, sunflower seeds
- 90 drops liquid stevia

Directions:
1. Take a container and put in all of the listed ingredients
2. Combine them well
3. Pour scant 2 tablespoons of the mixture into as many muffin molds as you prefer
4. Chill for about twenty minutes and pop them out
5. Serve and enjoy!

Nutritional Info: , Total Carbohydrates: 2g , Fiber: 0g , Protein: 2.53g , Fat: 14g

THE MOST ELEGANT PARSLEY SOUFFLÉ EVER

Time To Prepare: five minutes

Time to Cook: six minutes

Yield: Servings 5

Ingredients:
- 1 fresh red chili pepper, chopped
- 1 tablespoon fresh parsley, chopped
- 2 tablespoons coconut cream
- 2 whole eggs
- Sunflower seeds to taste

Directions:
1. Preheat the oven to 390 degrees F

2. Almond butter 2 soufflé dishes
3. Place the ingredients to a blender and mix thoroughly
4. Split batter into soufflé dishes and bake for about six minutes
5. Serve and enjoy!

Nutritional Info: , Calories: 108 , Fat: 9g , Carbohydrates: 9g , Protein: 6g

TROPICAL FRUIT CRISP

Time To Prepare: ten minutes

Time to Cook: fifteen minutes

Yield: Servings 6

Ingredients:

For the Filling:
- 1 big mango (cut into chunks)
- 1 big pineapple (cut into chunks)
- 1/8 teaspoon of ground cinnamon
- 1/8 teaspoon of ground ginger
- 2 tablespoons of coconut oil
- 2 tablespoons of coconut sugar

For the Topping:
- ¾ cup of almonds
- ½ teaspoon of ground allspice
- ½ teaspoon of ground cinnamon
- ½ teaspoon of ground ginger
- 1/3 cup of unsweetened coconut, shredded

Directions:
1. Preheat your oven to 375 degrees F.
2. To make the filling: melt the coconut oil in a pan on medium-low heat and cook the coconut sugar for a couple of minutes while stirring.
3. Put in the rest of the ingredients then cook for minimum five minutes. Stir.
4. Take away the contents from heat and move it to a baking dish.
5. For the topping: Combine all ingredients in a mixer and pulse until a coarse meal forms.
6. Put the topping over the filling.
7. Bake for minimum fifteen minutes or until the top becomes golden brown.

Nutritional Info: , Calories: 265 , Fat: 12.4g , Carbohydrates: 38g , Sugar: 23.3g , Protein: 4.3g , Sodium: 17mg

TROPICAL POPSICLES

Time To Prepare: 10 Minutes

Time to Cook: 10 Minutes

Yield: Servings 6

Ingredients:
- ½ tsp. Black Pepper
- 2 Kiwi, cut
- 2 tbsp. Coconut Oil
- 2 tsp. Turmeric
- 3 cups Pineapple, chopped

Directions:
1. First, place all the ingredients needed to make the popsicles excluding the kiwi in a high-speed blender for a couple of minutes or until you get a smooth mixture.
2. After this, pour the smoothie into the popsicle molds.
3. Next, insert the kiwi slices into the molds and then put the frames in the freezer until set.
4. Tip: If you desire texture, you can blend it less.

Nutritional Info: , Calories: 101 Kcal , Protein: 0.5g , Carbohydrates: 15g , Fat:4g

TURMERIC MILKSHAKE

Time To Prepare: five minutes

Time to Cook: 0 minutes

Yield: Servings 2

Ingredients:
- 1 tablespoon of ground flaxseeds
- 1 teaspoon of turmeric
- 2 cups of unsweetened almond milk
- 2 frozen bananas
- 2 tablespoons of raw cocoa powder
- 3 tablespoons of raw honey

Directions:
1. Combine all ingredients into a high-speed blender, and blend until the desired smoothness is achieved.
2. Split between two serving glasses, and enjoy straight away.

Nutritional Info: , Total Carbohydrates: 74g , Fiber: 7g , Protein: 4g , Total Fat: 6g , Calories: 334

VANILLA CAKES

Time To Prepare: ten minutes

Time to Cook: fifteen minutes

Yield: Servings 8

Ingredients:

- .5 tsp. Baking soda
- .5 tsp. Salt
- 1 cup Agave sweetener
- 1 cup Almond milk
- 1 tbsp. Apple cider vinegar
- 2 cup Whole wheat flour
- 2 tsp. Baking powder
- C.5 cup warmed coconut oil
- tsp. Vanilla extract

Directions:
1. Ensure the oven is set to 350F.
2. Prepare two muffin pans (12 c) for use by greasing them.
3. Put in the apple cider vinegar into a measuring c that is big enough to hold minimum 2 c. Put in in the almond milk for a total of 1.5 c. Allow the results to curdle roughly five minutes or until done.
4. Put together the salt, baking soda, baking powder, sugar, and flour together in a big container and whisk well.
5. Separately, mix the vanilla, coconut oil, and curdled almond in its container before combining the two bowls and blending well. Put in the results to the muffin pans, dividing uniformly.
6. Put the muffin pans in your oven and allow them to cook for approximately fifteen minutes. You will know if it's all already cook when you can press down on the tops and spring back when pressed lightly.
7. Allow the cake pans to cool on a wire rack before removing the cakes for the best results.

Nutritional Info: , Calories: 336 kcal **,** Protein: 5.75 g **,** Fat: 16.25 g **,** Carbohydrates: 44.15 g

WATERMELON AND AVOCADO CREAM

Time To Prepare: 2 hours

Time to Cook: 0 minutes

Yield: Servings 4

Ingredients:
- 1 tablespoon honey
- 1 watermelon, peeled and chopped
- 2 avocados, peeled, pitted and chopped
- 2 cups coconut cream
- 2 teaspoons lemon juice

Directions:

Throw all the ingredients into a blender. Split it into bowls, and keep in your refrigerator for about two hours before you serve.

Nutritional Info: Calories 121 , Fat: 2 , Fiber: 2 , Carbohydrates: 6 , Protein: 5

WATERMELON SORBET

Time To Prepare: 5 Minutes

Time to Cook: fifteen Minutes

Yield: Servings 4

Ingredients:
- 1 Seedless Watermelon, cubed

Directions:
1. To start with, put the watermelon cubes in a baking sheet in a uniform layer.
2. Next, keep the sheet in the freezer for about two hours or until the watermelon is solid.
3. After this, move the frozen watermelon cubes in the high-speed blender and puree them until you get a smooth puree.
4. Next, pour the puree among the two loaf pans.

Nutritional Info: , Calories: 427Kcal , Protein:5.9g , Carbohydrates: 80g , Fat: 15.6g

YUMMY FRUITY ICE-CREAM

Time To Prepare: twenty minutes + 3-4 hours freezing

Time to Cook: 0 minutes

Yield: Servings 4

Ingredients:
- ½ cup of coconut cream
- ½ peeled and cut small banana
- 1 cup fresh strawberries, hulled and cut
- 2 tbsp. of shredded coconut

Directions:
1. In a powerful blender, put all together the ingredients and pulse till smooth.
2. Put it into an ice cream maker, then process in accordance with the manufacturer's directions.
3. Now, move into an airtight container. Freeze to set for minimum 3-4 hours, stirring after every thirty minutes.

Nutritional Info: , Calories: 103 , Fat: 8.2g , Carbohydrates: 8.2g , Protein: 1.2g , Fiber: 2g

Stephanie Bennett is an American health coach, foodie, and author based in New York. She enjoys sharing simple, delicious recipes with her readers, and coming up with new ways to help people live a healthier life.

MOROCCAN STYLE COUSCOUS

Time To Prepare: ten minutes

Time to Cook: ten minutes

Yield: Servings 4

Ingredients:
- ½ teaspoon ground cardamom
- ½ teaspoon red pepper
- 1 cup chicken stock
- 1 cup yellow couscous
- 1 tablespoon butter
- 1 teaspoon salt

Directions:
1. Toss butter in the pan and melt it.
2. Put in couscous and roast it for a minute over the high heat.
3. Then put in ground cardamom, salt, and red pepper. Stir it well.
4. Pour the chicken stock and bring the mixture to boil.
5. Simmer couscous for five minutes with the closed lid.

Nutritional Info: Calories 196 , Fat: 3.4 , Fiber: 2.4 , Carbs: 35 , Protein: 5.9

MUSHROOM MILLET

Time To Prepare: ten minutes

Time to Cook: fifteen minutes

Yield: Servings 3

Ingredients:
- ¼ cup mushrooms, cut
- ½ cup millet
- ¾ cup onion, diced
- 1 cup of water
- 1 tablespoon olive oil
- 1 teaspoon butter
- 1 teaspoon salt
- 3 tablespoons milk

Directions:
1. Pour olive oil in the frying pan then put the onion.
2. Put in mushrooms and roast the vegetables for about ten minutes over the moderate heat. Stir them occasionally.
3. In the meantime, pour water in the pan.
4. Put in millet and salt.

5. Cook the millet with the closed lid for fifteen minutes over the moderate heat.
6. Then put in the cooked mushroom mixture in the millet.
7. Put in milk and butter. Mix up the millet well.

Nutritional Info: Calories 198 , Fat: 7.7 , Fiber: 3.5 , Carbs: 27.9 , Protein: 4.7

ONION AND ORANGE HEALTHY SALAD

Time To Prepare: ten minutes

Time to Cook: 0 minutes

Yield: Servings 3

Ingredients:
- ¼ cup of fresh chives, chopped
- 1 cup olive oil
- 1 red onion, thinly cut
- 1 teaspoon of dried oregano
- 3 tablespoon of red wine vinegar
- 6 big orange
- 6 tablespoon of olive oil
- Ground black pepper

Directions:
1. Peel the orange and cut each of them in 4-5 crosswise slices
2. Move the oranges to a shallow dish
3. Sprinkle vinegar, olive oil and drizzle oregano
4. Toss
5. Chill for thirty minutes
6. Position cut onion and black olives on top
7. Garnish with an additional drizzle of chives and a fresh grind of pepper
8. Serve and enjoy!

Nutritional Info: , Calories: 120 , Fat: 6g , Carbohydrates: 20g , Protein: 2g

PARMESAN ROASTED BROCCOLI

Time To Prepare: ten minutes

Time to Cook: twenty minutes

Yield: Servings 6

Ingredients:
- ½ teaspoon of Italian seasoning
- 1 tablespoon of lemon juice
- 1 tablespoon parsley, chopped

- 3 tablespoons of olive oil
- 3 tablespoons of vegan parmesan, grated
- 4 cups of broccoli florets
- Pepper and salt to taste

Directions:
1. Preheat the oven to 450 degrees F. Apply cooking spray on your pan.
2. Keep the broccoli florets in a freezer bag.
3. Now put in the Italian seasoning, olive oil, pepper, and salt.
4. Seal your bag. Shake it. Coat well.
5. Pour your broccoli on the pan. It must be in a single layer.
6. Bake for about twenty minutes. Stir midway through.
7. Take out from the oven. Drizzle parsley and parmesan.
8. Sprinkle some lemon juice.
9. You can decorate with lemon wedges if you wish.

Nutritional Info: Calories 96 , Carbohydrates: 4g , Cholesterol: 2mg , Total Fat: 8g , Protein: 2g , Sugar: 1g , Fiber: 1g , Sodium: 58mg , Potassium: 191mg

QUINOA SALAD

Time To Prepare: ten minutes

Time to Cook: 0 minutes

Yield: Servings 2

Ingredients:
- ¼ tsp sea salt
- ½ cup quinoa (uncooked)
- 1 carrot
- 1 tbsp. apple cider vinegar
- 1 tbsp. flaxseed oil
- 2 brussels sprouts

Directions:
1. Wash quinoa meticulously.
2. Dice the carrots and brussels sprouts to minuscule pieces.
3. Cook the quinoa based on the instruction on the packaging.
4. Mix flaxseed oil, sea salt, and apple cider vinegar.
5. Sauté brussels sprouts and carrots on a small amount of olive oil for a few minutes.
6. After both brussels sprouts and carrots, and quinoa are ready, combine them all in a container.
7. Put in the dressing and mix meticulously.
8. Serve warm.

Nutritional Info: , Calories: 280 kcal , Protein: 10.15 g , Fat: 12.52 g , Carbohydrates: 31.99 g

RED CABBAGE WITH CHEESE

Time To Prepare: five minutes

Time to Cook: twelve minutes

Yield: Servings 4

Ingredients:
- ¼ cup & 1 tbsp. of extra virgin olive oil
- ¼ tsp of freshly ground pepper
- ¼ tsp of salt
- 1 cup of walnuts
- 1 Tbsp. of crumbled blue cheese
- 1 tbsp. of Dijon mustard
- 1 tsp of butter
- 2 thinly cut scallions
- 3 tbsp. of pure maple syrup
- 3 tbsp. of red wine vinegar
- 8 cups of red cabbage, thinly cut

Directions:

For the vinaigrette:
1. Combine the blue cheese, ¼ cup of olive oil, mustard, vinegar, salt, and pepper in a food processor or blender until the mixture has a creamy consistency.

For the salad:
1. Put a parchment paper near the stove.
2. Heat 1 tbsp. Of oil on moderate heat in a moderate-sized frying pan and mix in the walnuts, cooking them for approximately 2 minutes.
3. Now mix salt and pepper, sprinkle maple syrup and cook for approximately three to five minutes while stirring the mixture up to the nuts are uniformly coated.
4. Move to the paper and pour the rest of the syrup over them using a spoon. Separate the nuts and cool down for approximately five minutes.
5. In a big container, put in the cabbage and scallions and toss them with the vinaigrette. Put in the walnuts and blue cheese as toppings.

Nutritional Info: Calories 232 , Fat: 19 gram Saturated , Fat: 4 gram , Sodium: 267 gram , Carbs: 12 gram , Fiber: 2 gram sugar , 8 gram Added sugar 5 gram , Protein: 4 gram

RICE WITH PISTACHIOS

Time To Prepare: ten minutes

Time to Cook: twenty minutes

Yield: Servings 6

Ingredients:

- ¼ cup of raw pistachios (or more for decoration)
- ½ cup of chopped and packed dill leaves
- ½ teaspoon of turmeric
- 1 ½ cups of Basmati rice (rinsed in a colander and soaked in water for approximately 30 minutes, or more)
- 1 teaspoon of vegetable oil
- 1 thinly cut medium onion
- 2 dry baby leaves
- 3 cups of vegetable stock or water
- 5 pods of slightly crushed green cardamom
- Ground black pepper (to taste)
- Salt, to taste

Directions:
1. In a big deep cooking pan, warm the oil and put in the cardamom. Heat it for approximately 1 minute until it turns smildly brown and put in the onion. Sauté for approximately 1-2 minutes.
2. Mix in the dill leaves, turmeric and pistachios. Then put in the rice and stir-fry for approximately one minute.
3. Combine the vegetable stock, black pepper and salt to taste, stir it well and bring it to its boiling point.
4. Cover the pan using lid and cook on moderate to low heat for approximately fifteen minutes.
5. Take it off from the heat then set aside the rice (covered) for approximately ten minutes. Then fluff it using a fork and put in more pistachios as decorate, if you desire.
6. Enjoy!

Nutritional Info: , Calories: 90 kcal , Protein: 3.36 g , Fat: 5.08 g , Carbohydrates: 8.39 g

ROASTED CARROTS

Time To Prepare: ten minutes

Time to Cook: forty minutes

Yield: Servings 4

Ingredients:
- ¼ teaspoon ground pepper
- ½ teaspoon rosemary, chopped
- ½ teaspoon salt
- 1 onion, peeled & cut
- 1 teaspoon thyme, chopped
- 2 tablespoons of extra-virgin olive oil
- 8 carrots, peeled & cut

Directions:
1. Preheat the oven to 425 degrees F.
2. Combine the onions and carrots by tossing in a container with rosemary, thyme, pepper, and salt. Spread on your baking sheet.

3. Roast for forty minutes. The onions and carrots must be browning and soft.

Nutritional Info: Calories 126 , Carbohydrates: 16g , Total Fat: 6g , Protein: 2g , Fiber: 4g , Sugar: 8g , Sodium: 286mg

ROASTED CURRIED CAULIFLOWER

Time To Prepare: five minutes

Time to Cook: thirty minutes

Yield: Servings 4

Ingredients:
- ¾ teaspoon salt
- 1 and ½ tablespoon olive oil
- 1 big head cauliflower, cut into florets
- 1 teaspoon cumin seeds
- 1 teaspoon curry powder
- 1 teaspoon mustard seeds

Directions:
1. Preheat the oven to 375 degrees F
2. Grease a baking sheet with cooking spray
3. Take a container and place all ingredients
4. Toss to coat well
5. Position the vegetable on a baking sheet
6. Roast for thirty minutes
7. Serve and enjoy!

Nutritional Info: , Calories: 67 , Fat: 6g , Carbohydrates: 4g , Protein: 2g

ROASTED PARSNIPS

Time To Prepare: five minutes

Time to Cook: thirty minutes

Yield: Servings 4

Ingredients:
- 1 tablespoon of extra-virgin olive oil
- 1 teaspoon of kosher salt
- 1½ teaspoon of Italian seasoning
- 2 lbs. parsnips
- Chopped parsley for decoration

Directions:
1. Preheat the oven to 400 degrees F.
2. Peel the parsnips. Cut them into one-inch chunks.
3. Now toss with the seasoning, salt, and oil in a container.

4. Spread this on your baking sheet. It must be in a single layer.
5. Roast for half an hour Stir every ten minutes.
6. Move to a plate. Decorate using parsley.

Nutritional Info: Calories 124 , Carbohydrates: 20g , Total Fat: 4g , Protein: 2g , Fiber: 4g , Sugar: 5g , Sodium: 550mg

ROASTED PORTOBELLOS WITH ROSEMARY

Time To Prepare: five minutes

Time to Cook: fifteen minutes

Yield: Servings 4

Ingredients:
- ¼ cup extra virgin olive oil
- 1 clove garlic, minced
- 1 sprig rosemary, torn
- 2 tablespoons fresh lemon juice
- 8 portobello mushroom, trimmed
- Salt and pepper, to taste

Directions:
1. Preheat the oven to 450 degrees F
2. Take a container and put in all ingredients
3. Toss to coat
4. Put the mushroom in a baking sheet stem side up
5. Roast in your oven for fifteen minutes
6. Serve and enjoy!

Nutritional Info: , Calories: 63 , Fat: 6g , Carbohydrates: 2g , Protein:1g

SHOEPEG CORN SALAD

Time To Prepare: ten minutes

Time to Cook: 0 minute

Yield: Servings 4

Ingredients:
- ¼ cup Greek yogurt
- ½ cup cherry tomatoes halved
- 1 cup shoepeg corn, drained
- 1 jalapeno pepper, chopped
- 1 tablespoon chives, chopped
- 1 tablespoon lemon juice

- 3 tablespoons fresh cilantro, chopped

Directions:
1. In the salad container, mix up together shoepeg corn, cherry tomatoes, jalapeno pepper, chives, and fresh cilantro.
2. Put in lemon juice and Greek yogurt. Mix yo the salad well.
3. Put in your fridge and store it for maximum 1 day.

Nutritional Info: Calories 49 , Fat: 0.7 , Fiber: 1.2 , Carbs: 9.4 , Protein: 2.7

SPICED SWEET POTATO BREAD

Time To Prepare: fifteen minutes

Time to Cook: 45-55 minutes

Yield: Servings 2

Ingredients:

For dry Ingredients :
- ¼ teaspoon sea salt
- 1 cup coconut flour
- 1 teaspoon ground mace
- 2 tablespoons ground cinnamon
- 2 teaspoons baking powder
- 2 teaspoons baking soda
- 2 teaspoons ground nutmeg

Wet Ingredients:
- 1 cup almond butter
- 2 teaspoons organic almond extract
- 4 big sweet potatoes, peeled, thinly cut
- 4 tablespoons coconut oil
- 8 big eggs
- 8 tablespoons melted grass fed butter, unsalted

Directions:
1. Grease 2 loaf pans of 9 x 5 inches with coconut oil. Coat the bottom of the pan using parchment paper. Set aside.
2. Put a medium deep cooking pan on moderate heat. Put in sweet potatoes. Pour enough water to immerse the sweet potatoes. Cook until the sweet potatoes are soft.
3. Remove the heat and drain the sweet potatoes.
4. Put in the sweet potatoes back into the pan. Mash with a potato masher until the desired smoothness is achieved. Allow it to cool completely.
5. Put all together the dry ingredients into a container and mix thoroughly.
6. Put in eggs into a big container and whisk well. Put in sweet potatoes, butter, almond extract and almond butter and whisk until well blended.
7. Put in the dry ingredients into the container of wet ingredients and whisk until well blended.

8. Split the batter into the prepared loaf pans.
9. Bake in a preheated oven at 350°F for approximately 45 -55 minutes or a toothpick when inserted in the middle of the loaf comes out clean.
10. Remove from oven and cool to room temperature.
11. Slice using a sharp knife into slices of 1-inch thickness.

Nutritional Info: , Calories: 1738 kcal **,** Protein: 27 g **,** Fat: 145.92 g **,** Carbohydrates: 89.58 g

SPICY BARLEY

Time To Prepare: seven minutes

Time to Cook: 42 minutes

Yield: Servings 5

Ingredients:
- ½ teaspoon cayenne pepper
- ½ teaspoon chili pepper
- ½ teaspoon ground black pepper
- 1 cup barley
- 1 teaspoon butter
- 1 teaspoon olive oil
- 1 teaspoon salt
- 3 cups chicken stock

Directions:
1. Put barley and olive oil in the pan.
2. Roast barley on high heat for a minute. Stir it well.
3. Then put in salt, chili pepper, ground black pepper, cayenne pepper, and butter.
4. Put in chicken stock.
5. Close the lid and cook barley for forty minutes over the medium-low heat.

Nutritional Info: Calories 152 **,** Fat: 2.9 **,** Fiber: 6.5 **,** Carbs: 27.8 **,** Protein: 5.1

SPICY ROASTED BRUSSELS SPROUTS

Time To Prepare: five minutes

Time to Cook: thirty minutes

Yield: Servings 4

Ingredients:
- ½ cup kimchi with juice
- 1 and ¼ pound Brussels sprouts, cut into florets
- 2 tablespoons olive oil
- Salt and pepper, to taste

Directions:
1. Set the oven to 425 F.

2. Toss the Brussels sprouts with pepper, salt, and oil.
3. Bake using your oven for about twenty-five minutes
4. Remove from oven and mix with kimchi
5. Return to the oven
6. Cook for five minutes
7. Serve and enjoy!

Nutritional Info: , Calories: 135 , Fat: 7g , Carbohydrates: 16g , Protein: 5g

SPICY WASABI MAYONNAISE

Time To Prepare: fifteen minutes

Time to Cook: 0 minute

Yield: Servings 4

Ingredients:
- ½ tablespoon wasabi paste
- 1 cup mayonnaise

Directions:
1. Take a container and mix wasabi paste and mayonnaise

Mix thoroughly
2. Allow it to chill, use as required
3. Serve and enjoy

Nutritional Info: , Calories: 388 , Fat: 42g , Carbohydrates: 1g , Protein: 1g

STIR-FRIED ALMOND AND SPINACH

Time To Prepare: ten minutes

Time to Cook: fifteen minutes

Yield: Servings 2

Ingredients:
- 1 tablespoon coconut oil
- 3 tablespoons almonds
- 34 pounds spinach
- Salt to taste

Directions:
1. Put oil to a big pot and place it on high heat
2. Put in spinach and allow it to cook, stirring regularly
3. Once the spinach is cooked and soft, sprinkle with salt and stir
4. Put in almonds and enjoy!

Nutritional Info: , Calories: 150 , Fat: 12g , Carbohydrates: 10g , Protein: 8g

STIR-FRIED FARROS

Time To Prepare: five minutes

Time to Cook: thirty-five minutes

Yield: Servings 2

Ingredients:
- ½ cup farro
- ½ teaspoon ground coriander
- ½ teaspoon paprika
- ½ teaspoon turmeric
- 1 ½ cup water
- 1 carrot, grated
- 1 tablespoon butter
- 1 teaspoon chili flakes
- 1 teaspoon salt
- 1 yellow onion, cut

Directions:
1. Put farro in the pan. Put in water and salt.
2. Close the lid and boil it for half an hour
3. In the meantime, toss the butter in the frying pan.
4. Heat it and put in cut onion and grated carrot.
5. Fry the vegetables for about ten minutes over the moderate heat. Stir them with the help of spatula occasionally.
6. When the farro is cooked, put in it in the roasted vegetables and mix up well.
7. Cook stir-fried farro for five minutes over the moderate to high heat.

Nutritional Info: Calories 129 , Fat: 5.9 , Fiber: 3 , Carbs: 17.1 , Protein: 2.8

TENDER FARRO

Time To Prepare: 8 minutes

Time to Cook: forty minutes

Yield: Servings 4

Ingredients:
- 1 cup farro
- 1 tablespoon almond butter
- 1 tablespoon dried dill
- 1 teaspoon salt
- 3 cups beef broth

Directions:
1. Put farro in the pan.

2. Put in beef broth, dried dill, and salt.
3. Close the lid and put the mixture to boil.
4. Then boil it for a little more than half an hour over the medium-low heat.
5. When the time is done, open the lid and put in almond butter.
6. Mix up the cooked farro well.

Nutritional Info: Calories 95 , Fat: 3.3 , Fiber: 1.3 , Carbs: 10.1 , Protein: 6.4

THYME WITH HONEY-ROASTED CARROTS

Time To Prepare: five minutes

Time to Cook: thirty minutes

Yield: Servings 4

Ingredients:
- ½ teaspoon of sea salt
- ½ teaspoon thyme, dried
- 1 tablespoon of honey
- 1/5 lb. carrots, with the tops
- 2 tablespoons of olive oil

Directions:
1. Preheat the oven to 425 degrees F.
2. Place parchment paper on your baking sheet.
3. Toss your carrots with honey, oil, thyme, and salt. Coat well.
4. Keep in a single layer. Bake in the oven for half an hour
5. Allow to cool before you serve.

Nutritional Info: Calories 85 , Carbohydrates: 6g , Cholesterol: 0mg , Total Fat: 8g , Protein: 1g , Sugar: 6g , Fiber: 1g , Sodium: 244mg

TOMATO BULGUR

Time To Prepare: seven minutes

Time to Cook: twenty minutes

Yield: Servings 2

Ingredients:
- ½ cup bulgur
- ½ white onion, diced
- 1 ½ cup chicken stock
- 1 teaspoon tomato paste
- 2 tablespoons coconut oil

Directions:

1. Toss coconut oil in the pan and melt it.
2. Put in diced onion and roast it until light brown.
3. Then put in bulgur and stir thoroughly.
4. Cook bulgur in coconut oil for about three minutes.
5. Then put in tomato paste and mix up bulgur until homogenous.
6. Put in chicken stock.
7. Close the lid and cook bulgur for fifteen minutes over the moderate heat.
8. The cooked bulgur should soak all liquid.

Nutritional Info: Calories 257 , Fat: 14.5 , Fiber: 7.1 , Carbs: 30.2 , Protein: 5.2

WHEATBERRY SALAD

Time To Prepare: ten minutes

Time to Cook: 50 minutes

Yield: Servings 2

Ingredients:
- ¼ cup fresh parsley, chopped
- ¼ cup of wheat berries
- 1 cup of water
- 1 tablespoon canola oil
- 1 tablespoon chives, chopped
- 1 teaspoon chili flakes
- 1 teaspoon salt
- 2 oz. pomegranate seeds
- 2 tablespoons walnuts, chopped

Directions:
1. Put wheat berries and water in the pan.
2. Put in salt and simmer the ingredients for about fifty minutes over the moderate heat.
3. In the meantime, mix up together walnuts, chives, parsley, pomegranate seeds, and chili flakes.
4. When the wheatberry is cooked, move it in the walnut mixture.
5. Put in canola oil and mix up the salad well.

Nutritional Info: Calories 160 , Fat: 11.8 , Fiber: 1.2 , Carbs: 12 , Protein: 3.4

APPLE AND TOMATO DIPPING SAUCE

Time To Prepare: ten minutes

Time to Cook: 0 minutes

Yield: Servings 2-4

Ingredients:
- ¼ cup of cider vinegar

- ¼ tsp of freshly ground black pepper
- ½ tsp of sea salt
- 1 garlic clove, finely chopped
- 1 large-sized shallot, diced
- 1 tbsp. natural tomato paste
- 1 tbsp. of extra-virgin olive oil
- 1 tbsp. of maple syrup
- 1/8 tsp of ground cloves
- 3 moderate-sized apples, roughly chopped
- 3 moderate-sized tomatoes, roughly chopped

Directions:
1. Put oil into a huge deep cooking pan and heat it up on moderate heat.
2. Put in shallot and cook until light brown for approximately 2 minutes.
3. Stir in the tomato paste, garlic, salt, pepper, and cloves for approximately half a minute. Then put in in the apples, tomatoes, vinegar, and maple syrup.
4. Bring to its boiling point then decrease the heat to allow it to simmer for approximately 30 minutes. Allow to cool for twenty additional minutes before placing the mixture into your blender. Combine the mixture until the desired smoothness is achieved.
5. Keep in a mason jar or an airtight container; place in your fridge for maximum 5 days.
6. Serve it on a burger or with fries.

Nutritional Info: , Calories: 142 kcal **,** Protein: 3 g **,** Fat: 3.46 g **,** Carbohydrates: 26.93 g

BALSAMIC VINAIGRETTE

Time To Prepare: ten minutes

Time to Cook: 0 minutes

Yield: Servings 2-4

Ingredients:
- ¼ tsp of freshly ground black pepper
- ½ cup of extra-virgin olive oil
- ½ cup of rice vinegar
- 1 clove of freshly minced garlic
- 1 tbsp. of honey or maple syrup
- 1 tsp of sea or kosher salt
- 2 tsp of Dijon mustard

Directions:
1. Put all ingredients in a mason jar and cover firmly. Shake thoroughly until all ingredients are blended.
2. Keep in your fridge for minimum 30 minutes before you serve to keep its freshness.
3. Serve with a salad or as your meat marinate.

Nutritional Info: , Calories: 147 kcal **,** Protein: 1.85 g **,** Fat: 13.21 g **,** Carbohydrates: 4.02 g

BEAN POTATO SPREAD

Time To Prepare: twenty-five minutes

Time to Cook: 0 minutes

Yield: Servings 7-8

Ingredients:
- ¼ cup sesame paste
- ½ teaspoon cumin, ground
- 1 cup garbanzo beans, drained and washed
- 1 tablespoon olive oil
- 2 tablespoons lime juice
- 2 tablespoons water
- 4 cups cooked sweet potatoes, peeled and chopped
- 5 garlic cloves, minced
- A pinch of salt

Directions:
1. Throw all the ingredients into a blender and blend to make a smooth mix.
2. Move to a container.
3. Serve with carrot, celery, or veggie sticks.

Nutritional Info: Calories 156 , Fat: 3g , Carbohydrates: 10g , Fiber: 6g , Protein: 8g

CASHEW GINGER DIP

Time To Prepare: five minutes

Time to Cook: 0 minutes

Yield: Servings 1

Ingredients:
- ¼ cup filtered water
- ¼ teaspoon salt
- ½ teaspoon ground ginger
- 1 cup cashews, soaked in water for about twenty minutes and drained
- 1 tablespoon extra-virgin olive oil
- 1 teaspoon lemon juice
- 2 garlic cloves
- 2 teaspoons coconut aminos
- Pinch cayenne pepper

Directions:
1. In a blender or food processor, put together the cashews, garlic, water, olive oil, aminos, lemon juice, ginger, salt, and cayenne pepper.
2. Put in the mix in a container.

3. Cover and place in your fridge until chilled. You can use store it for 4-5 days in your fridge.

Nutritional Info: Calories 124 , Fat: 9g , Carbohydrates: 5g , Fiber: 1g , Protein: 3g

CREAMY AVOCADO DRESSING

Time To Prepare: ten minutes

Time to Cook: 0 minutes

Yield: Servings 2-4

Ingredients:
- ½ cup of extra-virgin olive oil
- 1 clove of garlic, chopped
- 1 tsp of honey or maple syrup
- 2 small or 1 large-sized avocado, pitted and chopped
- 2 tsp of lemon or lime juice
- 3 tbsp. of chopped parsley
- 3 tbsp. of red wine vinegar
- Onion powder
- Some Kosher salt and ground black pepper

Directions:
1. Combine all ingredients into a blender, apart from the oil. As the ingredients are mixed, progressively put in the oil into the mixture. Blend until the desired smoothness is achieved or becomes liquidy.
2. Use as a vegetable or fruit salad dressing. Put in your fridge for maximum 5 days.

Nutritional Info: , Calories: 300 kcal , Protein: 4.09 g , Fat: 27.9 g , Carbohydrates: 11.41 g

CREAMY HOMEMADE GREEK DRESSING

Time To Prepare: ten minutes

Time to Cook: 0 minutes

Yield: Servings 2-4

Ingredients:
- ¼ cup non-dairy milk (e.g., almond, rice milk)
- ½ cup of high-quality mayonnaise, without preservatives
- ½ tsp dried basil
- ½ tsp dried oregano
- ½ tsp parsley
- ½ tsp thyme
- 1/3 cup of extra-virgin olive oil
- 1/4 cup of white wine vinegar

- 2 cloves of garlic, minced
- 2 tbsp. of lemon or lime juice
- 2 tsp of honey
- A few tablespoons of water
- Some Kosher salt and pepper

Directions:
1. Put all together ingredients in a mason jar and shake, cover firmly, and shake thoroughly. Place in your fridge for a few hours before you serve or serve instantly on your favorite vegetable or fruit salad.
2. Shake well before use. Put in your fridge for maximum 5 days.
3. You may put in a few tablespoons of water to tune the consistency as per your preference.

Nutritional Info: , Calories: 474 kcal , Protein: 2.08 g , Fat: 50.1 g , Carbohydrates: 5.31 g

CREAMY RASPBERRY VINAIGRETTE

Time To Prepare: ten minutes

Time to Cook: 0 minutes

Yield: Servings 2-4

Ingredients:
- ½ cup of raspberries
- 1 tbsp. of Dijon mustard
- 1 tbsp. of Greek yogurt
- 1/3 cup of extra-virgin olive oil
- 2 tbsp. of honey or maple syrup
- 2 tbsp. of raspberry vinegar

Directions:
1. Put all together the ingredients apart from the oil into a blender, in accordance with the ordered list. Cover and blend for ten seconds, by slowly increasing the speed.
2. After 10 seconds, reduce the speed and progressively put in the oil into the mixture. Keep the speed at a stable pace until all of the oil has been poured in. Blend until blended.
3. Store in a mason jar then place in your fridge for maximum 5 days. Serve with a vegetable or fruit salad.

Nutritional Info: , Calories: 151 kcal , Protein: 2.22 g , Fat: 9.47 g , Carbohydrates: 14.65 g

CREAMY SIAMESE DRESSING

Time To Prepare: ten minutes

Time to Cook: 0 minutes

Yield: Servings 2-4

Ingredients:
- ¼ cup of non-dairy milk (e.g., almond, rice, soymilk)

- ¼ cup of unsweetened peanut sauce
- 1 cup of mayonnaise
- 1 tbsp. of honey or maple syrup
- 1 tbsps. freshly chopped cilantro
- 2 tbsp. of unsalted peanuts
- 2 tbsp. rice vinegar

Directions:
1. Put all ingredients apart from the cilantro and peanuts into a blender and blend until the desired smoothness is achieved and creamy. Next, put in in the cilantro and peanuts and pulse the blender a few times until completely crushed and well blended. Put in a mason jar and bring it in your fridge.
2. Serve with a garden salad, pasta or as a dipping sauce.

Nutritional Info: , Calories: 525 kcal , Protein: 18.14 g , Fat: 45.55 g , Carbohydrates: 11.01 g

CUCUMBER AND DILL SAUCE

Time To Prepare: ten minutes

Time to Cook: 0 minutes

Yield: Servings 2-4

Ingredients:
- ¼ cup of lemon juice
- 1 cucumber, peeled and squeezed to remove surplus liquid
- 1 cup of freshly chopped dill
- 1 tsp of sea salt
- 450g of Greek yogurt

Directions:
1. In a moderate-sized container, put together the yogurt, cucumber, and dill then stir until well blended. Put in in the lemon juice and salt to taste.
2. Cover and place in your fridge for approximately 1-2 hours before you serve to keep its freshness. Best serve with Mediterranean food, chips, fish, or even bread.

Nutritional Info: , Calories: 97 kcal , Protein: 13.49 g , Fat: 2.1 g , Carbohydrates: 6.34 g

DAIRY-FREE CREAMY TURMERIC DRESSING

Time To Prepare: ten minutes

Time to Cook: 0 minutes

Yield: Servings 2-4

Ingredients:
- ½ cup of extra-virgin olive oil

- ½ cup of tahini
- 1 tbsp. of turmeric powder
- 2 tbsp. of lemon juice
- 2 tsp of honey
- Some sea salt and pepper

Directions:
1. In a container, whisk all ingredients until well blended.
2. Store in a mason jar and place in your fridge for maximum 5 days.

Nutritional Info: , Calories: 328 kcal , Protein: 7.3 g , Fat: 29.36 g , Carbohydrates: 12.43 g

HERBY RAITA

Time To Prepare: ten minutes

Time to Cook: 0 minutes

Yield: Servings 2-4

Ingredients:
- ¼ cup of freshly chopped mint
- ¼ tsp of freshly ground black pepper
- ½ tsp of sea salt
- 1 cup of Greek yogurt
- 1 large-sized cucumber, shredded
- 1 tsp of lemon juice

Directions:
1. Combine the cucumber with ¼ tsp of salt in a sieve and leave to drain for fifteen minutes. Shake to release any surplus liquid and move to a kitchen towel. Squeeze out as much liquid as you can using the paper towel.
2. Put the cucumber into a medium container then mix in the rest of the ingredients until well blended.
3. Put in your fridge for minimum 2 hours to keep its freshness. Best consume with spicy foods as it could relief the spiciness.

Nutritional Info: , Calories: 69 kcal , Protein: 4.33 g , Fat: 3.66 g , Carbohydrates: 4.93 g

HOMEMADE GINGER DRESSING

Time To Prepare: ten minutes

Time to Cook: 0 minutes

Yield: Servings 2-4

Ingredients:
- ¼ cup of chopped celery
- ¼ cup of honey or maple syrup
- ¼ cup of water

- ½ cup of chopped carrots
- ½ tsp of white pepper
- 1 cup of chopped onion
- 1 cup of extra-virgin olive oil
- 1 tsp of freshly minced garlic
- 1 tsp of kosher salt
- 2 ½ tbsp. of unsalted, gluten-free soy sauce
- 2 tbsp. of ketchup
- 2/3 cup of rice vinegar
- 6 tbsp. of freshly grated ginger

Directions:
1. Put the onion, ginger, celery, carrots, and garlic into a blender. Blend until the mixture are fine but still lumpy from the small vegetable chunks.
2. Put in in the vinegar, water, ketchup, soy sauce, honey or maple syrup, lemon juice, salt, and pepper. Pulse until the ingredients are well blended.
3. Slowly put in the oil while blending, until everything is thoroughly combined. The mixture must be runny but still grainy.
4. Serve with a winter salad.

Nutritional Info: , Calories: 389 kcal , Protein: 2.71 g , Fat: 32.08 g , Carbohydrates: 22.14 g

HOMEMADE LEMON VINAIGRETTE

Time To Prepare: ten minutes

Time to Cook: 0 minutes

Yield: Servings 2-4

Ingredients:
- ¼ tsp of sea salt
- ½ tsp of Dijon mustard, without preservatives
- ½ tsp of lemon zest
- 1 tsp of honey or maple syrup
- 2 tbsp. of freshly squeezed lemon juice
- 3 tbsp. of extra-virgin olive oil
- Freshly ground black pepper

Directions:
1. Whisk all together the ingredients apart from olive oil and black pepper in a small container. Then progressively put in 3 tbsp. of olive oil while continuously whisking until well blended. Put in some ground black pepper to taste.
2. Put mason jar and place in your fridge for maximum 3 days.
3. Serve with a garden salads.

Nutritional Info: , Calories: 68 kcal , Protein: 1.69 g , Fat: 6.06 g , Carbohydrates: 1.71 g

HOMEMADE RANCH

Time To Prepare: ten minutes

Time to Cook: 0 minutes

Yield: Servings 2-4

Ingredients:
- ¼ cup of Greek yogurt
- ¼ tsp Kosher salt
- ½ cup of natural mayonnaise, without preservatives
- ½ tsp of dried dill
- ½ tsp of dried parsley
- ½ tsp of garlic powder
- ½ tsp of onion powder
- ¾ cup of non-dairy milk
- 1/8 tsp Freshly ground black pepper
- 2 tsp of dried chives

Directions:
1. Combine all ingredients apart from the milk into a medium container. Mix together until well blended.
2. Put in in the milk and mix thoroughly.
3. Pour in a mason jar or an airtight container. Serve instantly or place in your fridge for maximum 2 hours to keep the freshness. Put in your refrigerator for maximum 5 days.
4. Serve with a garden or fruit salad.

Nutritional Info: , Calories: 482 kcal , Protein: 3.55 g , Fat: 51.98 g , Carbohydrates: 1.63 g

HONEY BEAN DIP

Time To Prepare: five minutes

Time to Cook: 0 minutes

Yield: Servings 3-4

Ingredients:
- ¼ teaspoon ground cumin
- ¼ teaspoon salt
- 1 (14-ounce) can each of kidney beans and black beans
- 1 tablespoon apple cider vinegar
- 1 teaspoon lime juice
- 2 cherry tomatoes
- 2 garlic cloves
- 2 tablespoons filtered water
- 2 teaspoons raw honey
- Freshly ground black pepper to taste

- Pinch cayenne pepper to taste

Directions:
1. In a blender or food processor, put together the beans, garlic, tomatoes, water, vinegar, honey, lime juice, cumin, salt, cayenne pepper, and black pepper.
2. Blend until it becomes smooth. Put in the mix in a container.
3. Cover and place in your fridge to chill. You can place in your fridge for maximum 5 days.

Nutritional Info: Calories 158 , Fat: 1g , Carbohydrates: 33g , Fiber: 8g , Protein: 9g

SOY WITH HONEY AND GINGER GLAZE

Time To Prepare: ten minutes

Time to Cook: 0 minutes

Yield: Servings 2-4

Ingredients:
- ¼ cup of honey
- 1 tbsp. of rice vinegar
- 1 tsp of freshly grated ginger
- 2 tbsp. gluten-free soy sauce

Directions:
1. Put all together the ingredients into a small container and whisk well.
2. Serve with a vegetables, chickens, or seafood.
3. Keep the glaze in a mason jar, firmly covered, and place in your fridge for maximum four days.

Nutritional Info: , Calories: 90 kcal , Protein: 2.32 g , Fat: 1.54 g , Carbohydrates: 17.99 g

STRAWBERRY POPPY SEED DRESSING

Time To Prepare: ten minutes

Time to Cook: 0 minutes

Yield: Servings 2-4

Ingredients:
- ¼ cup of raspberry vinegar
- ¼ tsp of ground ginger
- ¼ tsp of sea salt
- ½ tsp of onion powder
- ½ tsp of poppy seeds
- 1/3 cup of extra-virgin olive oil

- 1/3 cup of honey
- 2 tbsp. of freshly squeezed orange juice

Directions:

1. Put all ingredients, apart from the poppy seeds and oil into a blender. Blend until the desired smoothness is achieved and creamy. Next, progressively put the oil into the mixture until blended. Put in in the poppy seeds and stir thoroughly.
2. Put in a mason jar then place in your fridge before you serve. Keep for maximum 3 days.
3. Serve with your garden salads.

Nutritional Info: , Calories: 167 kcal , Protein: 1.84 g , Fat: 9.35 g , Carbohydrates: 18.89 g

TAHINI DIP

Time To Prepare: ten minutes

Time to Cook: 0 minutes

Yield: Servings 2-4

Ingredients:

- ¼ cup of tahini
- ½ tsp of maple syrup
- 1 small grated or thoroughly minced clove of garlic (this is optional)
- 1 tbsp. of apple cider vinegar
- 1 tbsp. of freshly squeezed lemon juice
- 1 tbsp. of tamari
- 1 tsp of finely grated ginger, or ½ tsp of ground ginger
- 1 tsp of turmeric
- 1/3 cup of water

Directions:

1. Blend or whisk all ingredients together. Place the dressing in an airtight container then place in your fridge for approximately 5 days.
2. Enjoy!

Nutritional Info: , Calories: 120 kcal , Protein: 4.77 g , Fat: 9.63 g , Carbohydrates: 5.12 g

TOMATO AND MUSHROOM SAUCE

Time To Prepare: ten minutes

Time to Cook: 0 minutes

Yield: Servings 2-4

Ingredients:

- ½ cup of water
- 1 moderate-sized leek, chopped
- 2 moderate-sized carrots, chopped
- 2 stalks of celery, chopped

- 2 tsp of dried oregano
- 4 cloves of garlic, crushed
- 450g of button mushrooms, diced
- 5 tbsp. of coconut milk
- 680g of unsalted tomato puree
- Black pepper, seasoning
- Some sea salt, seasoning

Directions:

1. In a big frying pan, place a few tablespoons of water and heat on moderate heat. Once it sizzles, put in in the mushrooms and Sautee for approximately five minutes, stir once in a while.
2. Next, put in in the leek, carrots, and celery. Stir thoroughly and cook for approximately five minutes or until the vegetables are soft. Put in more water if required.
3. Mix in the tomato puree with ½ cup of water and dried oregano. Bring to its boiling point and then decrease the heat to allow it to simmer for approximately fifteen minutes.
4. Remove from heat and mix in the garlic, coconut milk, and salt and pepper to taste.
5. Put in an airtight container, then store for maximum four days in your fridge or freeze for maximum 1 month. Serve with a pasta.

Nutritional Info: , Calories: 467 kcal , Protein: 16.91 g , Fat: 3.81 g , Carbohydrates: 109.68 g

ALMOND AND HONEY HOMEMADE BAR

Time To Prepare: fifteen minutes + thirty minutes refrigerator time

Time to Cook: fifteen minutes

Yield: Servings 8

Ingredients:

- ¼ cup almond butter
- ¼ cup honey
- ¼ cup sugar (or another sweetener to your taste in adjusted amount)
- ¼ cup sunflower seeds
- ½ teaspoon vanilla extract
- 1 cup oats
- 1 cup whole-grain puffed cereal (unsweetened)
- 1 tbsp. flaxseeds
- 1 tbsp. sesame seeds
- 1/3 cup apricots (dried and chopped)
- 1/3 cup currants
- 1/3 cup raisins (chopped)
- 1/8 tsp salt
- A ¼ cup of almonds

Directions:
1. Preheat your oven to 350 degrees Fahrenheit.
2. Place a baking paper to an 8-inch pan or coat it with cooking spray/oil.
3. Combine the almonds, oats, and seeds and spread the mixture on a rimmed baking sheet.
4. Bake the mixture until you notice that the oats are mildly toasted (for approximately ten minutes).
5. Move the mixture to a container.
6. Put in cereal, raisins, currants, and apricots to the container.
7. Toss thoroughly to blend.
8. Mix honey, almond butter, vanilla, salt, and sugar in a deep cooking pan.
9. Heat on moderate heat. Stir regularly for 2-5 minutes until you see light bubbles.
10. Once you notice the bubbles, pour the mixture over the dry mixture with apricots and oats you prepared previously.
11. Mix thoroughly using a spatula. There mustn't be any dry spots.
12. Move the new mixture to the previously prepared pan.
13. Push it to the pan to make a firm and flat layer.
14. Place in your refrigerator for half an hour
15. Chop the layer into eight equal bars or squares, to your taste.
16. Consume instantly or place in your refrigerator up to seven days.

Nutritional Info: , Calories: 213 kcal , Protein: 6.92 g , Fat: 9.59 g , Carbohydrates: 32.33 g

ALMONDS AND BLUEBERRIES YOGURT SNACK

Time To Prepare: ten minutes

Time to Cook: 0 minutes

Yield: Servings 2

Ingredients:
- 1 ½ cups nonfat Greek yogurt
- 1 cup blueberries
- 20 almonds, chopped

Directions:
1. Take 2 bowls and put in ¾ cup yogurt into each container.
2. Split the blueberries among the bowls and stir.
3. Drizzle half the almonds in each container before you serve.

Nutritional Info: , Calories: 223 kcal , Protein: 6.57 g , Fat: 9.45 g , Carbohydrates: 30.82 g

ANTI-INFLAMMATORY KEY LIME PIE

Time To Prepare: twenty minutes + thirty-five minutes refrigerator time

Time to Cook: 0

Yield: Servings 8

Ingredients:
- ½ cup honey
- ½ cup Medjool dates, chopped and pitted
- 1 cup unsweetened shredded coconut
- 1 cup walnuts
- 1 teaspoon lime zest
- 1/4 teaspoon sea salt
- 3 firm avocados
- 3 tablespoons lime juice
- Lime slices
- Pinch of sea salt

Directions:
1. Use a food processor to put all together the walnuts, coconut, and the salt, then pulse until crudely ground.
2. Place the dates and pulse until the mixture resembles bread crumbs, trying to stick together.
3. Push the mixture into the edges and bottom of a non-stick greased 9-inch pie pan. Use your fingers or the back of a spoon to press the crust into a uniform layer. Bring the crust into the freezer for minimum fifteen minutes while preparing the filling.
4. Use the food processor again and mix the avocado, honey, lime juice, lime zest, and salt. Process until the desired smoothness is achieved.
5. Pour the filling into the now-chilled piecrust and place it in your fridge for about twenty minutes.
6. Decorate using fresh lime slices and serve cold. Store any left overs in your fridge.

Nutritional Info: , Calories: 273 kcal , Protein: 4.19 g , Fat: 18.4 g , Carbohydrates: 28.49 g

ANTS ON A LOG

Time To Prepare: five minutes

Time to Cook: 0 minutes

Yield: Servings 2

Ingredients:
- 3 tablespoons of almond butter
- 3 tablespoons of raisins
- 6 celery sticks

Directions:
1. Spread half a tablespoon of almond butter on each celery stick.
2. Top with half a tablespoon of raisins on each celery stick.
3. Split the celery sticks between two plates, and enjoy!

Nutritional Info: , Total Carbohydrates: 17g , Fiber: 2g , Net Carbohydrates: , Protein: 4g , Total Fat: 14g , Calories: 201

APPLE CRISP

Time To Prepare: fifteen minutes

Time to Cook: twenty-five minutes

Yield: Servings 6-8

Ingredients:

Topping:
- 1 ½ cups old-fashioned rolled oats
- 1 teaspoon salt
- ½ cup stevia
- 2 teaspoons ground cinnamon
- 1 cup nuts, crudely chopped
- 3 tablespoon melted coconut oil.
- 1/3 cup almond meal
- 2/3 cup shredded, unsweetened coconut
- 1/4 teaspoon ground nutmeg

Apple filling:
- ½ cup stevia
- 1 tablespoon ground cinnamon
- 1 teaspoon vanilla
- 1/4 cup arrowroot flour
- 1/4 teaspoon salt
- 10 tart apples
- 2 tablespoons fresh-squeezed lemon juice
- 3 tablespoons melted coconut oil
- The zest of 1 orange

Directions:
1. Set the oven to 350 F then grease a 9 by a 13-inch baking pan with coconut oil.
2. Put together the topping ingredients in a container, then mix and save for later.
3. Combine the filling ingredients (except for the apples) in a second big container.
4. Leave the skins on the apples, if you wish. Core them and slice super slim (1/8 inch thick).
5. Toss the apples in the filling ingredients to coat uniformly. Put the apple mixture in a baking pan and spread the topping over it all, pushing down tightly.
6. Put in your oven with a pan underneath to catch any drips.
7. Bake for about twenty-five minutes or until the topping is brown and juices are bubbling. Apples must be tender.
8. Cool slightly on a rack then serve.

Nutritional Info: , Calories: 446 kcal , Protein: 6.15 g , Fat: 27.39 g , Carbohydrates: 57.45 g

APPLE SAUCE TREAT

Time To Prepare: ten minutes

Time to Cook: 0 minutes

Yield: Servings 1

Ingredients:
- ½ teaspoon cinnamon
- 1 ½ teaspoons toasted slivered almonds
- 1/4 cup low Fat cottage cheese
- 1/4 cup unsweetened applesauce

Directions:
1. Combine the cottage cheese and applesauce in a container, stirring well.
2. Drizzle with cinnamon and mix thoroughly.
3. Drizzle the top with almonds, pick up your spoon, and enjoy.

Nutritional Info: , Calories: 225 kcal , Protein: 16.24 g , Fat: 14.17 g , Carbohydrates: 8.54 g

AVOCADO AND EGG SANDWICH

Time To Prepare: ten minutes

Time to Cook: 0 minutes

Yield: Servings 2

Ingredients:
- ½ lime juice
- 1 avocado (ripe)
- 1 egg, organic
- 1 scallion
- 2 radishes
- 2 slices of who wheat, seed bread
- A pinch of salt (sea or Himalayan)
- Black pepper – to your taste
- Mixed seeds – to your choice

Directions:
1. Peel the avocado.
2. Boil the egg (soft boiled).
3. Chop the radishes to thin slices.
4. Dice the scallion (finely).
5. Mix avocado, salt, and lime juice in a container. Mash the mixture meticulously.
6. Spread the mixture onto the bread.
7. Put in some radish.
8. Put tender boiled eggs on top.

9. Put in some scallion, seeds, and pepper.

Nutritional Info: , Calories: 342 kcal , Protein: 12.36 g , Fat: 22.99 g , Carbohydrates: 26.54 g

AVOCADO HUMMUS

Time To Prepare: fifteen minutes

Time to Cook: 0 minutes

Yield: Servings 4

Ingredients:
- .25 cup Sunflower seeds
- .25 cup Tahini
- .25 tsp. Pepper
- .5 cup Cilantro
- .5 cup Coconut oil
- .5 Lemon juice
- .5 tsp. Salt
- 1 clove pressed garlic
- 3 Avocados
- 5 tsp. Cumin

Directions:
1. Halve the avocados, take off the pits, then spoon out the flesh.
2. Put all together ingredients in a blender and stir until super smooth.
3. Put in water, lemon juice, or oil if you need to loosen the mixture bit.

Nutritional Info: , Calories: 651 kcal , Protein: 9.62 g , Fat: 64.05 g , Carbohydrates: 19.95 g

AVOCADO WITH TOMATOES AND CUCUMBER

Time To Prepare: ten minutes

Time to Cook: 0 minutes

Yield: Servings 2

Ingredients:
- ¼ cup cilantro
- ¼ cup olives – to your choice
- ½ red onion
- 1 cucumber
- 1 lemon
- 1 Tbsp. turmeric
- 1/8 cup parsley
- 2 avocados

- 4 Roma tomatoes
- Salt and pepper – to your taste

Directions:
1. Dice the tomatoes, cucumber, avocado, and olives.
2. Cut the cilantro, parsley, and onion.
3. Put in the above ingredients into a container.
4. Squeeze the lemon juice then put in to the vegetables.
5. Put in olive oil, turmeric, salt, and pepper.
6. Toss thoroughly.
7. Consume instantly after putting in lemon juice and olive oil.
8. If you prefer to consume the salad later, put in the dressing instantly before consuming it.

Nutritional Info: , Calories: 480 kcal , Protein: 11.57 g , Fat: 35.27 g , Carbohydrates: 39.77 g

BAKED VEGGIE TURMERIC NUGGETS

Time To Prepare: ten minutes

Time to Cook: twenty-five minutes

Yield: Servings 24

Ingredients:
- ¼ tsp. Black pepper powder
- ¼ tsp. Sea salt
- ½ cup Almond meal
- ½ tsp. Turmeric powder
- 1 big Whole egg
- 1 cup Chopped carrots
- 1 tsp. Minced garlic
- 2 cups Broccoli florets
- 2 cups Cauliflower florets

Directions:
1. Preheat your oven to 400°F.
2. Get a parchment-lined baking sheet ready.
3. Pour cauliflower, turmeric, broccoli, carrots, black pepper, garlic, and sea salt in the blender and blitz until it's smooth.
4. Pour in the egg and almond meal and stir until it's blended.
5. Pour the paste into a mixing container. Scoop out a small amount onto your hand and make a circular disc. Put this disc on the baking sheet and repeat the pulse until the mixing container is empty.
6. Slide into the oven then bake for minimum fifteen minutes on one before flipping and baking for about ten minutes on the other side.
7. Serve with a side of Paleo ranch sauce.

Nutritional Info: , Calories: 12 kcal , Protein: 0.88 g , Fat: 0.52 g , Carbohydrates: 1.12 g

BERRY DELIGHT

Time To Prepare: fifteen minutes

Time to Cook: 0 minutes

Yield: Servings 6

Ingredients:
- ¼ cup of raw honey
- 1 cup of fresh organic blackberries
- 1 cup of fresh organic blueberries
- 1 cup of fresh organic raspberries
- 1 tablespoon of cinnamon

Directions:
1. Mix all the berries together in a big container, put in in the honey, and slowly stir.
2. Drizzle with the cinnamon.

Nutritional Info: , Total Carbohydrates: 20g , Fiber: 3g , Net Carbohydrates: , Protein: 1g , Total Fat: 0g , Calories: 78

BERRY ENERGY BITES

Time To Prepare: ten minutes

Time to Cook: 0 minutes

Yield: Servings 6

Ingredients:
- ¼ cup of dried blueberries
- ½ - 1 cup of almond milk
- ½ cup of coconut flour
- 1 tablespoon of coconut sugar
- 1 teaspoon of cinnamon

Directions:
1. In a huge mixing container, put together the coconut flour, cinnamon, coconut sugar, and blueberries, and mix thoroughly.
2. Put in the almond milk slowly until a firm dough is formed.
3. Form into bite-sized balls and place in your fridge for thirty minutes so they can harden up.
4. Store leftovers in your fridge.

Nutritional Info: , Total Carbohydrates: 18g , Fiber: 1g , Net Carbohydrates: , Protein: 1g , Total Fat: 1g , Calories: 80

BLUEBERRY & CHIA FLAX SEED PUDDING

Time To Prepare: ten minutes

Time to Cook: fifteen minutes

Yield: Servings 4

Ingredients:
- ¼ cup of blueberries
- 2 cups of almond milk
- 3 tablespoons of chia seeds
- 3 tablespoons of ground flaxseed

Directions:
1. Warm a pan on moderate heat then put all together of the ingredients apart from the blueberries.
2. Stir all the ingredients until the pudding is thick, this will take around three minutes.
3. Place the pudding into a container then top with blueberries.

Nutritional Info: , Total Carbohydrates: 23g , Fiber: 12g , Net Carbohydrates: , Protein: 7g , Total Fat: 15g , Calories: 243

BOILED OKRA AND SQUASH

Time To Prepare: five minutes

Time to Cook: five minutes

Yield: Servings 1

Ingredients:
- ½ cup of okra, cut in 1" cubes
- ½ cup of squash, cut in 1" cubes
- 1 clove garlic, minced
- 2/3 cup Vegetable stock or fish stock, plain water may be used as well
- Salt to taste

Directions:
1. Boil the liquid in high heat.
2. Put in the okra and squash. Bring to its boiling point. Put in the garlic. Reduced the heat and simmer for minimum five minutes or until the squash is soft.
3. Put in salt to taste and serve hot.

Nutritional Info: , Calories: 117 kcal , Protein: 8.2 g , Fat: 6.25 g , Carbohydrates: 7.82 g

BROWNIES AVOCADO

Time To Prepare: ten minutes

Time to Cook: twenty-five minutes

Yield: Servings 6-8

Ingredients:
- ½ cup almond meal
- 1 ½ teaspoon instant coffee (with or without caffeine, as you wish)
- 2 teaspoons ground cinnamon
- ½ teaspoon salt
- 2 cups nuts or seeds, chopped
- 1 avocado
- 1 apple, cored and chopped, with the skin on
- 1 cup cooked and diced sweet potato
- 4 tablespoons ground chia seeds
- 1 teaspoon vanilla
- ½ cup almond butter
- ½ cup coconut butter, softened
- 1/4 cup coconut oil
- 2 1/4 cup stevia
- 3/4 cup cocoa powder

Directions:
1. Set the oven to 350F then line a 9 by 13-inch pan with parchment. Allow it to overlap the sides to make handles for lifting the brownies out when done.
2. In a container, mix the almond meal, cocoa, coffee, cinnamon, salt, and nuts. Whisk and save for later.
3. Bring the remaining ingredients in a food processor and mix until the desired smoothness is achieved. Put in the ingredients in the container and pulse. This combination must be lumpy.
4. Pour into pan and bake for minimum twenty-five minutes.
5. Allow to cool and chill in your fridge for a couple of hours before cutting. The baked product will be a little gooey, so refrigerating it makes the brownies easier to cut. The chilled results will be fairly crumbly.

Nutritional Info: , Calories: 591 kcal , Protein: 11.03 g , Fat: 53.8 g , Carbohydrates: 26.58 g

BRUSCHETTA

Time To Prepare: 60 minutes

Time to Cook: 0 minutes

Yield: Servings 4

Ingredients:
- ¼ cup of extra virgin olive oil

- ¼ teaspoon of ground black pepper
- 1 red onion, diced
- 1 teaspoon of sea salt
- 2 cloves of garlic, minced
- 2 tablespoons of balsamic vinegar
- 4 medium tomatoes, diced

Directions:
1. Put all together the ingredients into a big container, and stir slowly.
2. Place in your fridge for an hour before you serve on gluten-free toast (toast is not included in nutritional information)

Nutritional Info: , Total Carbohydrates: 8g , Fiber: 2g , Net Carbohydrates: , Protein: 1g , Total Fat: 14g , Calories: 156

BRUSSELS SPROUT CHIPS

Time To Prepare: ten minutes

Time to Cook: ten minutes

Yield: Servings 4

Ingredients:
- 2 cups Brussels sprout leaves
- 2 tablespoons ghee
- Kosher salt
- Lemon zest

Directions:
1. Set the oven to 350F, then cover two cookie sheets using parchment paper.
2. Place the leaves in a huge container and pour melted ghee over the top, and put in salt.
3. Bake for minimum 8 to ten minutes or until the leaves are crunchy. If they are tender at all, put them back in your oven.
4. While still hot, drizzle the lemon zest over the leaves. Serve warm.

Nutritional Info: , Calories: 42 kcal , Protein: 3.13 g , Fat: 1.68 g , Carbohydrates: 4.77 g

BUTTERED BANANA CHICKPEA COOKIES

Time To Prepare: ten minutes

Time to Cook: twelve minutes

Yield: Servings 8

Ingredients:
- ¼-tsp cinnamon
- ¼-tsp salt

- ⅓-cup chocolate chips
- ⅓-cup coconut sugar
- ½-cup creamy peanut butter
- 1-pc small banana, very ripe
- 1-tsp baking powder
- 2-Tbsps ground flaxseed
- 2-tsp vanilla extract
- fifteen-oz. chickpeas, washed and drained

Directions:
1. Preheat the oven to 350F. Grease a baking pan with cooking spray.
2. Mix in all the ingredients apart from the chocolate chips in your blender. Combine the batter for two minutes, or until turning into a smooth consistency.
3. Mix in the chocolate chips. Ladle the batter to make cookies. Put the cookies in the pan, and bake for about twelve minutes.

Nutritional Info: , Calories: 372 , Fat: 12.4g , Protein: 18.6g , Sodium: 174mg , Total Carbohydrates: 58.1g , Fiber: 11.6g , Net Carbohydrates: 46.5g

CANDIED DATES

Time To Prepare: five minutes

Time to Cook: 0 minutes

Yield: Servings 2

Ingredients:
- 2 tablespoons of dark cocoa nibs
- 2 tablespoons of peanut butter
- 4 pitted Medjool dates

Directions:
1. Cut the pitted dates in half, and spread half a tablespoon of peanut butter on each date.
2. Top each date with half a tablespoon of dark cocoa nibs.
3. Split the candied dates between two plates, and enjoy!

Nutritional Info: , Total Carbohydrates: 20g , Fiber: 3g , Net Carbohydrates: , Protein: 5g , Total Fat: 12g , Calories: 187

CARROT STICKS WITH AVOCADO DIP

Time To Prepare: ten minutes

Time to Cook: 0 minutes

Yield: Servings 6

Ingredients:

- ½ cup cilantro, firmly packed
- ½ onion
- 1 big avocado, pitted
- 1 tablespoon of chili-garlic sauce or chili sauce
- 2 tablespoon olive oil
- 6 ounces shelled edamame
- Juice of one lemon
- Salt and pepper

Directions:
1. Put the edamame, cilantro, onion, and chili sauce in a blender or food processor. Pulse it to cut and mix the ingredients. Put in the avocado and the lemon juice. Slowly put in the olive oil as you blend. Move to a jar.
2. Scoop 2 spoons and serve with carrot sticks.

Nutritional Info: , Calories: 154 kcal , Protein: 5.16 g , Fat: 11.96 g , Carbohydrates: 8.44 g

CASHEW "HUMUS"

Time To Prepare: ten minutes

Time to Cook: 0 minutes

Yield: Servings 1

Ingredients:
- ¼ Cup Water
- ¼ Teaspoon Sea Salt, Fine
- ½ Teaspoon Ground Ginger
- 1 Cup Cashews, Raw & Soaked in Water for fifteen Minutes & Drained
- 1 Tablespoon Olive Oil
- 1 Teaspoon Lemon juice, Fresh
- 2 Cloves Garlic
- 2 Teaspoon Coconut Aminos
- Pinch Cayenne Pepper

Directions:
1. Blend all ingredients together, and ensure to scrape the sides.
2. Continue to combine until the desired smoothness is achieved, and then place in your fridge it before you serve.

Nutritional Info: , Calories: 112 , Protein: 2.9 Grams , Fat: 8.8 Grams , Carbohydrates: 5.3 Grams

CASHEW CHEESE

Time To Prepare: 2 hours

Time to Cook: 0 minutes

Yield: Servings 6

Ingredients:
- ¼ cup of fresh basil
- 1 cup of raw cashews
- 1 tablespoon of nutritional yeast
- Juice of ½ lemon
- Salt and pepper to taste

Directions:
1. In a1 cup of water, soak the cashew for minimum 2 hours. Drain.
2. Put the cashews, lemon juice, nutritional yeast, and fresh basil into a food processor and pulse until the desired smoothness is achieved. Put in 1 tablespoon of water at a time to make it creamy, but not runny.
3. Flavor it with pepper and salt, then spread it on gluten-free bread or toast.
4. Store in an airtight jar in your fridge.

Nutritional Info: , Total Carbohydrates: 126g , Fiber: 1g , Net Carbohydrates: , Protein: 4g , Total Fat: 10g , Calories: 126

CAULIFLOWER SNACKS

Time To Prepare: ten minutes

Time to Cook: 60 minutes

Yield: Servings 4

Ingredients:
- 1 head of cauliflower
- 1 teaspoon salt
- 4 tablespoons extra virgin olive oil

Directions:
1. Set the oven to 425F, then prepare two cookie sheets by lining them using parchment paper.
2. Trim off the cauliflower florets and discard the core. Chop the florets into golf-ball-sized pieces.
3. Put the cauliflower in a container, and pour olive oil over them and drizzle with salt. Mix to coat. Spread in a single layer, not touching.
4. Roast approximately 1 hour flipping the cauliflower three to four times until a golden-brown color is achieved. Serve warm.

Nutritional Info: , Calories: 91 kcal , Protein: 2.93 g , Fat: 7.7 g , Carbohydrates: 3.29 g

CEREAL CHIA CHIPS

Time To Prepare: ten minutes

Time to Cook: thirty minutes

Yield: Servings 10

Ingredients:
- ¼-cup rolled oats, gluten-free
- ½-cup maple syrup
- ½-cup white quinoa, uncooked
- ¾-cup pecans, chopped
- 2-Tbsps chia seeds
- 2-Tbsps coconut oil
- 2-Tbsps coconut sugar
- A pinch of sea salt (not necessary)

Directions:
1. Preheat the oven to 325°F. Coat a baking pan using parchment paper.
2. Mix in the first six ingredients in a mixing container. Mix thoroughly until meticulously blended. Set aside.
3. Pour the oil and syrup in a small deep cooking pan placed on moderate to low heat. Heat the mixture for about three minutes, stirring once in a while.
4. Fold in the dry ingredients; stir thoroughly to coat completely.
5. Pour the mixture in the baking pan, and spread to a uniform layer using a spoon.
6. Place the pan in your oven. Bake for fifteen minutes. Turn the pan around to cook uniformly. Bake for 8-ten minutes until the mixture turns golden brown.
7. Allow cooling completely before breaking the chips into bite-size pieces.

Nutritional Info: , Calories: 157 , Fat: 5.2g , Protein: 7.8g S , Sodium: 25mg , Total Carbohydrates: 22.1g , Fiber: 2.5g , Net Carbohydrates: 19.6g

CHEWY BLACKBERRY LEATHER

Time To Prepare: fifteen minutes

Time to Cook: 5-6 hours

Yield: Servings 8

Ingredients:
- ¼ cup of raw honey
- 1 tbsp. of fresh mint leaves
- 1 tsp. of ground cinnamon
- 1/8 tsp. of fresh lemon juice
- 2 cups of fresh blackberries

Directions:
1. Set the oven to 170F. Coat baking sheet using parchment paper.
2. Use a food processor to put all ingredients and pulse till smooth.
3. Take the mixture onto the readied baking sheet and, using the backside of a spoon, smooth the top.
4. Bake for approximately 5-6 hours.
5. Chop the leather into equal-sized strips.
6. Now, roll each rectangle to make fruit rolls.

Nutritional Info: , Calories: 49 , Fat: 0.2g , Carbohydrates: 12.5g , Protein: 0.6g , Fiber: 2.1g

CHIA CASHEW CREAM

Time To Prepare: 2 hours and five minutes

Time to Cook: 0 minutes

Yield: Servings 1

Ingredients:
- ¼-cup quinoa, cooked
- ¼-tsp vanilla powder
- ¾-cup cashew milk
- 2-Tbsps chia seeds
- 2-Tbsps hemp hearts
- 2-Tbsps maple syrup or a dash of liquid stevia
- A pinch of cinnamon

Directions:
1. Mix all the ingredients in a jar. Mix thoroughly until meticulously blended. Cover the jar and place in your fridge for about two hours.
2. To serve, top with your desired toppings.

Nutritional Info: , Calories: 258 , Fat: 8.6g , Protein: 12.9g , Sodium: 123mg , Total Carbohydrates: 34.2g , Fiber: 2g , Net Carbohydrates: 32.2g

COCO CHERRY BAKE-LESS BARS

Time To Prepare: ten minutes

Time to Cook: 0 minutes

Yield: Servings 6

Ingredients:
- ¼-cup pure maple syrup
- ⅓ -cup coconut, unsweetened and shredded
- ⅓ -cup dried cherries or cranberries
- ⅓ -cup ground flaxseed
- ½-cup almond butter
- 1-cup old-fashioned oats
- 1-Tbsp almond milk
- 1-Tbsp vanilla extract
- 3-scoops vanilla plant-based Protein powder

Directions:
1. Coat a loaf pan using parchment paper.
2. Mix in the first four ingredients in your blender. Blend until the mixture becomes powdery.

3. Move the mixture to a mixing container. Put in in all the rest of the ingredients. Mix thoroughly until meticulously blended.
4. Put the mixture in the pan, and press down onto a consistently flat surface.
5. Freeze for thirty minutes before cutting into six bars.

Nutritional Info: , Calories: 193 , Fat: 6.4g , Protein: 9.6g , Sodium: 200mg , Total Carbohydrates: 27.1g , Fiber: 3g , Net Carbohydrates: 24.1g

COCONUT PORRIDGE

Time To Prepare: twenty minutes

Time to Cook: ten minutes

Yield: Servings 2

Ingredients:
- 1 tbsp. coconut oil
- 1 tsp cinnamon
- 1 vanilla bean
- 2 cups oats
- 2 tbsp. maple syrup
- 2 tsp ginger
- 2 tsp turmeric
- 330ml vaporized coconut milk
- 750 ml of water
- Coconut milk
- Fresh, shredded coconut (for serving)

Directions:
1. Mix 750 ml water and turmeric in a container. Allow it to sit for about ten minutes.
2. Combine all ingredients apart from coconut milk and shredded coconut in a deep cooking pan.
3. Heat it on medium heat while stirring continuously, and cook for eight minutes.
4. Allow it to cool for about ten minutes.
5. Split into serving bowls.
6. Put in coconut milk and shredded coconut on top.
7. Put in some extra cinnamon to your taste.
8. Eat warm.

Nutritional Info: , Calories: 417 kcal , Protein: 20.63 g , Fat: 16.8 g , Carbohydrates: 83.03 g

COTTAGE CHEESE WITH APPLE SAUCE

Time To Prepare: five minutes

Time to Cook: 0 minutes

Yield: Servings 2

Ingredients:
- ½ teaspoon cinnamon powder
- 5-6 tablespoons cottage cheese
- two to three tablespoons applesauce or more if required

Directions:
1. Split the cottage cheese into 2 bowls.
2. Spread applesauce over the cottage cheese.
3. Drizzle ¼ teaspoon cinnamon powder on each before you serve.

Nutritional Info: , Calories: 79 kcal , Protein: 8.09 g , Fat: 3.45 g , Carbohydrates: 3.92 g

CUCUMBER ROLLS HORS D'OEUVRES

Time To Prepare: twenty minutes

Time to Cook: 0 minutes

Yield: Servings 8-10

Ingredients:
- ¼ cup fresh dill, finely chopped
- ½ cup capers
- ½ cup fresh parsley + extra to decorate, finely chopped
- 1 teaspoon Himalayan pink salt
- 2 big organic English cucumbers or 4 normal cucumbers
- 5-6 ripe avocadoes, peeled, pitted, mashed
- For the avocado spread:
- Freshly cracked pepper to taste

Directions:
1. Peel the cucumbers and cut thin slices along the length on a mandolin slicer.
2. Put the cucumber slices on your countertop.
3. To make the avocado spread: Put in all the ingredients of avocado spread into a container and stir until well blended.
4. Spread the avocado mixture uniformly and thinly on the cucumber slices.
5. Begin rolling from one of the shorter ends to the other end and place on a serving platter with its seam side facing down.
6. Repeat the above step with the rest of the cucumber slices.
7. Serve instantly as the cucumbers tend to get soggy after a while.

Nutritional Info: , Calories: 227 kcal , Protein: 3.77 g , Fat: 19.88 g , Carbohydrates: 12.99 g

CUCUMBER YOGURT

Time To Prepare: five minutes

Time to Cook: 0 minutes

Yield: Servings 1

Ingredients:
- 1 cup cucumbers, skin removed and chopped in chunks
- 1 teaspoon fresh dill, chopped fine
- 1/4 cup fat-free Greek yogurt
- 2 tablespoons chopped cashews
- 2 teaspoons fresh-squeezed lemon juice

Directions:
1. Peel and cut the cucumbers, then put them in a container.
2. Put in the cashews, yogurt, lemon juice, and dill.
3. Mix thoroughly, grab a spoon, and enjoy.

Nutritional Info: , Calories: 300 kcal , Protein: 11.35 g , Fat: 23.55 g , Carbohydrates: 14.13 g

DELECTABLE COOKIES

Time To Prepare: twenty minutes

Time to Cook: fifteen-twenty minutes

Yield: Servings 6

Ingredients:
- 1 cup of almonds
- ¼ cup of arrowroot flour
- 1 tbsp. of coconut flour
- 1 tsp. ground turmeric
- Salt, to taste
- Freshly ground black pepper, to taste
- 1 organic egg
- ¼ cup of olive oil
- 3 tbsp. of raw honey
- 1 tsp. of organic vanilla extract
- 1 1/3 cups of almond flour

Directions:
1. Use a food processor to put the almonds and pulse till chopped roughly
2. Move the chopped almonds in a big container.
3. Place the flours and spices and mix thoroughly.
4. In another container, put the rest of the ingredients then beat till well blended.
5. Put the flour mixture into the egg mixture and mix till well blended.

6. Position a plastic wrap over the cutting board.
7. Put the dough over the cutting board.
8. Use your hands to pat into approximately 1-inch thick circle.
9. Gently chop the circle in 6 wedges.
10. Set the scones onto a cookie sheet in a single layer.
11. Bake for approximately fifteen-20 minutes.

Nutritional Info: , Calories: 335 , Fat: 27.7g , Carbohydrates: 17.6g , Protein: 9g , Fiber: 4.8g

DRIED DATES & TURMERIC TRUFFLES

Time To Prepare: fifteen minutes

Time to Cook: 0 minutes

Yield: Servings 4

Ingredients:
- ¼-tsp black pepper
- ⅓ -cup walnuts
- ½-cup rolled oats
- ¾-cup dates, pitted
- 1-Tbsp turmeric powder + more for rolling

Directions:
1. Mix in all the ingredients, excluding the dates in a food processor. Blend until meticulously blended.
2. Put in the dates progressively until forming into the dough.
3. Shape and roll balls from the mixture. Roll each ball with the additional turmeric powder until coating fully.
4. Store the truffles in an airtight jar until ready to serve.

Nutritional Info: , Calories: 95 , Fat: 3.1g , Protein: 4.7g , Sodium: 62mg , Total Carbohydrates: 13.8g , Fiber: 2g , Net Carbohydrates: 11.8g

EASY GUACAMOLE

Time To Prepare: ten minutes

Time to Cook: 0 minutes

Yield: Servings 3

Ingredients:
- ½ Teaspoon Sea Salt
- 1 Teaspoon Garlic Powder
- 4 Avocados, Halved & Pitted

Directions:

1. Scoop your avocado flesh out, placing it in a container.
2. Put in in your salt and garlic powder mashing until it's creamy. You can place in your fridge it, and it'll keep for two days.

Nutritional Info: , Calories: 358 , Protein: 7.3 Grams , Fat: 32.2 Grams , Carbohydrates: 13.7 Grams

EASY PEASY GINGER DATE

Time To Prepare: twenty minutes

Time to Cook: ten minutes

Yield: Servings 8

Ingredients:
- ¼ cup Almond milk
- ¾ cup Dates
- 1 or 1 ½ cup Almonds or almond flour
- 1 tsp. Ground ginger

Directions:
1. Preheat your oven to 350ºF.
2. If you're using fresh almonds, put it through a blender to turn it to almond flour. Blitz for a couple of minutes or so until it looks and feels smooth.
3. Do not blitz for too long, or you might end up making nut butter. Now that you have your almond powder put it in a container and set it aside.
4. Pour the dates and almond milk into your blender and pulse for five minutes. If it doesn't resemble a paste, pulse for another two minutes.
5. Pour in the ground ginger and almond flour. Pulse for three to four minutes to combine.
6. Place the mixture to a baking dish and bake for approximately twenty minutes.
7. Take out of the oven and leave to cool before cutting into bits.
8. Serve or store.

Nutritional Info: , Calories: 55 kcal , Protein: 1.24 g , Fat: 0.99 g , Carbohydrates: 11.24 g

ENERGETIC OAT BARS

Time To Prepare: ten minutes

Time to Cook: twenty-five minutes

Yield: Servings 6

Ingredients:
- ½ cup of gluten-free rolled oats
- ¾ cup fresh blueberries
- 1 peeled and mashed banana
- 1 tbsp. of chopped walnuts
- 1 tbsp. of fresh pomegranate juice

- 1 tbsp. of sunflower seeds
- 2 tbsp. of flax seeds
- 2 tbsp. of pitted and chopped finely dates
- 2 tbsp. of raisins

Directions:
1. Set the oven to 350F. Lightly, oil an 8-inch baking dish.
2. In a huge mixing container, put all ingredients and mix till well blended.
3. Put the mixture into the readied baking dish uniformly.
4. Bake for approximately twenty-five minutes. Remove from the oven then cool.
5. Using a knife, split the bars into the size your desired pieces then serve.

Nutritional Info: , Calories: 88 , Fat: 2.3g , Carbohydrates: 18.2g , Protein: 2.3g , Fiber: 2.8g

ENERGY DATES BALLS

Time To Prepare: ten minutes

Time to Cook: twenty-five minutes

Yield: Servings 7

Ingredients:
- ¼ cup of fresh lemon juice
- ½ cup of shredded sweetened coconut
- 1 cup of pitted and chopped dates
- 1 cup of toasted almonds

Directions:
1. Coat a big baking sheet using a parchment paper. Keep aside.
2. Use a food processor to add almonds and pulse till chopped crudely.
3. Put in dates and lemon juice and pulse till a tender dough forms.
4. Make equal sized balls from the mixture.
5. In a shallow, dish place shredded coconut.
6. Roll the balls in shredded coconut uniformly.
7. Place the balls onto the baking sheet in a single layer.
8. Place in your fridge to set completely before you serve.

Nutritional Info: , Calories: 173 , Fat: 7.9g , Carbohydrates: 23g , Protein: 3.8g , Fiber: 4.3g

FLAVORSOME ALMONDS

Time To Prepare: ten minutes

Time to Cook: fifteen minutes

Yield: Servings 8

Ingredients:
- ¼ tsp. of cayenne pepper
- ¼ tsp. of ground cumin

- ½ tsp. of chili powder
- ½ tsp. of ground cinnamon
- 1 tbsp. of filtered water
- 1 tsp. of extra-virgin olive oil
- 2 cups of whole almonds
- 3 tbsp. of raw honey
- Salt, to taste

Directions:
1. Preheat your oven to 350 degrees F.
2. Position the almonds onto a big rimmed baking sheet in a single layer.
3. Roast for approximately ten minutes.
4. In the meantime, in a microwave-safe container, put in honey and microwave on Hugh for approximately half a minute.
5. Remove from microwave and mix in oil and water.
6. In a small container, combine all spices.
7. Take away the almonds from the oven, put in it into the container of honey mixture, and stir until blended well.
8. Move the almond mixture onto the baking sheet in a single layer.
9. Drizzle with spice mixture uniformly.
10. Roast for approximately 3-4 minutes.
11. Take off from oven and keep aside to cool to room temperature and serve.
12. You can preserve these roasted almonds in an airtight jar.

Nutritional Info: , Calories: 168 , Fat: 12.5g , Carbohydrates: 11.8g , Protein: 5.1g , Fiber: 3.1g

FLOURLESS & FLAKY MUFFIN MUNCHIES

Time To Prepare: twenty-five minutes

Time to Cook: twenty minutes

Yield: Servings 4

Ingredients:
- ⅛-tsp baking soda
- ¼-cup peanut butter or allergy-friendly substitution
- ¼-cup pure maple syrup or honey
- ¼-tsp salt
- ½-cup quick oats or quinoa flakes, loosely packed
- ¾-tsp baking powder
- 1-cup white beans, cooked
- 1-pc medium mashed banana, very ripe
- 2-tsp pure vanilla extract

- A handful of mini chocolate chips, crushed walnuts, shredded coconut, pinch cinnamon, etc. (not necessary)

Directions:
1. Preheat your oven to 350 F. Coat 8-muffin cups with glassine.
2. Mix all the ingredients in your blender. Blend to a smooth consistency. Pour the mixture into the muffin cups at ⅔ full.
3. Place the cups in your oven, and bake for about twenty minutes.
4. Allow the muffins to sit and cool for about twenty minutes.

Nutritional Info: , Calories: 119 , Fat: 3.9g , Protein: 8.9g , Sodium: 102mg , Total Carbohydrates: 14.4g , Fiber: 2.5g , Net Carbohydrates: 11.9g

GINGER FLOUR BANANA GINGER BARS

Time To Prepare: ten minutes

Time to Cook: forty minutes

Yield: Servings 4-6

Ingredients:
- 1 ½ tbsp. Grated ginger
- 1 cup Coconut flour
- 1 tsp. Baking soda
- 1 tsp. Ground cardamom
- 1/3 cup Honey or maple syrup
- 1/3 cup melted butter
- 2 big Ripe bananas
- 2 tsp. Apple cider vinegar
- 2 tsp. Cinnamon
- 6 medium While eggs

Directions:
1. Preheat your oven to 350ºF.
2. Coat a glass baking dish using parchment paper. If you do not have any paper, just grease the pan.
3. Put all the ingredients apart from the baking soda and apple cider vinegar through a food processor and pulse until it's all mixed up.
4. Now put in the last two ingredients and blitz once before pouring the mix into the glass dish.
5. Bake up to a toothpick inserted into the center comes out clean. This usually takes forty minutes.

Nutritional Info: , Calories: 1407 kcal , Protein: 42.18 g , Fat: 100.26 g , Carbohydrates: 88.33 g

GINGER TURMERIC , PROTEIN: BARS

Time To Prepare: ten minutes + 20 cooling time

Time to Cook: twenty-five minutes

Yield: Servings 7

Ingredients:
- ½ cup coconut
- 1 cup cashews
- 1 scoop turmeric Protein bone broth
- 1 Tbsp. ginger
- 1/3 cup sunflower butter
- 2 Tbsp. maple syrup

Directions:
1. Put in coconut pieces and cashews to a blender or food processor. Use the pulse option to obtain a coarse mixture.
2. Put in butter, broth, maple syrup, and ginger and pulse the mixture to make a coarse, yet even and fairly sticky mass.
3. Evenly put the mixture to a baking pan (8x8 inches) with your hands or a spoon. Push tightly to the baking pan.
4. Bring it in a fridge and allow it to cool for about twenty minutes.
5. Chop the mixture into even squares.
6. You can consume instantly or store in a glass container in the refrigerator (up to 7 days).

Nutritional Info: 107 kcal , Protein: 1.15 g , Fat: 9.59 g , Carbohydrates: 4.63 g

HUMMUS DEVILED EGGS

Time To Prepare: ten minutes

Time to Cook: 0 minutes

Yield: Servings 6

Ingredients:
- ½ cup hummus
- 6 hard-boiled eggs
- Paprika

Directions:
1. Cut the hardboiled eggs in half along the length and remove the yolk.
2. Fill the egg whites with hummus and drizzle with paprika before you serve.

Nutritional Info: , Calories: 179 kcal , Protein: 11.03 g , Fat: 12.41 g , Carbohydrates: 5.14 g

HUMMUS WITH CELERY

Time To Prepare: fifteen minutes

Time to Cook: 0 minutes

Yield: Servings 4

Ingredients:
- 3 cloves of garlic, crushed
- 2 tablespoons extra virgin olive oil
- ½ teaspoon salt
- ½ teaspoon cumin
- 1 (fifteen–ounce) can chickpeas
- two to three tablespoons water
- Dash of paprika
- 6 stalks celery, cut into two-inch pieces
- 3 tablespoons salsa
- 1/4 cup lemon juice
- 1/4 cup tahini

Directions:
1. Using a food processor mix the lemon juice and tahini for approximately one minute, until it is smooth. Scrape the sides down and process for 30 more seconds.
2. Put in the garlic, olive oil, salt, and cumin. Blend for approximately one minute.
3. Drain the chickpeas, put the half of them on the food processor, and blend for one more minute. Scrape down the sides, put in the other half of the chickpeas, and pulse until smooth, approximately 2 minutes. If it like a little too thick, put in water, 1 tablespoon at a time until you reach the desired consistency.
4. Fill the celery sticks with hummus and drizzle paprika on top.
5. Serve with salsa for dipping.

Nutritional Info: , Calories: 240 kcal , Protein: 9.27 g , Fat: 14.51 g , Carbohydrates: 21.01 g

KALE CHIPS

Time To Prepare: ten minutes

Time to Cook: 2 hours

Yield: Servings 8

Ingredients:
- ½ teaspoon sea salt
- 1 cup cashews, soaked and softened in water about 2 hours
- 1 cup grated sweet potato
- 2 bunches of curly kale with stems removed, washed and torn into bite-sized pieces
- 2 tablespoons honey
- 2 tablespoons nutritional yeast (found at health food stores)

- 2 tablespoons water
- The juice of 1 lemon

Directions:
1. Place the kale in a huge container and save for later.
2. In a blender or food processor, process the sweet potato, softened cashews yeast, lemon juice, honey, salt, and water until the desired smoothness is achieved. Place the mixture on the kale and toss with your hands to coat the leaves.
3. Spread the kale leaves out on a big cookie sheet in a single cover without touching.
4. Set the oven to its lowest setting.
5. Prop the oven door slightly ajar and dehydrate the chips for approximately 2 hours flipping the cookie sheet and watching to ensure the chips do not burn.
6. When crunchy, take it out of the oven and allow to cool. Store in an airtight container.

Nutritional Info: , Calories: 40 kcal , Protein: 2.19 g , Fat: 0.87 g , Carbohydrates: 6.39 g

LEMONY GINGER COOKIES

Time To Prepare: fifteen minutes + thirty minutes chill time

Time to Cook: 10-twelve minutes

Yield: Servings 25

Ingredients:
- ½ cup arrowroot flour
- ½ teaspoon baking soda
- 1 ½ cup coconut butter, softened
- 1 ½ cups stevia
- 1 teaspoon nutritional yeast
- 2 teaspoons vanilla
- 3 inches of ginger root, peeled and diced
- 3/4 teaspoon salt
- Zest of 1 lemon

Directions:
1. Set the oven to 350F, then line two or three cookie sheets using parchment paper.
2. Combine the arrowroot flour, stevia, salt, soda, and yeast in a container.
3. In another container, put the rest of the ingredients and mix thoroughly.
4. Put in the dry ingredients progressively until well blended. If the dough is too soft, put an additional one to 2 tablespoons of arrowroot powder. The dough will stiffen when chilled, so be careful.
5. Cover the dough in parchment and push it flat. Chill for half an hour
6. Take a chunk of the chilled dough and flatten it between two pieces of parchment until it is 1/8 inch thick. Sprinkle with a little arrowroot powder and slice into shapes.
7. Put on baking sheets approximately 1 inch apart and bake ten to twelve minutes. Cool on cookie sheets for fifteen minutes before removing.

Nutritional Info: , Calories: 112 kcal , Protein: 0.44 g , Fat: 11.3 g , Carbohydrates: 2.49 g

LOW CHOLESTEROL-LOW CALORIE BLUEBERRY MUFFIN

Time To Prepare: ten minutes

Time to Cook: twenty-five minutes

Yield: Servings 12

Ingredients:
- ½ cup skim milk or non-fat milk
- ½ cup white sugar
- 1 and ½ cup of flour, all-purpose
- 1 cup blueberries, fresh
- 1 egg white
- 1 tablespoon coconut oil
- 2 tablespoons melted margarine
- 2 teaspoons baking powder
- Pinch of salt

Directions:
1. Set the oven to 205C.
2. Grease a 12-cup muffin pan using oil.
3. In a small container, put the blueberries. Put in ¼ cup of the flour and mix it together. Set aside.
4. In another container, whisk the egg white and the coconut oil. Put in the melted margarine.
5. In a different container, mix all together the dry ingredients and sift. Sift again over the egg white mixture. Mix to moisten the flour. The flour should look lumpy, so do not overmix.
6. Fold in the blueberries. Separate the blueberries, so that each scoop will have blueberries. Scoop the mixture into the muffin pans. Fill only up to two-thirds of the pan.
7. Bake for about twenty-five minutes or until the muffin turns golden brown.

Nutritional Info: , Calories: 114 kcal , Protein: 2.66 g , Fat: 5.34 g , Carbohydrates: 14.25 g

MANDARIN COTTAGE CHEESE

Time To Prepare: five minutes

Time to Cook: 0 minutes

Yield: Servings 1

Ingredients:
- ½ cup canned mandarin oranges
- ½ cup low-fat cottage cheese
- 1 ½ tablespoons slivered almonds

Directions:

1. Put the cottage cheese in a container.
2. Drain the mandarin oranges, put them atop the cottage cheese, and drizzle with almonds.

Nutritional Info: , Calories: 360 kcal **,** Protein: 26.24 g **,** Fat: 21.37 g **,** Carbohydrates: 15.22 g

MINI PEPPER NACHOS

Time To Prepare: five minutes

Time to Cook: ten minutes

Yield: Servings 8

Ingredients:
- .25 tsp. Red pepper flakes
- .5 cup Tomato, chopped
- .5 tsp. Oregano
- 1 tbsp. Chili powder
- 1 tsp. Cumin, ground
- 1 tsp. Garlic powder
- 1 tsp. Paprika
- 16 oz. Ground beef
- 16 oz. Mini peppers, seeded, halved
- 5 tsp. Pepper
- 5 tsp. Salt
- cup Cheddar cheese, shredded

Directions:
1. Mix seasonings together in a container.
2. On moderate heat, brown the meat, be sure all the clumps are broken up.
3. Stir in the spices and continue to sauté until the seasoning has gone through all of the meat.
4. Heat the oven to 400F.
5. Put the peppers in a single line. They can touch.
6. Coat with the beef mix.
7. Drizzle with cheese.
8. Bake for minimum ten minutes or until cheese has melted.
9. Pull out of the oven and top with the toppings.

Nutritional Info: , Calories: 240 kcal **,** Protein: 11.01 g **,** Fat: 18.2 g **,** Carbohydrates: 9.49 g

MUSHROOM CHIPS

Time To Prepare: ten minutes

Time to Cook: 45-60 minutes

Yield: Servings 2-4

Ingredients:
- 16 ounces of king oyster mushrooms

- 2 tablespoons ghee
- Kosher salt and ground pepper to taste

Directions:
1. Set the oven to 300F, then line two cookie sheets using parchment paper.
2. Cut every mushroom in half along the length, then cut with a mandolin into 1/8 inch slices or strips. Put them on cookie sheets with some room in between. Melt the ghee and brush it over the mushrooms, then flavor with the salt and pepper.
3. Bake for minimum 45 minutes to an hour, until they are completely crunchy. Store in airtight containers.

Nutritional Info: , Calories: 62 kcal , Protein: 5.58 g , Fat: 2 g , Carbohydrates: 7.97 g

g

ANTI-INFLAMMATORY SPRING PEA SOUP

Time To Prepare: five minutes

Time to Cook: fifteen minutes

Yield: Servings 6

Ingredients:
- ½ tsp. Black pepper powder
- ½ tsp. ground cumin
- 1 liter Vegetable stock
- 1 medium Chopped onion
- 2 tbsp. Coconut oil
- 2 tsp. Celtic sea salt
- 700 g. Fresh peas
- Chopped flat-leaf parsley
- Chopped mint leaves
- Fresh lemon juice
- Grated nutmeg
- Toasted sunflower seeds

Directions:
1. Warm the coconut oil in a pan set on moderate heat.
2. Mix in onions and stir fry for approximately five minutes.
3. Put in the stock and raise the heat. Throw in fresh peas and cook for five minutes. If you're using frozen peas, it should take half the time.
4. Pour in the lemon juice, salt, pepper, herbs, and spices. Stirring continuously
5. Remove the heat and allow it to cool before running it through a food processor to whatever consistency you prefer.
6. Serve with sunflower seed sprinkles and mint or parsley leaves.
7. Enjoy!

Nutritional Info: Calories: 115 kcal , Protein: 5 g , Fat: 5.91 g , Carbohydrates: 11.8 g

ANTI-INFLAMMATORY SWEET POTATO SOUP

Time To Prepare: twenty minutes

Time to Cook: thirty minutes

Yield: Servings 8

Ingredients:
- 1 13.66-ounce can lite coconut milk
- 1 big zucchini, cut width-wise
- 1 garlic clove
- 1 liter low-sodium vegetable stock
- 1 tablespoon sweet yellow curry powder
- 1 teaspoon black pepper
- 1 teaspoon cayenne pepper
- 1 teaspoon turmeric
- 1 white onion
- 2 moderate-sized white potatoes,
- 3 moderate-sized sweet potatoes,
- 3/4 tablespoons salt
- 4 cups of hot water
- 4 tablespoons olive oil
- A pinch of cinnamon
- A pinch of cloves

Directions:
1. Prepare every one of your vegetables by cutting, cleaning & cubing. Put in a safe spot.
2. To a large pot, include 4 tablespoons of additional virgin olive oil. Allow it to heat up swiftly; at that point, include your white onion. Allow it to sweat for minimum five minutes on low warmth.
3. Put in all your flavoring & garlic. Give it a decent mix; at that point, including the potatoes.
4. Allow these cook on moderate heat for around five minutes to get a pleasant darker shading. Continue blending to abstain from consuming.
5. Put in your stalk & water, warm it to the point of boiling & then stew for around 20-twenty-five minutes. Part of the way through the stewing procedure, include your zucchini.
6. After 20-twenty-five minutes, include your coconut milk. Before pouring the soup to the blender, do a fork content to guarantee your potatoes are cooked.
7. Use your blender to purée the soup. Embellishment with lemon juice, dark pepper & herbs & flavors of your preference.

Nutritional Info: Calories: 281 kcal , Protein: 4.1 g , Fat: 20.22 g , Carbohydrates: 23.8 g

BACON & CHEESE SOUP

Time To Prepare: fifteen minutes

Time to Cook: forty minutes

Yield: Servings 6

Ingredients:
- ½ cup sour cream, for serving
- ½ teaspoon cumin
- ½ teaspoon onion powder
- ½ teaspoon paprika
- 1 cup heavy cream
- 1 cup shredded cheddar cheese
- 1 pound of lean ground beef
- 1 tablespoon coconut oil, for cooking
- 1 teaspoon garlic powder
- 1 yellow onion, chopped
- 6 cups beef broth
- 6 slices uncured bacon

Directions:
1. Put in the coconut oil to a frying pan and cook the bacon until crunchy. Allow the bacon to cool and cut into little pieces. Set aside.
2. Once cooked, put in the lean ground beef to the same frying pan with the bacon fat and cook until browned.
3. Put in the onions and cook for an extra two to three minutes.
4. Put in all the ingredients minus the bacon, heavy cream, sour cream and cheese to a stockpot and stir. Cook for about twenty-five minutes.
5. Warm the heavy cream, and then put in the warmed cream and cheese and serve with the bacon and a spoonful of sour cream.

Nutritional Info: Calories: 498 , Carbohydrates: 5g , Fiber: 1g Net , Carbohydrates: 4g , Fat: 34g , Protein: 41g

BEEF AND VEGGIE SOUP

Time To Prepare: ten minutes

Time to Cook: twenty minutes

Yield: Servings 8

Ingredients:
- ½ cup heavy whipping cream
- ½ cup onion, chopped
- 1 (8 ounces / 227 g) package cream cheese, softened
- 1 pound (454 g) ground beef

- 1 tablespoon ground cumin
- 1 teaspoon chili powder
- 2 (10 ounces / 284 g) cans diced tomatoes and green chiles
- 2 (14.5 ounces / 411 g) cans beef broth
- 2 cloves garlic, minced
- 2 teaspoons salt, or to taste

Directions:
1. Position the ground beef, chopped onion, and garlic in a pot, stir until blended well. Cook on moderate to high heat for five to seven minutes or until the beef is thoroughly browned. Stir continuously.
2. Discard the grease extract from the beef, then put in chili powder and cumin, and cook for an extra two minutes. Stir continuously.
3. Put in the cream cheese to the pot and cook for three to five minutes more, then fold in the tomatoes and green chiles, beef broth, heavy whipping cream, and salt, and cook for about ten minutes to cook through. Keep stirring during the cooking.
4. Serve the soup in a big serving container. Allow to stand for a couple of minutes before you serve.

Nutritional Info: calories: 288 , total fat: 24g , carbs: 5.4g , protein: 13.4g , Cholesterol: 85mg , Sodium: 1310mg

BROCCOLI CHEDDAR & BACON SOUP

Time To Prepare: ten minutes

Time to Cook: ten minutes

Yield: Servings 6

Ingredients:
- ¼ teaspoon black pepper
- ½ teaspoon salt
- ½ white onion, chopped
- 1 cup broccoli florets finely chopped
- 1 cup heavy cream
- 1 cup shredded cheddar cheese
- 2 cloves garlic, chopped
- 2 cups chicken broth
- 3 slices cooked bacon, crumbled for serving

Directions:
1. Put in all the ingredients minus the heavy cream, cheddar cheese and bacon to a stockpot on moderate heat.
2. Heat to a simmer and cook for 5 minutes.
3. Warm the cream, and then put in the warm cream and cheddar cheese. Whisk until the desired smoothness is achieved.
4. Serve with crumbled bacon.

Nutritional Info: Calories: 220 , Carbohydrates: 4g , Fiber: 1g Net , Carbohydrates: 3g , Fat: 18g , Protein: 11g

BROCCOLI SOUP WITH GORGONZOLA CHEESE

Time To Prepare: ten minutes

Time to Cook: thirty minutes

Yield: Servings 4

Ingredients:
- ½ cup 18% cream
- 1 big broccoli, divided into little roses
- 1 flat teaspoon of sweet pepper
- 1 onion, diced
- 1 tablespoon of chopped fresh basil
- 1 tablespoon of chopped parsley
- 1 tablespoon of oil
- 150 g Gorgonzola cheese, diced
- 2 potatoes, peeled and diced
- 4 tablespoons of almond flakes roasted in a dry pan
- 5 garlic cloves, chopped
- 750 ml broth
- a pinch of sugar
- pumpkin oil (not necessary)
- salt and pepper

Directions:
1. In a big deep cooking pan, warm the oil on moderate heat, put the onion and garlic, and fry it until the vitrified glass onion.
2. Then put the broccoli with potatoes, pour the broth and cook for approximately fifteen-twenty minutes until the vegetables become tender. Put in basil, parsley, sugar, pepper, and pepper to taste.
3. Put in cheese and cream, and when the cheese dissolves, blend with a blender until the desired smoothness is achieved. Sprinkle with salt and pepper if required.
4. Serve the soup sprinkled with almond flakes and sprinkled with pumpkin oil.

Nutritional Info: Calories: 382 kcal , Protein: 13.06 g , Fat: 18.93 g , Carbohydrates: 41.65 g

BROWN RICE AND SHITAKE MISO SOUP WITH SCALLION

Time To Prepare: ten minutes

Time to Cook: forty-five minutes

Yield: Servings 4

Ingredients:
- ½ teaspoon salt
- 1 (1½-inch) piece fresh ginger, peeled and cut
- 1 cup medium-grain brown rice
- 1 cup thinly cut shiitake mushroom caps
- 1 garlic clove, minced
- 1 tablespoon white miso
- 2 scallions, thinly cut
- 2 tablespoons finely chopped fresh cilantro
- 2 tablespoons sesame oil

Directions:
1. In a large pot, heat the oil on moderate to high heat.
2. Put in the mushrooms, garlic, and ginger and sauté until the mushrooms start to tenderize, approximately five minutes.
3. Place the rice and stir to uniformly coat with the oil.
4. Put in 2 cups of water and salt and place it to its boiling point.
5. Reduce the heat then cook until the rice is soft, thirty to forty minutes.
6. Use a little of the soup broth to tenderize the miso, then mix it into the pot until well mixed.
7. Stir in the scallions and cilantro, then serve.

Nutritional Info: Calories: 265 , Total Fat: 8g , Total Carbohydrates: 43g , Sugar: 2g , Fiber: 3g , Protein: 5g , Sodium: 456mg

BUFFALO SAUCE AND TURKEY SOUP

Time To Prepare: five minutes

Time to Cook: ten minutes

Yield: Servings 4

Ingredients:
- ⅓ cup buffalo sauce
- 2 cups turkey, cooked, shredded
- 3 tablespoons butter, melted
- 4 cups chicken broth
- 4 ounces (113 g) cream cheese
- 4 tablespoons cilantro, chopped
- From The Cupboard:
- Salt and freshly ground black pepper, to taste

Directions:
1. Place the buffalo sauce, cream cheese, and melted butter in a blender, and process until the desired smoothness is achieved.

2. Pour the buffalo sauce mixture in a deep cooking pan, and put in the chicken broth. Heat the soup using high heat until hot and nearly boil off but not boil. Keep stirring during the heating.
3. Put in the shredded turkey, and drizzle with salt and black pepper. Cook for five minutes or until the desired smoothness is achieved. Stir continuously.
4. Ladle the soup into a big container and top with chopped cilantro before you serve.

Nutritional Info: calories: 409 , total fat: 29.7g , net carbs: 9.2g , protein: 26.4g

BUTTERNUT SQUASH SOUP WITH SHRIMP

Time To Prepare: ten minutes

Time to Cook: twenty minutes

Yield: Servings 4

Ingredients:
- ¼ cup slivered almonds (not necessary)
- ¼ teaspoon freshly ground black pepper
- 1 cup unsweetened almond milk
- 1 garlic clove, cut
- 1 pound cooked peeled shrimp, thawed if required
- 1 small red onion, finely chopped
- 1 teaspoon salt
- 1 teaspoon turmeric
- 2 cups peeled butternut squash cut into ¼-inch dice
- 2 tablespoons finely chopped fresh flat-leaf parsley
- 2 teaspoons grated or minced lemon zest
- 3 cups vegetable broth
- 3 tablespoons unsalted butter

Directions:
1. In a large pot, melt the butter on high heat.
2. Put in the onion, garlic, turmeric, salt, and pepper and sauté until the vegetables are tender and translucent, five to seven minutes.
3. Put in the broth and squash and bring to its boiling point.
4. Reduce the heat and cook until the squash has tenderized, approximately five minutes.
5. Put in the shrimp and almond milk and cook until thoroughly heated, approximately 2 minutes.
6. Drizzle with the almonds (if using), parsley, and lemon zest before you serve.

Nutritional Info: Calories: 275 , Total Fat: 12g , Total Carbohydrates: 12g , Sugar: 3g , Fiber: 2g; , Protein: 30g , Sodium: 1665mg

CANNELLINI BEAN SOUP

Time To Prepare: twenty-five minutes

Time to Cook: thirty minutes

Yield: Servings 6

Ingredients:
- 1 bunch red Swiss chard
- 1 cannellini beans
- 1 clove garlic (minced)
- 1 onion (chopped)
- 1 tablespoon extra-virgin olive oil
- 1/4 teaspoon nutmeg (grated)
- 1/8 teaspoon red pepper flakes (crushed)
- 2 ounces Parmesan cheese rind
- 2 slices smoked bacon (chopped)
- 2 tablespoons chopped sun-dried tomatoes
- 5 big sage leaves (minced)
- 5 leaves basil (chopped)
- 6 cups chicken broth

Directions:
1. Cook the bacon with garlic, onion, nutmeg, and red pepper flakes for five minutes.
2. Pour in beans, chicken broth, sun-dried tomatoes, and Parmesan cheese rind, simmering for about ten minutes.
3. Put in the cut chard and chard leaves into the soup.
4. Simmer and then put in into bowls with a sprinkle of oil and Parmesan cheese.

Nutritional Info: Calories: 215 kcal , Carbohydrates: 23 g , Fat: 10 g , Protein: 9.7 g

CARROT BROCCOLI STEW

Time To Prepare: ten minutes

Time to Cook: forty-five minutes

Yield: Servings 3

Ingredients:
- 1 cup Broccoli, florets
- 1 cup Carrots, cut
- 1 cup Heavy Cream
- 3 cups Chicken broth
- Salt and black pepper to taste

Directions:

1. Put in florets, cream, carrots, salt, and chicken broth; toss thoroughly. Secure the lid and cook on Meat/Stew mode for forty minutes on High. When ready, do a quick pressure release.
2. Move into serving bowls and drizzle black pepper on top.

Nutritional Info: Calories 145 , Protein: 1.5g , Carbs: 1.2g

CARROT, GINGER & TURMERIC SOUP

Time To Prepare: fifteen minutes

Time to Cook: forty minutes

Yield: Servings 8

Ingredients:
- ¼ cup full-fat unsweetened coconut milk
- ¾ pound carrots, peeled and chopped
- 1 sweet yellow onion, chopped
- 1 teaspoon ground turmeric
- 2 cloves garlic, chopped
- 2 teaspoons grated ginger
- 6 cups vegetable broth
- Pinch of sea salt & pepper, to taste

Directions:
1. Put in all the ingredients minus the coconut milk to a stockpot on moderate heat and bring to its boiling point. Reduce to a simmer and cook for forty minutes or until the carrots are soft.
2. Use an immersion blender and blend the soup until the desired smoothness is achieved. Mix in the coconut milk.
3. Enjoy immediately and freeze any remainings.

Nutritional Info: Calories: 73 , Carbohydrates: 7g , Fiber: 2g Net , Carbohydrates: 5g , Fat: 3g , Protein: 4g

CAULIFLOWER AND CLAM CHOWDER

Time To Prepare: ten minutes

Time to Cook: ten minutes

Yield: Servings 6

Ingredients:
- ½ teaspoon dried thyme
- 1 small yellow onion
- 1½ cups heavy whipping cream
- 3 (6.5-ounce / 184-g) cans chopped clams
- 3 tablespoons butter

- 4 cups chopped cauliflower
- From the cupboard:
- Salt and freshly ground black pepper, to taste

Directions:
1. Split the clams and clam juice into two bowls. Thin the clam juice with water to make 2 cups of juice.
2. Place the onion and butter in an instant pot and press the Sauté bottom, then sauté for a couple of minutes or until the onion is translucent.
3. Put in the clam juice and cauliflower into the instant pot. Place the lid on and press the Manual button, and set the temperature to 375ºF (190ºC), then cook for five minutes.
4. Quick Release the pressure, then open the lid and mix in the heavy cream and clams.
5. Push the Sauté bottom and cook for about three minutes or until the clams are opaque and firm, then drizzle with thyme, salt, and black pepper. Stir to mix thoroughly.
6. Ladle the chowder in a big container and serve warm.

Nutritional Info: calories: 252 , total fat: 17.3g , total carbs: 8.9g , fiber: 2.1g , net carbs: 6.8g , protein: 17.1g

CAULIFLOWER, COCONUT MILK, AND SHRIMP SOUP

Time To Prepare: five minutes

Time to Cook: 2 hours and fifteen minutes

Yield: Servings 4

Ingredients:
- 1 (13.5-ounce / 383-g) can unsweetened full-fat coconut milk
- 1 cup shrimp, peeled, deveined, tail off, and cooked
- 1 cup water
- 2 cups riced cauliflower
- 2 tablespoons chopped fresh cilantro leaves, divided
- 2 tablespoons red curry paste
- From the cupboard:
- Salt and freshly ground black pepper, to taste

Directions:
1. Put in the riced cauliflower, red curry paste, coconut milk, 1 tablespoon cilantro, water, then drizzle with salt and black pepper. Combine the mixture to blend well.
2. Place the slow cooker lid on and cook on HIGH for about two hours.
3. Place the shrimp on a clean working surface, then drizzle salt and black pepper to season.
4. Place the shrimp in the slow cooker and cook for fifteen minutes more.
5. Move the soup into a big container and top with the rest of the cilantro leaves before you serve.

Nutritional Info: calories: 268 , total fat: 21.3g , total carbs: 7.8g , fiber: 3.2g , net carbs: 4.6g , protein: 16.1g

CELERY SOUP

Time To Prepare: ten minutes

Time to Cook: twenty minutes

Yield: Servings 4

Ingredients:
- ½ cup brown onion, chopped
- ½ cup full-fat milk
- ½ pound with Salsiccia links, casing removed and cut
- ½ teaspoon dried chili flakes
- ½ teaspoon ground black pepper
- 1 carrot, chopped
- 1 garlic clove, pressed
- 2 teaspoon coconut oil
- 3 cups celery, chopped
- 3 cups roasted vegetable broth
- Kosher salt, to taste

Directions:
1. Simply throw all of the above ingredients into your Instant Pot; gently stir until blended.
2. Secure the lid. Choose "Soup/Broth" mode and High pressure; cook for about twenty-five minutes. Once cooking is complete, use a quick pressure release; cautiously remove the lid.
3. Ladle into four soup bowls and serve hot. Enjoy!

Nutritional Info: 150 Calories , 5.9g Fat , 5.9g Total Carbs , 16.4g Protein , 4.1g Sugars

CHEESY BROCCOLI SOUP

Time To Prepare: five minutes

Time to Cook: twenty minutes

Yield: Servings 4

Ingredients:
- 1 cup broccoli, cut into florets
- 1 cup chicken broth
- 1 cup heavy whipping cream
- 1 cup shredded Cheddar cheese, plus more for topping
- 2 tablespoons butter
- From the cupboard:
- Salt and freshly ground black pepper, to taste

Directions:

1. Place the butter in a deep cooking pan, and melt on moderate heat.
2. Put in and sauté the broccoli for four to five minutes or until tender.
3. Stir in the chicken broth and heavy whipping cream over the broccoli, and drizzle with salt and black pepper. Cook for approximately fifteen minutes or until the soup is smooth and thickened. Keep stirring during the cooking.
4. Lower the heat to low and gently fold in the Cheddar cheese. Keep stirring until well blended.
5. Ladle the soup into a big container. Spread more cheese over the soup before you serve.

Nutritional Info: calories: 386 , total fat: 37.3g , total carbs: 3.8g , fiber: 1.1g , net carbs: 2.7g , protein: 9.8g

CHEESY CHICKEN SOUP

Time To Prepare: twenty minutes

Time to Cook: 33-40 minutes

Yield: Servings 6

Ingredients:
- ¼ teaspoon black pepper
- ½ cup shredded cheddar cheese
- ½ teaspoon cumin
- ½ teaspoon salt
- 1 cup whipped cream cheese
- 1 tablespoon coconut oil, for cooking
- 1 teaspoon chili powder
- 1 yellow onion, chopped
- 2 boneless, skinless chicken breasts
- 2 cloves garlic, chopped
- 2 cups chicken broth
- 2 cups water

Directions:
1. Heat a big frying pan on moderate heat with a ½ tablespoon of the coconut oil.
2. Brown the chicken breasts until thoroughly cooked. Set aside.
3. Put in the garlic and onion to a big stockpot with the rest of the 1 tablespoon of the coconut oil and sauté until translucent over low to moderate heat. This should take about three to five minutes.
4. Put in this chicken broth and water.
5. Whisk in the cream cheese and keep whisking over low to moderate heat until blended.
6. Put in in the spices and bring to its boiling point.
7. While the water is boiling, chop the chicken into bite-sized pieces and put in to the stockpot.
8. Reduce to a simmer and cook for half an hour.
9. Mix in the cheddar cheese before you serve.

Nutritional Info: Calories: 157 , Carbohydrates: 5g , Fiber: 1g Net , Carbohydrates: 4g , Fat: 7g , Protein: 17g

CHEESY TOMATO AND BASIL SOUP

Time To Prepare: five minutes

Time to Cook: fifteen minutes

Yield: Servings 12

Ingredients:
- ¼ teaspoon ground black pepper
- 1 tablespoon dried basil
- 1 teaspoon dried oregano
- 1 teaspoon salt
- 2 (14 ounces / 397 g) canned whole tomatoes, diced
- 2 garlic cloves, minced
- 2 tablespoons coconut oil
- 4 cups chicken broth
- 4 ounces (113 g) red onions, finely diced
- 5 ounces (142 g) grated Parmesan cheese, plus more for decoration
- 8 ounces (227 g) cream cheese, softened
- Fresh basil, chopped, for decoration

Directions:
1. Grease a nonstick frying pan with coconut oil, and sauté the onions, basil, oregano, and garlic in the frying pan for about four minutes or until aromatic.
2. Put in the cream cheese and fully whisk until no clump, then fold in the chicken broth, and put in the cheese, tomatoes, salt, and pepper. Stir to blend well.
3. Cover the lid and bring them to a simmer on moderate heat for eight minutes. Move the soup into a blender, then blitz until it becomes thick.
4. Lightly pour the soup into a big serving container and sprinkle with Parmesan cheese and basil as decorate.

Nutritional Info: calories: 146 , total fat: 12g , net carbs: 3g , fiber: 1g , protein: 6g

CHICKEN AND CAULIFLOWER CURRY STEW

Time To Prepare: fifteen minutes

Time to Cook: 4 hours

Yield: Servings 7

Ingredients:
- ¼ cup fresh cilantro, chopped
- ⅓ cup coconut oil
- 1 green bell pepper, chopped
- 1 pound (454 g) cauliflower, chopped into little pieces

- 1.5pounds (680 g) skinless, boneless chicken thighs, cut into bite-sized pieces
- 14 ounces (397 g) unsweetened coconut milk
- 2 tablespoons curry powder
- 2 tablespoons ginger garlic paste
- Salt and ground black pepper, to taste

Directions:
1. Warm half of the coconut oil in a nonstick frying pan on moderate heat, then sauté the garlic ginger paste and curry powder for a minutes or until aromatic.
2. Put in the chicken pieces, and drizzle with salt and pepper. sauté for another ten minutes or until the chicken is mildly browned. Remove from the frying pan and set aside in warm.
3. Warm another half of coconut oil in the frying pan, then sauté the cauliflower and bell pepper on moderate to high heat for one to two minutes.
4. Then fold in the coconut milk and reduce the heat to low. Cover with lid and stew for about forty-five minutes.
5. Drizzle with salt and pepper, then put in the sautéed chicken. Move the stew to a big platter and serve with cilantro on top as decorate.

Nutritional Info: calories: 782 , total fat: 68g , net carbs: 9g , fiber: 5g , protein: 33g

CHICKEN AND KALE SOUP

Time To Prepare: five minutes

Time to Cook: 4 hours

Yield: Servings 4

Ingredients:
- 1 (7-ounce / 198-g) bunch kale, trimmed and chopped
- 1 big chicken breast, cut into little strips
- 2 tablespoons olive oil
- 3 tablespoons fresh ginger, grated
- 6 cups chicken stock
- 6 garlic cloves, finely chopped
- From the cupboard:
- Salt and freshly ground black pepper, to taste

Directions:
1. Grease the insert of the slow cooker with olive oil.
2. Combine the chicken breast, stock, kale, ginger, garlic, ginger, salt, and black pepper in the slow cooker.
3. Place the slow cooker lid on and cook on HIGH for 4 hours.
4. Ladle the stew in a big container and serve warm.

Nutritional Info: calories: 168 , total fat: 7.6g , total carbs: 8.3g , fiber: 2.1g , net carbs: 6.2g , protein: 18.7g

CHICKEN CHILI BLANCO

Time To Prepare: ten minutes

Time to Cook: twenty minutes

Yield: Servings 4

Ingredients:
- ¼ teaspoon cayenne pepper
- 1 tablespoon ghee
- 1 teaspoon chili powder
- 2 (4-ounce) cans diced mild green chiles with their liquid
- 2 scallions, cut
- 2 small onions, chopped
- 2 teaspoons dried oregano
- 4 cups chicken broth or vegetable broth
- 4 cups shredded cooked chicken
- 4 cups white beans, drained and washed well
- 4 teaspoons ground cumin
- 6 garlic cloves, minced

Directions:
1. In a huge soup pot on moderate heat, melt the ghee.
2. Put in the onions and garlic, and sauté for five minutes.
3. Place the chiles, and cook for a couple of minutes, stirring.
4. Mix in the beans, broth, cumin, oregano, chili powder, and cayenne pepper. Heat it until it simmers.
5. Put in the chicken, bring to a simmer, decrease the heat to moderate-low, and cook for about ten minutes. Serve instantly, sprinkled with the scallions.

Nutritional Info: Calories: 304 , Total Fat: 4g , Saturated Fat: 2g , Cholesterol: 0mg , Carbohydrates: 46g , Fiber: 12g , Protein: 21g

CHICKEN TORTILLA SOUP

Time To Prepare: ten minutes

Time to Cook: twenty minutes

Yield: Servings 8-10

Ingredients:
- 1 teaspoon cayenne pepper or to taste
- 2 cups onions, chopped
- 2 teaspoons chili powder
- 2 teaspoons cumin powder
- 2 teaspoons dried oregano
- 2 teaspoons garlic powder

- 4 cups carrots, cut
- 4 cups celery, cut
- 4 cups water
- 4 teaspoons olive oil
- 6 cups rotisserie chicken, skinless, chopped or shredded
- 8 cloves garlic, minced
- 8 cups chicken broth
- 8 medium tomatoes, chopped
- Avocado, peeled, pitted, chopped
- For the topping: Use any (not necessary)
- Fresh cilantro, chopped
- Greek yogurt
- Pepper powder to taste
- Salt to taste
- Tortilla chips, crumbled

Directions:
1. Put a soup pot on moderate heat. Put in oil.
2. When the oil is warmed, put the onion and celery and sauté until slightly soft.
3. Put in garlic and sauté for a few seconds until aromatic. Stir in the tomatoes and cook until tender. Remove the heat.
4. Move into a blender. Put in water and blend until the desired smoothness is achieved.
5. Put back the mixed mixture into the pot. Put in the remaining ingredients and stir.
6. If it's beginning to boil, reduce the heat then simmer until vegetables are tender.
7. Ladle into soup bowls before you serve.

Nutritional Info: Calories: 1593 kcal , Protein: 147.22 g , Fat: 102.27 g , Carbohydrates: 13.17 g

CHICKPEA CURRY SOUP

Time To Prepare: ten minutes

Time to Cook: twenty-five minutes

Yield: Servings 4

Ingredients:
- ¼ cup extra-virgin olive oil or coconut oil
- 1 (fifteen-ounce) can chickpeas, drained and washed
- 1 big apple, cored, peeled, and slice into ¼-inch dice
- 1 cup full-fat coconut milk
- 1 medium onion, finely chopped
- 1 teaspoon salt
- 2 garlic cloves, cut
- 2 tablespoons finely chopped fresh cilantro
- 2 teaspoons curry powder
- 3 cups peeled butternut squash cut into ½-inch dice

- 3 cups vegetable broth

Directions:
1. In a large pot, heat the oil on high heat.
2. Put in the onion and garlic and sauté until the onion starts to brown, six to eight minutes.
3. Place the apple, curry powder, and salt and sauté to toast the curry powder, one to two minutes.
4. Place the squash and broth then bring to its boiling point.
5. Reduce the heat then cook until the squash is soft about ten minutes.
6. Mix in the coconut milk.
7. Use an immersion blender to purée the soup in the pot until the desired smoothness is achieved.
8. Mix in the chickpeas and cilantro, heat through for one to two minutes, before you serve.

Nutritional Info: Calories: 469 , Total Fat: 30g , Total Carbohydrates: 45g , Sugar: 14g , Fiber: 10g , Protein: 12g , Sodium: 1174mg

CLEAR CLAM CHOWDER

Time To Prepare: ten minutes

Time to Cook: fifteen minutes

Yield: Servings 4

Ingredients:
- ¼ teaspoon freshly ground black pepper
- ½ teaspoon dried thyme
- ½ teaspoon salt
- 1 (10-ounce) can clams
- 1 (8-ounce) bottle clam juice
- 1 small red onion, cut into ¼-inch dice
- 2 celery stalks, thinly cut
- 2 cups vegetable broth
- 2 garlic cloves, cut
- 2 medium carrots, cut into ½-inch pieces
- 2 tablespoons unsalted butter

Directions:
1. In a large pot, melt the butter on high heat.
2. Put in the carrots, celery, onion, and garlic and sauté until slightly softened two to three minutes.
3. Pour the broth and clam juice, then bring it to its boiling point.
4. Reduce the heat and cook until the carrots are soft, three to five minutes.
5. Mix in the clams and their juices, thyme, salt, and pepper, heat through for two to three minutes, before you serve.

Nutritional Info: Calories: 156 , Total Fat: 7g , Total Carbohydrates: 7g , Sugar: 3g , Fiber: 1g , Protein: 14g , Sodium: 981mg

COCONUT CASHEW SOUP WITH BUTTERNUT SQUASH

Time To Prepare: ten minutes

Time to Cook: twenty minutes

Yield: Servings 6

Ingredients:
- ½ tsp. salt
- ¾ cup toasted cashews
- 1 (14-ounce) can full-fat coconut milk
- 1 cup mung bean sprouts
- 1 small butternut squash, halved, diced
- 1 small Napa cabbage, shredded
- 1 white onion, diced
- 1½ tbsp. Ginger, peeled and minced
- 2 carrots, chopped
- 2 cups green beans, trimmed
- 2 red chili peppers, seeded and diced
- 2 tbsp. coconut oil
- 3 cups vegetable broth
- 3 garlic cloves, peeled and minced
- 4 tablespoons toasted coconut shavings
- Freshly ground black pepper

Directions:
1. In a huge soup pot on moderate heat, melt the coconut oil.
2. Place the cashews and sauté for a couple of minutes. Take off from the pan and save for later.
3. Place the peppers, garlic, and onion, and sauté for minimum 6 minutes. Then put the ginger and carrots, and sauté for minimum 3 minutes, or until the carrots and squash start to become tender.
4. Stir in the cabbage, green beans, broth, coconut milk, and salt, flavor with pepper. Simmer for fifteen minutes. Remove the heat.
5. Mix in the bean sprouts and coconut shavings.
6. Pour into soup bowls and serve instantly.

Nutritional Info: Calories: 340 , Total Fat: 25g , Saturated Fat: 20g , Cholesterol: 0mg , Carbohydrates: 23g , Fiber: 5g , Protein: 7g

COCONUT CURRIED BAN-APPLE SOUP

Time To Prepare: ten minutes

Time to Cook: 10-fifteen minutes

Yield: Servings 4

Ingredients:
- ¼ cup toasted coconut, for decoration
- 1 big potato 1 Granny Smith apple
- 1 celery heart
- 1 cup coconut milk
- 1 ripe banana
- 1 sweet onion
- 1 teaspoon curry powder
- 1 teaspoon salt
- 2 cups Basic Vegetable Stock or low-sodium canned vegetable stock
- 2 tablespoons chopped fresh cilantro, for decoration

Directions:
1. Place the vegetable stock in a soup pot.
2. Peel the banana and potato, cut them, and place them in the soup pot. Core the apple, cut it, and put in it to the soup pot. Cut the celery heart and onion and put in them to the soup pot.
3. Put the soup to its boiling point, then reduce the heat and simmer for ten to fifteen minutes. Put in the coconut milk, curry powder, and salt.
4. Place the hot soup in a blender and purée.
5. Serve the soup hot. Decorate using toasted coconut and cilantro.

Nutritional Info: Calories: 344 , Fat: 19 g , Protein: 6 g , Sodium: 886 mg , Fiber: 7 g , Carbohydrates: 40 g

CREAM OF MUSHROOM SOUP

Time To Prepare: twenty minutes

Time to Cook: thirty minutes

Yield: Servings 6

Ingredients:
- 5 cups mushrooms (cut)
- 1 tablespoon sherry
- 3 tablespoons butter
- 3 tablespoons flour
- 1 cup half-and-half
- Salt
- Ground black pepper
- 1½ cups chicken broth
- ½ cup onion (chopped)
- 1/8 teaspoon dried thyme

Directions:

1. Cook mushrooms with onion and thyme in the broth until soft.
2. Puree the mixture.
3. Whisk some flour in a pan of melted butter. Put in half-and-half, vegetable puree, and seasoning. Boil until it becomes thick.
4. Put in sherry.

Nutritional Info: Calories: 148 kcal , Carbohydrates: 8.6 g , Fat: 11 g , Protein: 4 g

CREAMY & CULTURE TOMATO SAUCE

Time To Prepare: ten minutes

Time to Cook: fifteen-twenty minutes

Yield: Servings 6

Ingredients:
- ⅛ teaspoon dried thyme
- ⅛ teaspoon freshly ground black pepper
- ¼ cup tomato paste
- ¼ teaspoon chili powder
- ½ cup plain whole-milk yogurt
- ½ teaspoon salt
- 1 small onion, chopped
- 1 tablespoon ghee
- 1 teaspoon dried basil
- 1 teaspoon dried oregano
- 2 (14-ounce) cans diced tomatoes with their juice
- 2 cups vegetable broth
- 3 garlic cloves, chopped

Directions:
1. In a huge soup pot on moderate heat, melt the ghee.
2. Place the onion and garlic, and sauté for five minutes.
3. Stir in the basil, oregano, salt, chili powder, pepper, and thyme.
4. Place the tomatoes, broth, and tomato paste, and stir until blended. Heat to a simmer, turn the heat to low, and cook for five to ten minutes. Take away the pot from the heat. With an immersion blender (or in batches in a standard blender), purée the mixture in the pot until you have the desired consistency.
5. Put in the yogurt. Blend for a minute more. Serve instantly.

Nutritional Info: Calories: 157 , Total Fat: 6g , Saturated Fat: 3g , Cholesterol: 3mg , Carbohydrates: 25g , Fiber: 13g , Protein: 8g

CREAMY BROCCOLI SOUP

Time To Prepare: fifteen minutes

Time to Cook: 4 hours

Yield: Servings 7

Ingredients:
- ¼ teaspoon ground black pepper
- ½ teaspoon paprika powder
- ½ teaspoon salt
- ⅔ cup heavy whipping cream
- 1 pinch cayenne pepper
- 1 red onion, roughly chopped
- 1 tablespoon olive oil
- 2 cups chicken broth
- 20 ounces (567 g) broccoli, cut into stalks and florets
- 3 garlic cloves, chopped
- 3 tablespoons butter
- ounces (99 g) Cheddar cheese, shredded

Directions:
1. Warm 1 tablespoon of butter and olive oil in a deep cooking pan, then fry the broccoli stalks and chopped onion on moderate heat for five minutes until soft.
2. Put in the garlic and keep frying for a couple of minutes until mildly browned, then drizzle with cayenne pepper, paprika, salt, and ground black pepper. Cook for another one minutes.
3. Pour over the chicken broth. Cover the lid and leave to simmer for five minutes.
4. Take away the cooked vegetables from the deep cooking pan to a food processor and process. Lightly ladle the soup into the food processor while processing until creamy.
5. Melt the rest of the butter in the deep cooking pan, and fry the broccoli florets for five minutes until tender and soft.
6. Pour the soup from the food processor into the deep cooking pan. Blend to mix thoroughly. If the soup is too thick, you can put in some water to make it thinner.
7. Bring the soup to its boiling point, then reduce the heat and bring to a simmer using low heat for about three minutes.
8. Put in the Cheddar cheese and heavy whipping cream and cook for a couple of minutes more until the cheese melts.
9. Take away the soup from the deep cooking pan and serve warm.

Nutritional Info: calories: 266 , total fat: 23g , net carbs: 7g , fiber: 3g , protein: 8g

CREAMY CELERY AND CHICKEN BROTH

Time To Prepare: five minutes

Time to Cook: twenty minutes

Yield: Servings 4

Ingredients:
- ¼ cup celery, chopped
- ½ cup coconut cream
- 1 onion, chopped
- 2 chicken breasts, chopped
- 3 tablespoons butter
- 4 cups water
- From The Cupboard:
- Salt and freshly ground black pepper, to taste

Directions:
1. Place the butter in a deep cooking pan, and melt on moderate heat.
2. Put in and sauté the celery and onion for about three minutes or until the onion is translucent.
3. Put in the chicken, salt, black pepper, and water, and simmer for fifteen minutes. Keep stirring during the simmering.
4. Mix in the coconut cream. Pour the soup in a big container and serve warm.

Nutritional Info: calories: 398 , total fat: 24.4g , net carbs: 5.9g , protein: 29.3g

CREAMY LEEK SOUP

Time To Prepare: two minutes

Time to Cook: 8 minutes

Yield: Servings 4

Ingredients:
- ½ cup heavy cream
- ½ cup Monterey-Jack cheese, shredded
- ½ cup tomato purée
- ½ pound chorizo, cut
- 1 bay leaf
- 1 cup leeks, chopped
- 1 green chili, deseeded and finely chopped
- 1 tablespoon sesame oil
- 2 chicken bouillon cubes
- 2 cloves garlic, minced
- 4 cups water

Directions:
1. Push the "Sauté" button to heat up your Instant Pot. Once hot, heat the oil and sauté the leeks until soft.
2. Now, mix in chorizo, garlic, and green chili; carry on cooking until aromatic. Next, put in water, tomato puree, heavy cream, bouillon cubes, and bay leaf.

3. Secure the lid. Choose "Manual" mode and High pressure; cook for about six minutes. Once cooking is complete, use a natural pressure release; cautiously remove the lid.
4. Next, press the "Sauté" button and put in the cheese; allow it to simmer until the cheese is melted and thoroughly heated.

Nutritional Info: 428 Calories , 36g Fat , 6.1g Total Carbs , 18.9g Protein , 2.1g Sugars

CREAMY PARSNIP SOUP

Time To Prepare: twenty-five minutes

Time to Cook: 60 minutes

Yield: Servings 10

Ingredients:
- 1 big onion (diced)
- 1 cup whole milk
- 1 tablespoon brown sugar
- 1 tablespoon butter
- 1 tablespoon olive oil
- 1 teaspoon ground ginger
- ½ teaspoon ground allspice
- ½ teaspoon ground cardamom
- ½ teaspoon ground nutmeg
- 1/4 teaspoon cayenne pepper
- 2 pounds parsnips (peeled, cut)
- 3 carrots (peeled, cut)
- 3 cloves garlic (minced)
- 3 stalks celery (diced)
- 4 cups chicken stock
- Ground black pepper
- Salt

Directions:
1. Preheat your oven to 425 F.
2. Toss the parsnips and carrots with oil and seasoning in a container. Put them over a baking sheet.
3. Roast in oven until for half an hour
4. Cook the onion and celery in oil till golden brown, approximately seven minutes. Put in butter, brown sugar, garlic, and the parsnips and carrots, cooking for about ten minutes.
5. Season and stir. Put in the chicken stock to its boiling point until soft.
6. Puree the soup.
7. Put in milk and cream and simmer some more before you serve with seasoning.

Nutritional Info: Calories: 187 kcal , Carbohydrates: 24 g , Fat: 9 g , Protein: 3 g

CREAMY PUMPKIN PUREE SOUP

Time To Prepare: ten minutes

Time to Cook: forty-five minutes

Yield: Servings 3

Ingredients:
- 1 cup Heavy Cream
- 1 cup Pumpkin puree
- 2 cups Chicken broth
- 2 tbsp. Olive oil
- 4-5 Garlic cloves
- Salt and black pepper to taste

Directions:
1. In the Instant Pot, put in all ingredients.
2. Secure the lid and cook for forty minutes on Meat/Stew mode on High. When ready, press Cancel and do a quick pressure release.
3. Move to a blender and blend thoroughly. Pour into serving bowls to serve.

Nutritional Info: Calories 465 , Protein: 15.4g , Carbs: 6.2g , Fat: 43.5g

CREAMY TURKEY SOUP

Time To Prepare: fifteen minutes

Time to Cook: 4 hours

Yield: Servings 7

Ingredients:
- 1 carrot, chopped
- 1 cup cream cheese
- 1 pound turkey breast, cubed
- 1 stalk celery, chopped
- 1 teaspoon freshly chopped rosemary
- 3 cloves garlic, chopped
- 5 cups chicken broth
- Salt & black pepper, to taste

Directions:
1. Put in all the ingredients minus the cream cheese to the base of a slow cooker.
2. Cook on high for 4 hours.
3. Mix in the cream cheese until well blended.

Nutritional Info: Calories: 216 , Carbohydrates: 6g , Fiber: 1g Net , Carbohydrates: 5g , Fat: 14g , Protein: 17g

CREAMY TURMERIC CAULIFLOWER SOUP

Time To Prepare: ten minutes

Time to Cook: fifteen minutes

Yield: Servings 4

Ingredients:
- ¼ cup finely chopped fresh cilantro
- ¼ teaspoon freshly ground black pepper
- ¼ teaspoon ground cumin
- ½ teaspoon salt
- 1 (1¼-inch) piece fresh ginger, peeled and cut
- 1 cup full-fat coconut milk
- 1 garlic clove, peeled
- 1 leek, white part only, thinly cut
- 1½ teaspoons turmeric
- 2 tablespoons extra-virgin olive oil
- 3 cups cauliflower florets
- 3 cups vegetable broth

Directions:
1. In a large pot, heat the oil on high heat.
2. Put in the leek, and sauté until it just starts to brown, three to four minutes.
3. Put in the cauliflower, garlic, ginger, turmeric, salt, pepper, and cumin and sauté to lightly toast the spices, one to two minutes.
4. Pour the broth then bring to its boiling point.
5. Reduce the heat and cook until the cauliflower is soft about five minutes.
6. Use an immersion blender to purée the soup in the pot until the desired smoothness is achieved.
7. Stir in the coconut milk and cilantro, heat through, before you serve.

Nutritional Info: Calories: 264 , Total Fat: 23g , Total Carbohydrates: 12g , Sugar: 5g , Fiber: 4g , Protein: 7g , Sodium: 900mg

CROCK-POT TURKEY TACO SOUP

Time To Prepare: ten minutes

Time to Cook: 4 hours

Yield: Servings 6

Ingredients:
- 1 cup canned diced tomatoes (no sugar added)
- 1 cup whipped cream cheese

- 1 pound ground turkey
- 1 tablespoon chili powder
- 1 teaspoon cumin
- 1 teaspoon garlic powder
- 1 teaspoon onion powder
- 1 yellow onion, chopped
- 5 cups chicken bone broth (you can also use regular chicken broth)

Directions:
1. Put in all the ingredients to the base of a Crock-Pot minus the cream cheese and cover with the chicken broth.
2. Set on high and cook for 4 hours putting in in the cream cheese at the 3.5 hour mark.
3. Stir thoroughly before you serve.

Nutritional Info: Calories: 335, Carbohydrates: 6g, Fiber: 1gNet , Carbohydrates: 5g, Fat: 23g, Protein: 28g

DETOX CABBAGE SOUP

Time To Prepare: ten minutes

Time to Cook: thirty-five minutes

Yield: Servings 4

Ingredients:
- 1 tbs. freshly grated ginger root
- 2 big carrot
- 1 cup whole canned tomatoes with juice
- 1 whole head of cabbage
- 1 tbs. freshly grated turmeric root
- 3 celery stalks with leaves
- Enough water to immerse the vegetables
- 2 medium Russet potatoes
- Sea salt & black pepper to taste
- ½ medium onion
- 1/4 cup extra virgin olive oil

Directions:
1. Heat the oil in a large pot on moderate heat for a couple of minutes.
2. Put in the celery, onions, ginger, carrots & turmeric, then sauté on medium until translucent. Sprinkle with salt & pepper to taste.
3. With the heat still on moderate, dice the potatoes & generally slash the cabbage at that point put in to the pot alongside the whole tomatoes & juice.
4. While they cook, break separated the tomatoes using a fork or blade. Fill the pot with sufficient water to simply cover the cabbage.

5. Cover with a top & heat to the point of boiling. When bubbling, evacuate the top & cook for around thirty minutes or until the potatoes & cabbage are fork delicate. Put in the ice chest for as long as 5 days & in the cooler for as long as three months.

Nutritional Info: Calories: 359 kcal , Protein: 10.85 g , Fat: 12.68 g , Carbohydrates: 54.94 g

FENNEL AND PEAR SOUP

Time To Prepare: fifteen minutes

Time to Cook: twenty minutes

Yield: Servings 4

Ingredients:
- ⅛ Teaspoon ground nutmeg
- ¼ cup freshly squeezed lemon juice
- ¼ cup honey
- ¼ teaspoon freshly ground black pepper
- 1 teaspoon finely chopped fresh tarragon
- 1 teaspoon salt
- 2 fennel bulbs, trimmed and slice into ½-inch dice
- 2 shallots, halved
- 2 tablespoons extra-virgin olive oil
- 4 cups vegetable broth
- 4 pears, cored and slice into ½-inch dice

Directions:
1. In a large pot, heat the oil on high heat.
2. Put in the pears, fennel, and shallots, and sauté until the pears and fennel barely start to brown, approximately five minutes.
3. Pour the broth, then bring to its boiling point.
4. Reduce the heat to a simmer, then cook, once in a while stirring, until the fennel is soft, 5 to 8 minutes.
5. Stir in the lemon juice, honey, salt, pepper, and nutmeg.
6. Use an immersion blender to purée the soup in the pot until the desired smoothness is achieved.
7. Drizzle with the tarragon before you serve.

Nutritional Info: Calories: 328 , Total Fat: 9g , Total Carbohydrates: 60g , Sugar: 39g , Fiber: 10g , Protein: 7g , Sodium: 1413mg

FRENCH CARAMELIZED ONION SOUP

Time To Prepare: five minutes

Time to Cook: ten minutes

Yield: Servings 4

Ingredients:
- ½ stick butter, softened
- 4 cups chicken stock
- ½ teaspoon dried basil
- Kosher salt and ground black pepper, to taste
- ½ cup Swiss cheese, freshly grated
- 3/4 pound yellow onions, cut

Directions:
1. Push the "Sauté" button to heat up your Instant Pot. Once hot, melt the butter and sauté the onions until caramelized and soft.
2. Put in chicken stock, basil, salt, and black pepper.
3. Secure the lid. Choose "Manual" mode and High pressure; cook for about ten minutes. Once cooking is complete, use a quick pressure release; cautiously remove the lid.
4. Ladle the soup into separate bowls and top with grated cheese. Enjoy!

Nutritional Info: 228 Calories , 18g Fat , 5.3g Total Carbs , 10.5g Protein , 3.5g Sugars

GARLIC AND LENTIL SOUP

Time To Prepare: fifteen minutes

Time to Cook: fifteen minutes

Yield: Servings 4

Ingredients:
- ¼ cup chopped walnuts (not necessary)
- ¼ teaspoon freshly ground black pepper
- 1 (fifteen-ounce) can lentils, drained and washed
- 1 small white onion, cut into ¼-inch dice
- 1 tablespoon minced or grated orange zest
- 1 teaspoon ground cinnamon
- 1 teaspoon salt
- 2 garlic cloves, thinly cut
- 2 medium carrots, thinly cut
- 2 tablespoons extra-virgin olive oil
- 2 tablespoons finely chopped fresh flat-leaf parsley
- 3 cups vegetable broth

Directions:
1. In a large pot, heat the oil using high heat.
2. Put in the carrots, onion, and garlic and sauté until tender, five to seven minutes.
3. Place the cinnamon, salt, and pepper and stir to uniformly coat the vegetables, one to two minutes.
4. Pour the broth then bring to its boiling point.
5. Reduce the heat to a simmer, put in the lentils and cook until they are thoroughly heated about one minute.

6. Mix in the orange zest and serve, sprinkled with the walnuts (if using) and parsley.

Nutritional Info: Calories: 201 , Total Fat: 8g , Total Carbohydrates 22g , Sugar: 4g , Fiber: 8g , Protein: 11g , Sodium: 1178mg

GARLIC MUSHROOM & BEEF SOUP

Time To Prepare: ten minutes

Time to Cook: forty minutes

Yield: Servings 6

Ingredients:
- ½ cup heavy cream
- ½ cup whipped cream cheese
- 1 pound beef chuck, cubed
- 1 tablespoon coconut oil, for cooking
- 1 yellow onion, chopped
- 1½ cups cremini mushrooms
- 2 cloves garlic, chopped
- 6 cups beef broth
- Salt & pepper, to taste

Directions:
1. Put in the coconut oil to a frying pan and brown the beef.
2. Once cooked, put in the beef to the base of a stockpot with all of the ingredients minus the heavy cream. Mix thoroughly.
3. Heat to a simmer and whisk again until the cream cheese is mixed uniformly into the soup.
4. Cook for half an hour
5. Warm the heavy cream, and then put in to the soup.

Nutritional Info: Calories: 315, Carbohydrates: 5g, Fiber: 1gNet , Carbohydrates: 4g, Fat: 19g, Protein: 30g

GARLICKY CHICKEN SOUP

Time To Prepare: ten minutes

Time to Cook: fifteen minutes

Yield: Servings 6

Ingredients:
- ¼ teaspoon black pepper
- ½ cup whipped cream cheese
- 1 tablespoon butter for cooking
- 1 teaspoon salt
- 1 teaspoon thyme
- 2 boneless, skinless chicken breasts

- 3 cloves garlic, chopped
- 4 cups chicken broth

Directions:
1. Preheat a stockpot on moderate heat with the butter.
2. Put in the chicken and brown until completely thoroughly cooked. Turn off the heat.
3. Shred the chicken and put in it back to the stockpot together with the rest of the ingredients minus the cream cheese.
4. Heat to a simmer.
5. Put in in the cream cheese and whisk until there are no more clumps.
6. Simmer for about ten minutes before you serve.

Nutritional Info: Calories: 128 , Carbohydrates: 2g , Fiber: 0g Net , Carbohydrates: 2g , Fat: 6g , Protein: 16g

GOLDEN CHICKPEA AND VEGETABLE SOUP

Time To Prepare: fifteen minutes

Time to Cook: twenty minutes

Yield: Servings 6

Ingredients:
- 1 ½ cup Diced celery
- 1 ½ cup Sliced leeks
- 1 cup cooked chickpeas
- 1 cup diced carrots
- 1 cup Torn curly kale leaves
- 1 tbsp. Grated ginger
- 2 cloves minced garlic
- 2 cups Cauliflower florets
- 2 tbsp. Curry powder
- 2 tbsp. Minced organic parsley
- 2 tsp. Coconut oil
- 4 cups Bone broth

Directions:
1. Warm the coconut oil in a pot and put in the garlic and ginger. Sauté for one minute before you put in the turmeric and curry powder and sautéing for one more minute.
2. Throw in celery, leeks, carrots, and cauliflower, continuously stirring for approximately one minute.
3. Put in the bone broth and chickpeas. Cover the pot and leave to boil. Reduce the heat and allow it to simmer for minimum fifteen minutes.
4. Turn off heat and put in parsley and kale, leaving the heat to cook the leaves.
5. Drizzle salt and pepper.

6. Serve.

Nutritional Info: Calories: 142 kcal , Protein: 8.64 g , Fat: 4.79 g , Carbohydrates: 17.57 g

GREEK SPLIT PEA SOUP

Time To Prepare: fifteen minutes

Time to Cook: 2 hours

Yield: Servings 6

Ingredients:
- 1 pinch dried marjoram
- 1 potato (diced)
- 1½ pounds ham bone
- 2 onions (cut)
- 2 quarts cold water
- 2-1/4 cups dried split peas
- 3 carrots, (chopped)
- 3 stalks celery (chopped)
- Ground black pepper
- Salt

Directions:
1. Simmer the peas in a pot for a couple of minutes and then soak for an hour.
2. Put in ham bone, onion, marjoram, and seasoning.
3. Boil for 1½hours.
4. Remove bone and meat. Put in the meat (diced) to the soup.
5. Put the rest of the vegetables and cook until soft.

Nutritional Info: Calories: 310 kcal , Carbohydrates: 58 g , Fat: 20 g , Protein: 2 g

GREEN BLAST SOUP

Time To Prepare: ten minutes

Time to Cook: twenty minutes

Yield: Servings 4

Ingredients:
- ¼ cup chopped cashews (not necessary)
- ¼ cup extra-virgin olive oil
- ¼ teaspoon freshly ground black pepper
- 1 bunch Swiss chard, crudely chopped
- 1 fennel bulb, trimmed and thinly cut
- 1 garlic clove, peeled
- 1 teaspoon salt
- 2 leeks, white parts only, thinly cut

- 2 tablespoons apple cider vinegar
- 3 cups vegetable broth
- 4 cups crudely chopped kale
- 4 cups crudely chopped mustard greens

Directions:
1. In a large pot, heat the oil on high heat.
2. Put in the leeks, fennel, and garlic and sauté until tender, for approximately five minutes.
3. Put in the Swiss chard, kale, and mustard greens and sauté until the greens wilt, two to three minutes.
4. Pour the broth then bring to its boiling point.
5. Reduce the heat to a simmer and cook until the vegetables are completely tender and soft about five minutes.
6. Mix in the vinegar, salt, pepper, and cashews (if using).
7. Use an immersion blender to purée the soup in the pot until the desired smoothness is achieved before you serve.

Nutritional Info: Calories: 238 , Total Fat: 14g , Total Carbohydrates: 22g , Sugar: 4g , Fiber: 6g , Protein: 9g , Sodium: 1294mg

GUT-HEALING BONE BROTH

Time To Prepare: fifteen minutes

Time to Cook: 8 to one day

Yield: Servings 4

Ingredients:
- 1 medium onion, chopped
- 1 tablespoon apple cider vinegar
- 2 bay leaves
- 2 celery stalks, chopped
- 2 pounds beef marrow bones
- 3 medium carrots, chopped
- 4 garlic cloves
- Filtered water, to cover

Directions:
1. In a 6-quart slow cooker, mix the bones, garlic, carrots, celery, onion, bay leaves, and vinegar. Cover with filtered water. Set the cooker on low and simmer for minimum 8 hours and up to one day.
2. Skim off and discard any foam that forms on the surface. Ladle the broth through a fine-mesh sieve or cheesecloth to strain out the solids. Pour into airtight glass containers. The broth can be placed in the fridge for maximum one week; just boil it again before use. To freeze, let the broth fully cool and then fill jars up to an inch below the top to allow for expansion, and keep for four to 5 months.

Nutritional Info: Calories: 40 , Total Fat: 0g , Saturated Fat: 0g , Cholesterol: 0mg , Carbohydrates: 5g , Fiber: 0g , Protein: 6g

HAMBURGER & TOMATO SOUP

Time To Prepare: ten minutes

Time to Cook: 4 hours

Yield: Servings 6

Ingredients:
- ½ cup beef broth
- ½ cup no-sugar added marinara sauce
- ½ cup shredded cheddar cheese
- 1 pound lean ground beef
- 1 yellow onion, chopped
- 2 cloves garlic, chopped
- Salt & pepper, to taste

Directions:
1. Put in all the ingredients to a slow cooker minus the shredded cheese and cook on high for 4 hours.
2. Mix in the cheese before you serve.

Nutritional Info: Calories: 209 , Carbohydrates: 5g , Fiber: 1g Net , Carbohydrates: 4g , Fat: 9g , Protein: 26g

HARVEST STEW

Time To Prepare: fifteen minutes

Time to Cook: 60 minutes

Yield: Servings 6

Ingredients:
- ¼ cup flour
- ½ cup cut carrots
- ½ cup diced celery
- ¾ cup diced onions
- 1 bay leaf
- 1 leek, cleaned and diced
- 1 potato, peeled and diced
- 1 pound stewing beef cubes
- 2 cups diced zucchini
- 2 tablespoons olive oil
- 2 tablespoons Worcestershire sauce
- 2 tomatoes, chopped

- 3 sprigs fresh thyme
- 3 turnips, diced
- 4 cups low-sodium beef broth
- 6 garlic cloves, peeled
- Salt and pepper, to taste

Directions:
1. Brown the beef cubes in olive oil. Dust the flour on the meat and stir to coat and spread.
2. Put in the onions, carrots, celery, leek, garlic, zucchini, potato, turnips, tomatoes, bay leaf, thyme sprigs, and beef broth. Put to its boiling point, then reduce the heat and simmer for 60 minutes.
3. Take away the bay leaf and thyme sprigs. Put in the Worcestershire sauce, salt, and pepper. Serve hot.

Nutritional Info: Calories: 254 , Fat: 9.5 g , Protein: 20 g , Sodium: 514 mg , Fiber: 3.5 g , Carbohydrates: 22 g

HEARTY ROOT VEGETABLE SOUP

Time To Prepare: five minutes

Time to Cook: ten minutes

Yield: Servings 4

Ingredients:
- 1 bay leaf
- 1 carrot, cut
- 1 celery, diced
- 1 garlic clove, minced
- 1 parsnip, cut
- 1 tablespoon fresh parsley, roughly chopped
- 1 teaspoon fresh sage
- 2 cups cauliflower, cut into little florets
- 4 cups chicken stock
- 4 tablespoons olive oil
- Kosher salt and freshly ground black pepper, to taste

Directions:
1. Simply drop all of the above ingredients into your Instant Pot.
2. Secure the lid. Choose "Manual" mode and High pressure; cook for about ten minutes. Once cooking is complete, use a natural pressure release; cautiously remove the lid.
3. Taste, calibrate the seasonings and serve instantly. Enjoy!

Nutritional Info: 190 Calories , 15.6g Fat , 6.1g Total Carbs , 6.7g Protein , 2.6g Sugars

HUNGARIAN LENTIL SOUP

Time To Prepare: fifteen minutes

Time to Cook: 2 hours

Yield: Servings 8

Ingredients:
- 7 Cups Chicken Stock
- 3 Carrots (Diced)
- 2 Stalks Celery (Diced)
- 1 Teaspoon Garlic (Minced)
- 2 Bay Leaves
- 1 Sprig Fresh Parsley (Chopped)
- 2 Tablespoons Olive Oil
- 2 Large Onions (Cubed)
- Salt
- Ground Black Pepper
- 1½ Cups Lentils (Soaked, Rinsed, Drained)
- ½ Teaspoon Paprika
- ½ Cup Grated Parmesan Cheese
- 3½ Cups Crushed Tomatoes
- 3/4 Cup White Wine

Directions:
1. Sauté onions in oil until shiny and put in garlic, paprika, celery, and carrots, cooking for about ten minutes.
2. Mix in tomatoes, chicken stock, lentils, bay leaves, seasoning, and wine to boil.
3. Cook until the lentils are soft.
4. Top with parsley and Parmesan before you serve.

Nutritional Info: Calories: 258 kcal , Carbohydrates: 34 g , Fat: 6 g , Protein: 14 g

ITALIAN BEEF SOUP

Time To Prepare: ten minutes

Time to Cook: 4 hours

Yield: Servings 6

Ingredients:
- ½ cup diced tomatoes
- ½ cup shredded mozzarella cheese
- 1 cup beef broth
- 1 cup heavy cream
- 1 pound lean ground beef
- 1 tablespoon Italian seasoning
- 1 yellow onion, chopped
- 2 cloves garlic, chopped
- Salt & pepper, to taste

Directions:
1. Put in all the ingredients to a slow cooker minus the heavy cream and mozzarella cheese. Cook on high for 4 hours.
2. Warm the heavy cream, and then put in the warmed cream and cheese to the soup. Stir thoroughly before you serve.

Nutritional Info: Calories: 241 , Carbohydrates: 4g , Fiber: 1g Net , Carbohydrates: 3g , Fat: 14g , Protein: 25g

ITALIAN MODENA SOUP

Time To Prepare: two minutes

Time to Cook: 8 minutes

Yield: Servings 4

Ingredients:
- ½ cup Parmigiano-Reggiano cheese, shaved
- ½ teaspoon crushed chili
- 1 cup water
- 1 onion, chopped
- 1 tablespoon Italian seasonings
- 16 ounces Cotechino di Modena, cut
- 2 cups tomatoes, purée
- 2 tablespoons olive oil
- 3 cups roasted vegetable broth
- Sea salt and ground black pepper, to taste

Directions:
1. Push the "Sauté" button to heat up your Instant Pot. Once hot, heat the oil and sauté the onions until soft and translucent.
2. Now, put in the sausage and cook an additional three minutes,
3. Mix in tomatoes, broth, water, sea salt, black pepper, crushed chili, and Italian seasonings.
4. Secure the lid. Choose "Manual" mode and High pressure; cook for five minutes. Once cooking is complete, use a quick pressure release; cautiously remove the lid.
5. Top with shaved Parmigiano-Reggiano cheese and serve warm

Nutritional Info: 340 Calories , 27.9g Fat , 5g Total Carbs , 14.1g Protein , 2.6g Sugars

ITALIAN SUMMER SQUASH SOUP

Time To Prepare: ten minutes

Time to Cook: fifteen minutes

Yield: Servings 4

Ingredients:
- ½ cup shredded carrot

- 1 cup shredded yellow squash
- 1 cup shredded zucchini
- 1 garlic clove, minced
- 1 small red onion, thinly cut
- 1 tablespoon finely chopped fresh chives
- 1 teaspoon salt
- 2 tablespoons finely chopped fresh basil
- 2 tablespoons pine nuts
- 3 cups vegetable broth
- 3 tablespoons extra-virgin olive oil

Directions:
1. In a large pot, heat the oil using high heat.
2. Put in the onion and garlic and sauté until tender, five to seven minutes.
3. Put in the zucchini, yellow squash, and carrot and sauté until tender, one to two minutes.
4. Pour the broth and salt then bring to its boiling point.
5. Reduce the heat and cook until the vegetables are soft, one to two minutes.
6. Mix in the basil and chives and serve, sprinkled with the pine nuts.

Nutritional Info: Calories: 172 , Total Fat: 15g , Total Carbohydrates: 6g , Sugar: 3g , Fiber: 2g , Protein: 5g , Sodium: 1170mg

KUMARA & CHICKPEA SOUP

Time To Prepare: twenty-five minutes

Time to Cook: thirty-five minutes

Yield: Servings 6

Ingredients:
- 1 bay leaf
- 1 onion (chopped)
- 1 teaspoon dried basil
- 1 tomato (chopped)
- ½ teaspoon dried thyme
- 1/4 teaspoon paprika
- 2 cloves garlic (minced)
- 2 cups kumara (peeled, chopped)
- 2 tablespoons olive oil
- 200g garbanzo beans
- 3 cups chicken broth
- Ground black pepper
- Mixed vegetables
- Salt

Directions:
1. Sauté onion, garlic, and sweet potatoes in oil for five minutes.

2. Put in broth, bay leaf, herbs, and seasoning.
3. Boil until soft.
4. Put in tomato, beans, and chickpeas, simmering some more before you serve.

Nutritional Info: Calories: 197 kcal , Carbohydrates: 30 g , Fat: 6 g , Protein: 7.5 g

LAMB STEW

Time To Prepare: five minutes

Time to Cook: 8 hours

Yield: Servings 6

Ingredients:
- 1 lamb stock cube
- 1 onion, roughly chopped
- 2 pounds (907 g) boneless lamb, cut into cubes
- 2 tablespoons olive oil, plus more for greasing the frying pan
- 2 teaspoons dried rosemary
- 3 cups water
- 4 garlic cloves, finely chopped
- From the cupboard:
- Salt and freshly ground black pepper, to taste

Directions:
1. Position the lamb into a mildly greased nonstick frying pan, and cook using high heat for a couple of minutes or until browned.
2. Grease a slow cooker with olive oil, then put in the cooked lamb, stock cube, rosemary, onion, garlic, salt, black pepper, and 3 cups of water. Blend to blend well.
3. Place the slow cooker lid on and cook on LOW for eight hours.
4. Take away the cooked lamb stew from the slow cooker and serve warm.

Nutritional Info: calories: 252 , total fat: 9.5g , carbs: 4.9g , protein: 34.9g

LAMB TACO SOUP

Time To Prepare: ten minutes

Time to Cook: 4-6 hours minutes

Yield: Servings 6

Ingredients:
- ½ teaspoon cayenne pepper
- 1 cup diced tomatoes
- 1 cup shredded cheddar cheese
- 1 green bell pepper, chopped
- 1 pound ground lamb
- 1 teaspoon ground coriander

- 1 teaspoon ground cumin
- 1 teaspoon paprika
- 1 yellow onion, chopped
- 2 cloves garlic, chopped
- 4 cups beef broth
- Salt & pepper, to taste

Directions:
1. Put in all the ingredients to a slow cooker minus the shredded cheese and cook on high for four to 6 hours.
2. Mix in the shredded cheese before you serve.

Nutritional Info: Calories: 265 , Carbohydrates: 6g , Fiber: 1g Net , Carbohydrates: 5g , Fat: 13g , Protein: 30g

LEBANESE LENTIL SOUP

Time To Prepare: fifteen minutes

Time to Cook: 60 minutes

Yield: Servings 6

Ingredients:
- 1 cup brown lentils
- 1 lemon juiced
- 1 medium onion
- 1 tablespoon olive oil
- 2 medium carrots
- 2 teaspoons cinnamon
- 2 teaspoons cumin
- 3 stalks celery
- 4 cloves garlic
- 4 cups chicken broth low sodium
- 4 cups water
- 8 cups spinach
- salt& pepper to taste

Directions:
1. Over moderate heat, heat oil in a soup pot, Put in & cook carrots, celery & onions until become soft for seven minutes, put in pepper & salt to taste.
2. Stir cumin, cinnamon & garlic heat it for 30-60 minutes. Put in lentils & heat for a couple of minutes to slightly toast. Pour in the lemon juice, water & chicken broth, then bring the pot to its boiling point. When lentils are soft, decrease the heat to low & simmer, approximately 30-45 minutes.
3. Before you serve, mix in the spinach, cook until the color is green, now served to put in pepper, lemon juice & salt.

Nutritional Info: Calories: 102 kcal , Protein: 6.33 g , Fat: 4.58 g , Carbohydrates: 11.6 g

LEEK, CHICKEN AND SPINACH SOUP

Time To Prepare: ten minutes

Time to Cook: fifteen minutes

Yield: Servings 4

Ingredients:
- ¼ teaspoon freshly ground black pepper
- 1 tablespoon thinly cut fresh chives
- 1 teaspoon salt
- 2 cups shredded rotisserie chicken
- 2 leeks, white parts only, thinly cut
- 2 teaspoons grated or minced lemon zest
- 3 tablespoons unsalted butter
- 4 cups baby spinach
- 4 cups chicken broth

Directions:
1. In a large pot, melt the butter on high heat.
2. Put in the leeks and sauté until tender and starting to brown, three to five minutes.
3. Put in the spinach, broth, salt, and pepper and bring to its boiling point.
4. Reduce the heat and cook till the spinach wilts, one to two minutes.
5. Place the chicken and cook until warmed through one to two minutes.
6. Drizzle with the chives and lemon zest before you serve.

Nutritional Info: Calories: 256 , Total Fat: 12g , Total Carbohydrates: 9g , Sugar: 3g , Fiber: 2g , Protein: 27g , Sodium: 1483mg

LEMON CHICKEN SOUP

Time To Prepare: ten minutes

Time to Cook: 4 hours

Yield: Servings 4

Ingredients:
- ¼ cup freshly squeezed lemon juice
- 1 yellow onion, chopped
- 2 boneless, skinless chicken breasts
- 2 cloves garlic, chopped
- 2 tablespoons chives, chopped
- 6 cups chicken broth
- Salt & pepper, to taste

Directions:
1. Put in all the ingredients to a slow cooker and cook on high for 4 hours.

2. Once cooked, shred the chicken and stir back into the soup.

Nutritional Info: Calories: 171 , Carbohydrates: 6g , Fiber: 1g Net , Carbohydrates: 5g , Fat: 6g , Protein: 22g

MEDITERRANEAN STEW

Time To Prepare: ten minutes

Time to Cook: fifteen minutes

Yield: Servings 4

Ingredients:
- 1 (19-ounce) can cannellini beans, drained and washed
- 1 (fifteen½-ounce) can chickpeas, drained and washed
- 1 cup Basic Vegetable Stock or low-sodium canned vegetable stock
- 1 teaspoon dried oregano
- 1 teaspoon red pepper, crushed or to taste
- 1½ cups artichoke hearts, quartered
- 2 cups roasted tomatoes
- 3 cloves garlic, crushed and minced
- 3 tablespoons olive oil
- 4 tablespoons grated Parmesan cheese
- Chopped Italian parsley, for decoration
- Chopped sun-dried tomatoes, for decoration
- Crumbled feta cheese, for decoration
- Fresh oregano leaves, for decoration
- Freshly ground black pepper, to taste
- Garlic-seasoned croutons, for decoration
- Salt, to taste

Directions:
1. Warm the olive oil in a huge deep cooking pan on moderate heat and sauté the garlic for two to three minutes or until golden.
2. Lower the heat to moderate-low. Mix in the chickpeas, cannellini beans, roasted tomatoes, artichoke hearts, stock, Parmesan cheese, crushed red pepper, oregano, salt, and pepper. Cook and stir for approximately ten minutes. Serve in separate bowls, garnishing as you wish.

Nutritional Info: Calories: 445 , Fat: 16 g , Protein: 18 g , Sodium: 530 mg , Fiber: 12 g , Carbohydrates: 61 g

MINESTRONE SOUP WITH QUINOA

Time To Prepare: ten minutes

Time to Cook: twenty minutes

Yield: Servings 6

Ingredients:

- ½ cup quinoa, washed well
- ½ red bell pepper, diced
- ½ teaspoon salt
- 1 (14 oz.) can cannellini beans, drained and washed well
- 1 (14 oz.) can diced tomatoes with its juice
- 1 bay leaf
- 1 cup packed kale, stemmed and meticulously washed
- 1 medium white onion, diced
- 1 small zucchini, diced
- 1 tablespoon freshly squeezed lemon juice
- 1 tablespoon ghee
- 2 carrots, chopped
- 2 celery stalks, diced
- 2 garlic cloves, minced
- 2 teaspoons dried rosemary
- 2 teaspoons dried thyme
- 5 cups vegetable broth
- Freshly ground black pepper

Directions:

1. In a huge soup pot on moderate heat, put in the ghee, garlic, onion, carrots, and celery, and sauté for about three minutes.
2. Put in the zucchini and red bell pepper, and sauté for a couple of minutes.
3. Mix in the broth, tomatoes, beans, kale, quinoa, lemon juice, rosemary, thyme, bay leaf, and salt, and flavor with black pepper. Put it to a simmer, reduce the heat temperature, cover, and cook for fifteen minutes, or until the quinoa is cooked. Take away the bay leaf and discard it. Serve hot.

Nutritional Info: Calories: 319 , Total Fat: 5g , Saturated Fat: 2g , Cholesterol: 0mg , Carbohydrates: 42g , Fiber: 9g , Protein: 18g

MOONG DAAL

Time To Prepare: fifteen minutes

Time to Cook: thirty minutes

Yield: Servings 6

Ingredients:

- ½ Cup Tomatoes (Diced)
- ½ Dried Red Chili Pepper
- ½ Teaspoon Ginger Root (Grated)
- ½ Teaspoon Ground Turmeric
- 1 Pinch Asafoetida
- 1 Teaspoon Cumin Seed

- 1 Teaspoon Jalapeno (Diced)
- 1/4 Cup Cilantro (Chopped)
- 2 Cloves Garlic (Chopped)
- 2 Teaspoons Vegetable Oil
- 2½ Cups Moong Dal (Rinsed)
- 2½ Cups Water
- 3 Teaspoons Lemon Juice
- Salt

Directions:
1. Soak daal for thirty minutes before boiling in water with salt until thick.
2. Put in ginger, jalapeno, tomato, lemon juice, and turmeric.
3. Heat cumin seed and red Chile pepper in a pan before you put in asafoetida powder and garlic.
4. Combine with split peas and serve with cilantro.

Nutritional Info: Calories: 330 kcal , Carbohydrates: 57 g , Fat: 3 g , Protein: 21 g

MUSHROOM AND THYME SOUP

Time To Prepare: five minutes

Time to Cook: twenty minutes

Yield: Servings 4

Ingredients:
- ¼ cup butter
- 12 ounces (340 g) wild mushrooms, chopped
- 2 garlic cloves, minced
- 2 teaspoons thyme leaves
- 4 cups vegetable broth
- 5 ounces (142 g) crème fraiche
- From the cupboard:
- Salt and freshly ground black pepper, to taste

Directions:
1. Place the butter in a deep cooking pan and melt on moderate heat.
2. Put in the minced garlic and cook for a minutes or until aromatic.
3. Put in the chopped mushrooms, and drizzle with salt and black pepper. Stir to blend and cook for about ten minutes or until the mushrooms are soft.
4. Put in the vegetable broth and bring the soup to its boiling point. Stir continuously. Reduce the heat and simmer the soup for about ten minutes or until it becomes slightly thick.
5. Pour the soup in a blender, and pulse until smooth, then fold in the crème fraiche.
6. Move the soup in a big container and top with thyme leaves before you serve.

Nutritional Info: calories: 282 , total fat: 25.1g , net carbs: 6.3g , protein: 7.8g

ONION, KALE AND WHITE BEAN SOUP

Time To Prepare: fifteen minutes

Time to Cook: twenty-five minutes

Yield: Servings 4

Ingredients:
- ⅛ Teaspoon red pepper flakes (not necessary)
- ¼ cup extra-virgin olive oil
- ¼ teaspoon freshly ground black pepper
- 1 (fifteen½-ounce) can white beans, drained and washed
- 1 big onion, thinly cut
- 1 teaspoon finely chopped fresh rosemary
- 1 teaspoon salt
- 2 garlic cloves, thinly cut
- 3 cups stemmed kale leaves cut into ½-inch pieces
- 4 cups vegetable broth

Directions:
1. In a large pot, heat the oil on high heat.
2. Lower the heat to moderate, and put in the onion, garlic, salt, pepper, and red pepper flakes (if using). Sauté until the onion is golden, approximately ten minutes.
3. Put in the kale, and sauté until wilted, one to two minutes.
4. Pour the broth then bring to its boiling point.
5. Lower the heat to simmer, and cook until the kale is tender about five minutes.
6. Put in the beans and rosemary. Cook until the beans are warmed through minimum two to three minutes before you serve.

Nutritional Info: Calories: 285 , Total Fat: 15g , Total Carbohydrates: 28g , Sugar: 3g , Fiber: 9g , Protein: 13g , Sodium: 1368mg

PORK STEW

Time To Prepare: five minutes

Time to Cook: 8 hours

Yield: Servings 6

Ingredients:
- 1 onion, finely chopped
- 1 teaspoon dried mixed spices (homemade or store-bought)
- 2 pounds (907 g) pork loin, cut into cubes
- 2 tablespoons olive oil
- 3 cups chicken stock

- 4 garlic cloves, crushed
- From the cupboard:
- Salt and freshly ground black pepper, to taste

Directions:
1. Grease the insert of the slow cooker with olive oil.
2. Combine the pork, chicken stock, onion, dried mixed spices, garlic, salt, and black pepper in the slow cooker.
3. Place the slow cooker lid on and cook on LOW for eight hours.
4. Ladle the stew in a big container and serve warm.

Nutritional Info: calories: 381 , total fat: 18.3g , carbs: 9.2g , protein: 42.3g

PUMPKIN AND SAUSAGE SOUP

Time To Prepare: five minutes

Time to Cook: 33 minutes

Yield: Servings 4

Ingredients:
- ½ cup heavy whipping cream
- ½ cup pumpkin puree
- ½ teaspoon dried sage
- ½ teaspoon ground dried thyme
- ½ teaspoon red chili pepper flakes (not necessary)
- 1 garlic clove, minced
- 1 moderate-sized red onion, minced
- 1 pinch salt
- 1 small red bell pepper, diced
- 2 cups chicken broth
- 2 tablespoons butter, melted
- pounds (680 g) fresh sausage

Directions:
1. Sauté the sausage in a nonstick frying pan on moderate to high heat for a minutes, then put in the onion and bell pepper. Continue sautéing for about six minutes until the sausage is mildly browned and the onion is translucent.
2. Fold in the chili pepper flakes, thyme, sage, minced garlic, and salt, then put in the pumpkin puree, chicken broth, and heavy whipping cream.
3. Reduce the heat and bring them to a simmer using low heat for fifteen minutes or until it becomes thick.
4. Pour the cooked soup into a big serving container and put in the butter. Stir to mix thoroughly before you serve.

Nutritional Info: calories: 777 , total fat: 70g , net carbs: 7g , fiber: 2g , protein: 27g

PUMPKIN, COCONUT & SAGE SOUP

Time To Prepare: fifteen minutes

Time to Cook: thirty minutes

Yield: Servings 6

Ingredients:
- 1 cup canned pumpkin
- 1 cup full-fat coconut milk
- 1 teaspoon freshly chopped sage
- 2 cloves garlic, chopped
- 6 cups vegetable broth
- Pinch of salt & pepper, to taste

Directions:
1. Put in all the ingredients minus the coconut milk to a stockpot on moderate heat and bring to its boiling point. Reduce to a simmer and cook for half an hour
2. Put in the coconut milk and stir.

Nutritional Info: Calories: 146 , Carbohydrates: 7g , Fiber: 2g Net , Carbohydrates: 5g , Fat: 11g , Protein: 6g

QUICK MISO SOUP WITH WILTED GREENS

Time To Prepare: ten minutes

Time to Cook: five minutes

Yield: Servings 4

Ingredients:
- ½ teaspoon fish sauce
- 1 cup cut mushrooms
- 1 cup fresh baby spinach, meticulously washed
- 3 cups filtered water
- 3 cups vegetable broth
- 3 tablespoons miso paste
- 4 scallions, cut

Directions:
1. In a huge soup pot on high heat, put in the water, broth, mushrooms, and fish sauce, and bring to its boiling point. Turn off the heat.
2. In a small container, combine the miso paste with ½ cup of heated broth mixture to dissolve the miso. Mix the miso mixture back into the soup.
3. Mix in the spinach and scallions. Serve instantly.

Nutritional Info: Calories: 44 , Total Fat: 0 , Saturated Fat: 0g , Cholesterol: 0mg , Carbohydrates: 8g , Fiber: 1g , Protein: 2g

RED LENTIL DAL

Time To Prepare: ten minutes

Time to Cook: twenty minutes

Yield: Servings 6

Ingredients:
- ½ teaspoon salt
- 1 (14-ounce) can unsweetened coconut milk
- 1 bay leaf
- 1 cup red dried lentils, sorted and washed well
- 1 medium tomato, diced
- 1 medium white onion, diced
- 1 tablespoon coconut oil
- 1 teaspoon ground cumin
- 1 teaspoon ground ginger
- 1 teaspoon ground turmeric
- 1 teaspoon mustard seeds
- 1 teaspoon sesame seeds
- 2 garlic cloves, minced
- 2 tablespoons chopped fresh cilantro leaves
- 3 cups vegetable broth
- Dash ground cinnamon

Directions:
1. In a huge soup pot using high heat, combine the broth, lentils, and bay leaf, and place to its boiling point. Lessen the heat to moderate-low and simmer for about twenty minutes, or until the lentils are cooked.
2. In the meantime, in a moderate-sized deep cooking pan on moderate heat, sauté the onion and garlic in the coconut oil for a couple of minutes.
3. Put in the tomato, sesame seeds, ginger, cumin, turmeric, mustard seeds, salt, and cinnamon. Cook, regularly stirring, for five minutes.
4. Mix in the coconut milk, then put it to a simmer.
5. Remove and discard the bay leaf. Put in the coconut milk mixture to the lentils together with the cilantro, and stir until blended. Serve alone or over rice if you wish.

Nutritional Info: Calories: 283 , Total Fat: 6g , Saturated Fat: 5g , Cholesterol: 0mg , Carbohydrates: 32g , Fiber: 7g , Protein: 14g

RIBOLLITA

Time To Prepare: forty-five minutes

Time to Cook: 195 minutes

Yield: Servings 12

Ingredients:
- ½ Cup Olive Oil
- 1 Bunch Kale (Trimmed, Chopped)
- 1 Bunch Swiss Chard (Trimmed, Chopped)
- 1½ Cups Cabbage (Chopped)
- 12½ Inch-Thick Slices French Bread (Toasted)
- 2 Bay Leaves
- 2 Cups Dry Cannellini Beans (Rinsed)
- 2 Onions (Diced)
- 2 Potatoes (Peeled, Cut)
- 3 Carrots (Peeled, Sliced)
- 3 Large Stalks Celery (Chopped)
- 32 Ounce Chicken Broth
- 4 Cups Water
- 4 Sage Leaves
- 5 Cloves Garlic (Minced)
- Grated Parmesan Cheese
- Ground Black Pepper
- Ounce Tomatoes (Diced)
- Salt

Directions:
1. Boil beans in water for minimum five minutes and cool for 70 minutes.
2. Boil beans, garlic, sage leaves, bay leaves, and salt in chicken broth until soft.
3. Discard the leaves from half of the mixture.
4. Combine the remaining until the desired smoothness is achieved. Set aside.
5. Cook onions in oil, putting in carrots, potatoes, cabbage, celery, Swiss chard, and kale, tomatoes, and seasoning for about twenty minutes.
6. Put in the pureed bean and cook for forty minutes before you put in the rest of the mixture.
7. Put in toasted bread slices. Heat the soup for about twenty minutes.
8. Serve with Parmesan cheese and olive oil.

Nutritional Info: Calories: 418 kcal , Carbohydrates: 41.8 g , Fat: 22 g , Protein: 14 g

RICH ONION AND BEEF STEW

Time To Prepare: five minutes

Time to Cook: 10 hours

Yield: Servings 6

Ingredients:
- 1 beef stock cube

- 1 teaspoon dried mixed herbs (such as Italian seasoning)
- 2 onions, roughly chopped
- 2 pounds (907 g) boneless stewing beef, cut into cubes
- 3 cups water
- 3 tablespoons olive oil, divided
- 5 garlic cloves, crushed
- From the cupboard:
- Salt and freshly ground black pepper, to taste

Directions:
1. Grease the insert of the slow cooker with 2 tablespoons of olive oil. Coat a nonstick frying pan with the rest of the olive oil.
2. Heat the oil in the frying pan on moderate to high heat, then put the beef in the frying pan and sear for a couple of minutes or until medium-rare. Shake the frying pan continuously to sear the beef cubes uniformly.
3. Position the cooked beef in the slow cooker, then put in the stock cube, mixed herbs, garlic, onions, salt, black pepper, and water. Stir to mix thoroughly.
4. Place the slow cooker lid on and cook on LOW for ten hours.
5. Ladle the stew in a big container and serve warm.

Nutritional Info: calories: 199 , total fat: 6.3g , carbs: 1.9g , protein: 33.8g

ROASTED BUTTERNUT SQUASH APPLE SOUP

Time To Prepare: ten minutes

Time to Cook: forty minutes

Yield: Servings 4

Ingredients:
- 1 butternut squash
- 1 celery rib
- 1 cup water
- 1 small onion
- 1/4 teaspoon cinnamon
- 1/4 teaspoon ginger
- 1/4 teaspoon nutmeg
- 2 red, sweet apples
- 3 cups low-sodium chicken/vegetable stock
- 4 tablespoons olive oil
- Salt & pepper to taste

Directions:
1. Preheat your oven to 400°F.
2. Put diced apple on a one-sheet pan & put the diced butternut squash on the second sheet pan.

3. Allow season to squash olive oil & put in pepper & salt. Stir get everything mix thoroughly. Put in apple with one tablespoon olive oil & stir to coat.
4. Apple & Roast squash for around half an hour, until browned.
5. Heat olive oil (remaining 1 ½ tablespoons) in a big stockpot.
6. Sauté celery & onion for around seven minutes, until soft. Put in Pepper & salt to taste.
7. Put in vegetable or chicken stock & water & bring to a simmer.
8. Once the apple & squash are roasted, put in them to the pot. Put in cinnamon, nutmeg & ginger.
9. Now blend the soup until the desired smoothness is achieved. Season pepper & salt to taste.
10. Serve with desired toppings.

Nutritional Info: Calories: 251 kcal , Protein: 4.06 g , Fat: 15.93 g , Carbohydrates: 25.14 g

RUSSIAN CABBAGE SOUP (SHCHI)

Time To Prepare: ten minutes

Time to Cook: twenty minutes

Yield: Servings 6

Ingredients:
- ½ big head cabbage, shredded
- ½ teaspoon salt
- 1 (14 oz.) can diced tomatoes with its juice
- 1 bay leaf
- 1 big potato, peeled and diced
- 1 celery stalk, diced
- 1 medium white onion, diced
- 1 tablespoon ghee
- 2 carrots, shredded
- 3 garlic cloves, minced
- 6 cups vegetable broth
- Freshly ground black pepper

Directions:
1. In a huge soup pot using high heat, mix the broth, bay leaf, and potato, and bring to its boiling point. Lower the heat to low and simmer for fifteen minutes.
2. In the meantime, in a moderate-sized deep cooking pan on moderate heat, heat the ghee. Place the onion and garlic, and sauté for five minutes.
3. Put in the carrots, celery, and cabbage, and cook for a couple of minutes, stirring frequently. Move to the soup pot.
4. Mix in the tomatoes and salt, and flavor with pepper. Mix thoroughly and carry on simmering until all ingredients have become tender and cooked, approximately five minutes. Take off and discard the bay leaf, and serve instantly.

Nutritional Info: Calories: 180 , Total Fat: 3g , Saturated Fat: 2g , Cholesterol: 7mg , Carbohydrates: 20g , Fiber: 5g , Protein: 12g

SAFFRON AND SALMON SOUP

Time To Prepare: ten minutes

Time to Cook: twenty minutes

Yield: Servings 4

Ingredients:
- ¼ cup extra-virgin olive oil
- ¼ tsp. freshly ground black pepper
- ¼ tsp. saffron threads
- ½ cup dry white wine
- 1 lb. salmon fillets, cut into 1-inch pieces
- 1 tsp. salt
- 2 cups baby spinach
- 2 garlic cloves, thinly cut
- 2 leeks, white parts only, thinly cut
- 2 medium carrots, thinly cut
- 2 tablespoons chopped scallions, both white and green parts
- 2 tablespoons finely chopped fresh flat-leaf parsley
- 4 cups vegetable broth

Directions:
1. In a large pot, heat the oil using high heat.
2. Put in the leeks, carrots, and garlic and sauté until tender, five to seven minutes.
3. Pour the broth then bring to its boiling point.
4. Reduce the heat to a simmer then put in the salmon, salt, pepper, and saffron. Cook until the salmon is thoroughly cooked, minimum 8 minutes.
5. Put in the spinach, wine, scallions, and parsley and cook until the spinach has wilted, one to two minutes, before you serve.

Nutritional Info: Calories: 418 , Total Fat: 26g , Total Carbohydrates: 13g , Sugar: 4g , Fiber: 2g , Protein: 29g , Sodium: 1455mg

SLOW COOKER LAMB & CAULIFLOWER SOUP

Time To Prepare: ten minutes

Time to Cook: 4 hours

Yield: Servings 6

Ingredients:
- ½ teaspoon cracked black pepper
- ½ teaspoon salt
- 1 cauliflower head, cut into florets

- 1 cup heavy cream
- 1 pound ground lamb
- 1 tablespoon freshly chopped thyme
- 1 yellow onion, chopped
- 2 cloves garlic, chopped
- 5 cups beef broth

Directions:
1. Put in the ground lamb and cauliflower to the base of a stockpot.
2. Put in in the rest of the ingredients minus the heavy cream, and cook on high for 4 hours.
3. Warm the heavy cream before you put in to the soup. Use an immersion blender to combine the soup until creamy.

Nutritional Info: Calories: 263 , Carbohydrates: 6g , Fiber: 2g Net , Carbohydrates: 4g , Fat: 14g , Protein: 27g

SPICY ASIAN-STYLE SOUP

Time To Prepare: ten minutes

Yield: Servings 4

Ingredients:
- ½ cup soy milk
- ½ pound asparagus, diced
- 1 bay leaf
- 1 cup celery, diced
- 1 shallot, diced
- 1 tablespoon coconut aminos
- 1 teaspoon Taco seasoning
- 1/4 teaspoon freshly ground black pepper
- 2 chicken bouillon cubes
- 2 cloves garlic, diced
- 2 cups Crimini mushrooms
- 2 tablespoons butter, softened
- 4 cups water
- Sea salt and black pepper, to taste

Directions:
1. Push the "Sauté" button to heat up your Instant Pot. Once hot, melt the butter; then, sweat the shallot until tender.
2. Mix in garlic; cook an additional 40 seconds, stirring regularly.
3. Put in the rest of the ingredients.
4. Secure the lid. Choose "Manual" mode and High pressure; cook for seven minutes. Once cooking is complete, use a quick pressure release; cautiously remove the lid.
5. Ladle into separate bowls and serve warm. Enjoy!

Nutritional Info: 104 Calories , 7g Fat , 6.6g Total Carbs , 3.9g Protein , 3.5g Sugars

SPICY CABBAGE TURMERIC COCONUT SOUP

Time To Prepare: ten minutes

Time to Cook: twenty minutes

Yield: Servings 4

Ingredients:
- ½ teaspoon black pepper
- ½ teaspoon salt
- 1 head white cabbage
- 1 teaspoon cumin powder
- 1/4 cup coconut milk
- 2 cloves garlic
- 2 tablespoons coconut oil
- 2 teaspoons turmeric powder
- 3 cups vegetable/chicken stock

Directions:
1. Heat the oil in a frying pan on moderate heat.
2. Put in the cabbage & garlic & sauté until the cabbage is delicate.
3. Put in the stock, bubble, spread, & stew for about twenty minutes.
4. Turn off the heat, including the coconut milk & flavors.
5. Blend until the desired smoothness is achieved & season to taste. Serve, gulp & appreciate!

Nutritional Info: Calories: 207 kcal , Protein: 13.52 g , Fat: 10.79 g , Carbohydrates: 16.84 g

SPICY LIME-CHICKEN "TORTILLA-LESS" SOUP

Time To Prepare: ten minutes

Time to Cook: twenty minutes

Yield: Servings 6

Ingredients:
- ¼ teaspoon cayenne pepper
- ½ teaspoon salt
- 1 (14 oz.) can diced tomatoes, and it's juice
- 1 (4oz.) can diced green chiles
- 1 avocado, cut
- 1 jalapeño pepper, seeded and minced
- 1 medium white onion, diced
- 1 pound shredded cooked chicken

- 1 tablespoon avocado oil
- 1 teaspoon chili powder
- 1 teaspoon ground cumin
- 3 garlic cloves, minced
- 3 tablespoons freshly squeezed lime juice
- 6 cups chicken broth or vegetable broth
- Fresh cilantro, for decoration
- Freshly ground black pepper

Directions:
1. In a huge soup pot on moderate heat, heat the avocado oil.
2. Put in the garlic, onion, and jalapeño pepper, and sauté for five minutes.
3. Mix in the broth, chicken, tomatoes, green chiles, lime juice, chili powder, cumin, salt, and cayenne pepper, and flavor with black pepper. Put it to a simmer, and cook for about ten minutes.
4. Serve hot, topped with slices of avocado and decorated with cilantro.

Nutritional Info: Calories: 283 , Total Fat: 7g , Saturated Fat: 1g , Cholesterol: 47mg , Carbohydrates: 12g , Fiber: 3g , Protein: 29g

SPICY RAMEN NOODLES

Time To Prepare: fifteen minutes

Time to Cook: 0 minutes

Yield: Servings 4

Ingredients:
- ¼ cup chopped fresh cilantro
- ¼ cup cut scallion
- ¼ cup thinly cut cucumber
- 1 tablespoon coconut aminos
- 1 tablespoon freshly squeezed lime juice
- 1 tablespoon grated peeled fresh ginger
- 1 tablespoon raw honey
- 1 teaspoon chili powder
- 2 tablespoons rice vinegar
- 2 tablespoons sesame oil
- 2 tablespoons sesame seeds
- 8 ounces buckwheat noodles or rice noodles, cooked

Directions:
1. In a big serving container, meticulously mix the noodles, sesame seeds, cucumber, scallion, cilantro, sesame oil, vinegar, ginger, coconut aminos, honey, lime juice, and chili powder.
2. Split among 4 soup bowls and serve at room temperature.

Nutritional Info: Calories: 663 , Total Fat: 28g , Saturated Fat: 4g , Cholesterol: 0mg , Carbohydrates: 115g , Fiber: 39g , Protein: 21g

SPICY SEAFOOD STEW

Time To Prepare: ten minutes

Time to Cook: twenty minutes

Yield: Servings 6

Ingredients:
- ¼ cup freshly squeezed lime juice
- ½ cup chopped fresh cilantro
- ½ cup chopped yellow onion
- ½ cup coconut milk
- ½ cup diced green pepper
- ½ cup thinly cut scallions
- ¾ pound medium-size shrimp, shelled and deveined
- ¾ pound skinless firm-fleshed fish fillets, (cod, center-cut salmon, or halibut)
- 1 tablespoon minced garlic
- 1 teaspoon hot pepper sauce
- 2 tablespoons olive oil
- 3 cups canned peeled, chopped tomatoes, undrained
- Seasoned salt, to taste

Directions:
1. Warm the oil in a huge nonstick frying pan on moderate to high heat. Put in the onions, green pepper, garlic, and tomatoes. Put to a simmer while stirring once in a while, then cook for three to four minutes.
2. Put in the coconut milk, pepper sauce, lime juice, and seasoned salt. Set to a simmer and cook for minimum 2 minutes. Put in the fish and stir, being cautious not to break apart the fillets. Cook till the fish is thoroughly cooked, approximately eight minutes. Put in the shrimp and cook until opaque and thoroughly cooked, approximately five minutes.
3. To serve, use a slotted spoon to take equal amounts of the fish and shrimp to 4 shallow serving bowls. Place the sauce over the seafood and decorate with scallions and cilantro. Serve hot.

Nutritional Info: Calories: 219 , Fat: 11 g , Protein: 19g , Sodium: 375 mg , Fiber: 2 g , Carbohydrates: 10 g

SWEET POTATO AND BLACK BEAN CHILI

Time To Prepare: ten minutes

Time to Cook: twenty minutes

Yield: Servings 8

Ingredients:

- ¼ teaspoon cayenne pepper
- ¼ teaspoon dried oregano
- ½ teaspoon ground cinnamon
- 1 (28-ounce) can diced tomatoes with their juice
- 1 green bell pepper, diced
- 1 red bell pepper, diced
- 1 red onion, diced
- 1 tablespoon chili powder
- 1 tablespoon freshly squeezed lime juice
- 1 teaspoon cocoa powder
- 1 teaspoon ground cumin
- 1 teaspoon salt
- 2 cups vegetable broth
- 2 tablespoons avocado oil
- 3 cups black beans, drained and washed well
- 3 cups cooked sweet potato cubes
- 5 garlic cloves, minced

Directions:
1. In a huge soup pot on moderate heat, warm the avocado oil.
2. Place the onion and garlic, and sauté for a couple of minutes.
3. Mix in the red bell pepper and the green bell pepper, and sauté for approximately 3 minutes until tender.
4. Put in the sweet potato, beans, broth, tomatoes, lime juice, chili powder, cocoa powder, cumin, salt, cinnamon, cayenne pepper, and oregano, then stir until blended. Put to a simmer, and cook for fifteen minutes. Serve instantly.

Nutritional Info: Calories: 160 , Total Fat: 4g , Saturated Fat: 0g , Cholesterol: 0mg , Carbohydrates: 29g , Fiber: 6g , Protein: 8g

SWEET POTATO AND CORN SOUP

Time To Prepare: ten minutes

Time to Cook: twenty minutes

Yield: Servings 4

Ingredients:
- ¼ cup extra-virgin olive oil or coconut oil
- ¼ teaspoon freshly ground black pepper
- 1 cup broccoli florets
- 1 cup coconut milk or almond milk
- 1 cup frozen corn kernels
- 1 cup thinly cut mushrooms
- 1 medium zucchini, cut into ¼-inch dice
- 1 small onion, cut into ¼-inch dice

- 1 teaspoon salt
- 2 cups peeled sweet potatoes cut into ¼-inch dice
- 2 tablespoons finely chopped fresh flat-leaf parsley
- 4 cups vegetable broth

Directions:
1. In a large pot, heat the oil on high heat.
2. Put in the zucchini, broccoli, mushrooms, and onion and sauté until tender, 5 to 8 minutes.
3. Pour the broth and sweet potatoes and place it to its boiling point.
4. Lower the heat to a simmer and cook until the sweet potatoes are soft, five to seven minutes.
5. Put in the corn, coconut milk, parsley, salt, and pepper. Cook on low heat up to the corn is thoroughly heated before you serve.

Nutritional Info: Calories: 402 , Total Fat: 29g , Total Carbohydrates: 31g , Sugar: 9g , Fiber: 6g , Protein: 10g , Sodium: 1406mg

TEX-MEX CHICKEN SOUP

Time To Prepare: ten minutes

Time to Cook: 1 hour

Yield: Servings 4

Ingredients:
- ¼ cup roasted pumpkin seeds
- 1 teaspoon paprika powder
- 1 yellow onion, chopped
- 1¾ cups coconut cream
- 12 ounces (340 g) boneless chicken thighs
- 2 tablespoons coconut oil
- 3 tablespoons Tex-Mex seasoning
- 4 tablespoons lime juice
- Fresh cilantro, chopped
- Salt and ground black pepper, to taste

Directions:
1. Cook the chicken thighs in a pot of water, covered, for thirty minutes or until the chicken is completely fork-soft. Move the chicken to a container and reserve the chicken broth until ready to use.
2. Warm the coconut oil in a nonstick frying pan on moderate heat, then put in the onion and drizzle with Tex-Mex seasoning, salt, and pepper. sauté for five minutes until the onion is translucent.
3. Pour over the reserved chicken broth and coconut cream. Bring them to a simmer for about twenty minutes or until it becomes thick.
4. Put in the chicken, pumpkin seeds, paprika powder, lime juice, and cilantro to the soup. Stir to blend well before you serve.

Nutritional Info: calories: 730 , total fat: 63g , net carbs: 19g , fiber: 9g , protein: 23g

THAI CHICKEN NOODLE SOUP

Time To Prepare: ten minutes

Time to Cook: ten minutes

Yield: Servings 2-3

Ingredients:
- 6 cups low-sodium chicken broth
- 1 stalk lemongrass, minced
- 1 bay leaf
- 1 tablespoon ginger, grated
- 1 big carrot, cut
- 1 cup broccoli florets, trimmed
- 1 cup mushrooms, quartered
- ½ teaspoon. cayenne pepper
- 3 cloves garlic, minced
- 2 Tablespoon. gluten-free soy sauce
- Salt and black pepper (to taste)
- a handful of fresh cilantro, chopped
- 1-2 fresh chicken breasts, chopped
- 1/4 cup fresh lime juice
- 1/4 cup coconut milk
- 8-10 oz. gluten-free flat Thai rice noodles

Directions:
1. Boil noodles in accordance with package directions, or until firm to the bite. Drain and save for later.
2. Pour chicken broth in a big pot and bring to its boiling point using high heat. Put in chicken, broccoli, mushrooms, lemongrass, ginger, carrot, bay leaf. Turn heat to high and let the broth boil for a minute. Cover the pot and decrease the heat to moderate. Simmer the soup for 6 more minutes.
3. While the soup is simmering, mix in cayenne, garlic, lime juice, and soy sauce. Turn heat to low and put in the coconut milk; stir thoroughly.
4. Put cooked noodles into bowls. Pour soup over the noodles, then drizzle with cilantro.

Nutritional Info: Calories: 503 kcal , Protein: 48.11 g , Fat: 19.63 g , Carbohydrates: 35.9 g

THAI WINTER VEGETABLE SOUP

Time To Prepare: 60 minutes

Time to Cook: 6 hours

Yield: Servings 12

Ingredients:
- ½ Of Lemon Juice

- 1 Lime Juice
- 1 Piece Ginger (Peeled, Grated)
- 1 Teaspoon Cumin
- 14 Ounce Coconut Milk
- 14 Ounce Peeled Italian Plum Tomatoes
- 2 Large Onions (Peeled, Quartered)
- 2 Stalks Lemongrass (Split)
- 3 Carrots (Peeled, Chopped)
- 3 Cloves Garlic (Peeled, Chopped)
- 3 Red Bell Peppers (Quartered, Seeded)
- 4 Large Sweet Potatoes (Peeled, Cut)
- 4 Tablespoons Cilantro (Chopped)
- Ground Black Pepper
- Optional: 1 Green Chili Pepper (Chopped)
- Salt

Directions:
1. Cook the vegetables with ginger and chili before pouring in coconut milk.
2. Mix in cilantro, cumin, lemon juice, and seasoning, cooking for around six hours.
3. Remove lemongrass and blend until thick.
4. Put in lime juice, seasoning, and cilantro to serve.

Nutritional Info: Calories: 468 kcal , Carbohydrates: 81 g , Fat: fifteen g , Protein: 8.5 g

TOMATO AND BASIL SOUP

Time To Prepare: five minutes

Time to Cook: fifteen minutes

Yield: Servings 4

Ingredients:
- ¼ cup chopped fresh basil leaves
- ¼ cup heavy whipping cream
- 1 (14.5-ounce / 411-g) can diced tomatoes
- 2 ounces (57 g) cream cheese
- 4 tablespoons butter
- From the cupboard:
- Salt and freshly ground black pepper, to taste

Directions:
1. Position the diced tomatoes in a food processor. Process until the desired smoothness is achieved.
2. Melt the butter in a deep cooking pan on moderate heat. Put in the tomato purée, cream, and cheese. Cook for about ten minutes or until well blended. Keep stirring during the cooking.

3. Drizzle with chopped basil leaves, salt, and black pepper. Keep cooking for another five minutes or until the desired smoothness is achieved and the soup has become thick. Stir continuously.
4. Ladle the soup into a big container and serve warm.

Nutritional Info: calories: 238 , total fat: 22.1g , total carbs: 8.9g , fiber: 2.1g , net carbs: 6.8g , protein: 3.1g

TOMATO BISQUE SOUP

Time To Prepare: ten minutes

Time to Cook: forty minutes

Yield: Servings 6

Ingredients:
- 1 cup heavy cream
- 1 teaspoon freshly chopped thyme
- 2 tablespoons butter
- 3 cloves garlic, chopped
- 3 cups canned whole, peeled tomatoes
- 4 cups chicken broth
- Salt & black pepper, to taste

Directions:
1. Put in the butter to the bottom of a stockpot.
2. Put in in all the rest of the ingredients minus the heavy cream. Bring to its boiling point, and then simmer for forty minutes.
3. Warm the heavy cream, and then mix into the soup.

Nutritional Info: Calories: 144 , Carbohydrates: 4g , Fiber: 1g Net , Carbohydrates: 3g , Fat: 12g , Protein: 4g

TURKEY MEATBALL SOUP

Time To Prepare: fifteen minutes

Time to Cook: fifteen minutes

Yield: Servings 6

Ingredients:

For the Meatballs:
- ¼ teaspoon red pepper flakes
- ½ teaspoon dried oregano
- ½ teaspoon salt
- 1 pound ground turkey
- 1 tablespoon Dijon mustard
- 1 tablespoon ghee

- 1 teaspoon dried basil
- 1 teaspoon garlic powder
- Freshly ground black pepper

For the Soup:
- ½ teaspoon dried thyme
- 1 bay leaf
- 1 medium white onion, diced
- 2 carrots, diced
- 2 cups shredded kale leaves, stemmed and meticulously washed
- 2 garlic cloves, minced
- 6 cups vegetable broth

Directions:

To make the Meatballs:
1. In a moderate-sized container, put the turkey, mustard, basil, garlic powder, oregano, salt, and red pepper flakes, and flavor with pepper. With your hands, combine the ingredients until they are well blended.
2. Put in the ghee to a stockpot on moderate to high heat. Roll the meat mixture into 1-inch balls and layer across the bottom of the pot. Cook for minimum 2 minutes per side, until almost thoroughly cooked. Move the meatballs to a plate.

To make the Soup:
1. To the stockpot, put in the onion, carrots, garlic, and thyme. Cook for approximately 2 minutes, slowly stirring, until the onions are translucent.
2. Put in the broth, kale, bay leaf, and meatballs. Put to a simmer, lessen the heat to moderate-low and simmer for approximately fifteen minutes until the meatballs are thoroughly cooked, and the kale has tenderized. Remove and discard the bay leaf. Serve hot.

Nutritional Info: Calories: 259 , Total Fat: 14g , Saturated Fat: 5g , Cholesterol: 88mg , Carbohydrates: 9g , Fiber: 2g , Protein: 26g

TUSCAN STYLE SOUP

Time To Prepare: three minutes

Time to Cook: five minutes

Yield: Servings 4

Ingredients:
- ½ cup leeks, cut
- 1 carrot, trimmed and grated
- 1 zucchini, shredded
- 1/4 teaspoon ground black pepper
- 2 cups broth, if possible homemade
- 2 cups water
- 2 garlic cloves, minced

- 2 tablespoons butter, melted
- 4 cups broccoli rabe, broken into pieces
- Sea salt, to taste

Directions:
1. Push the "Sauté" button to heat up your Instant Pot; now, melt the butter. Cook the leeks for approximately 2 minutes or until tender.
2. Put in minced garlic and cook an additional 40 seconds.
3. Put in the rest of the ingredients. Secure the lid.
4. "Manual" mode and Low pressure; cook for about three minutes. Once cooking is complete, use a quick pressure release; cautiously remove the lid. Enjoy!

Nutritional Info: 95 Calories , 6.7g Fat , 5.2g Total Carbs , 4.2g Protein , 1.4g Sugars

VEGETABLE BEEF SOUP

Time To Prepare: ten minutes

Time to Cook: 4-6 hours

Yield: Servings 6

Ingredients:
- ½ cup diced tomatoes
- 1 pound lean ground beef
- 1 teaspoon freshly chopped rosemary
- 1 teaspoon freshly chopped thyme
- 1 yellow onion, chopped
- 1 zucchini, diced
- 2 cloves garlic, chopped
- 2 stalks celery, chopped
- 4 cups beef broth
- Salt & pepper, to taste

Directions:
1. Put in all the ingredients to a slow cooker and cook on high for four to 6 hours.
2. Stir thoroughly before you serve.

Nutritional Info: Calories: 185 , Carbohydrates: 5g , Fiber: 1g Net , Carbohydrates: 4g , Fat: 6g , Protein: 7g

VEGETARIAN GARLIC, TOMATO & ONION SOUP

Time To Prepare: fifteen minutes

Time to Cook: thirty minutes

Yield: Servings 6

Ingredients:

- ½ cup full-fat unsweetened coconut milk
- 1 bay leaf
- 1 teaspoon Italian seasoning
- 1 yellow onion, chopped
- 1½ cups canned diced tomatoes
- 3 cloves garlic, chopped
- 6 cups vegetable broth
- Fresh basil, for serving
- Pinch of salt & pepper, to taste

Directions:

1. Put in all the ingredients minus the coconut milk and fresh basil to a stockpot on moderate heat and bring to its boiling point. Reduce to a simmer and cook for half an hour
2. Take away the bay leaf, and then use an immersion blender to combine the soup until the desired smoothness is achieved. Mix in the coconut milk.
3. Decorate using fresh basil before you serve.

Nutritional Info: Calories: 104 , Carbohydrates: 6g , Fiber: 1g Net , Carbohydrates: 5g , Fat: 7g , Protein: 6g

WEDDING SOUP

Time To Prepare: fifteen minutes

Time to Cook: 60 minutes

Yield: Servings 6

Ingredients:

- ¼ bunch fresh parsley, chopped
- ¾ pound lean ground beef
- 1 cup rough chopped fresh spinach with stems removed
- 1 egg or ¼ cup egg substitute
- 1 yellow onion, chopped
- 2 quarts Rich Poultry Stock or low-sodium canned chicken stock
- 2 sprigs fresh basil, chopped
- 3 cloves garlic, minced
- 3 slices Italian bread, toasted
- 3 sprigs fresh oregano, chopped
- 4 ounces fresh grated Parmesan cheese
- Freshly cracked black pepper, to taste

Directions:

1. Preheat your oven to 375°F.
2. Wet the toasted Italian bread with water, then squeeze out all the liquid.

3. In a big container, combine the bread, beef, egg, onion, garlic, parsley, oregano, basil, pepper, and half of the Parmesan. Form the mixture into 1- to two-inch balls; put in a baking dish and cook for twenty minutes to half an hour. Take off from the oven and drain using paper towels.
4. Steam the spinach firm to the bite. In a big stockpot, mix the stock, spinach, and meatballs; simmer for half an hour
5. Ladle the soup into serving bowls then top with the rest of the cheese

Nutritional Info: Calories: 245 , Fat: 10 g , Protein: 26 g , Sodium: 1,021 mg , Fiber: 0.5 g , Carbohydrates: 9 g

WHITE VELVET CAULIFLOWER SOUP

Time To Prepare: ten minutes

Time to Cook: twenty minutes

Yield: Servings 6

Ingredients:
- 1 head cauliflower, chopped into 1-inch pieces
- 1 small celery root, peeled, cut into 1-inch pieces
- 1 small white onion, diced
- 1 tbsp. avocado oil
- 2 scallions, cut
- 2 tbsp. ghee
- 3 garlic cloves, minced
- 4 cups vegetable broth

Directions:
1. In a huge soup pot on moderate heat, heat the avocado oil.
2. Place the onion and garlic, and sauté for five minutes.
3. Place the celery root and cauliflower.
4. Raise the heat to moderate-high, then continue to sauté for minimum five minutes, or until the cauliflower starts to brown and caramelize the sides.
5. Mix in the broth and ghee and place it to its boiling point. Lessen the heat to moderate-low and simmer for about ten minutes. Take away the pot from the heat.
6. Use an immersion blender to or in batches in a standard blender, purée the soup until creamy. Serve instantly, sprinkled with the scallions.

Nutritional Info: Calories: 183 , Total Fat: 8g , Saturated Fat: 3g , Cholesterol: 0mg , Carbohydrates: 10g , Fiber: 3g , Protein: 9g

WHOLESOME CABBAGE SOUP

Time To Prepare: two minutes

Time to Cook: 8 minutes

Yield: Servings 4

Ingredients:
- ½ pound Capocollo, chopped
- ½ teaspoon cayenne pepper
- 1 bay leaf
- 1 celery stalk, chopped
- 1 cup tomatoes, puréed
- 1 cup water
- 1 onion, chopped
- 1 parsnip, chopped
- 1 pound cabbage, cut into wedges
- 2 cups broth, if possible homemade
- Coarse sea salt and ground black pepper, to your preference

Directions:
1. Put in all of the above ingredients to your Instant Pot.
2. Secure the lid. Choose "Manual" mode and High pressure; cook for about three minutes. Once cooking is complete, use a quick pressure release; cautiously remove the lid.
3. Ladle into four soup bowls and serve hot. Enjoy!

Nutritional Info: 258 Calories , 20.4g Fat , 6g Total Carbs , 9.9g Protein , 3.6g Sugars

ZESTY BROCCOLI SOUP

Time To Prepare: ten minutes

Time to Cook: twenty minutes

Yield: Servings 4

Ingredients:
- ½ teaspoon freshly squeezed lemon juice
- ½ teaspoon lemon zest
- ½ teaspoon salt
- 1 carrot, chopped
- 1 celery stalk, diced
- 1 head broccoli, roughly chopped
- 1 medium white onion, diced
- 1 tablespoon ghee
- 3 cups vegetable broth
- 3 garlic cloves, minced
- Freshly ground black pepper

Directions:
1. In a huge soup pot on moderate heat, melt the ghee.
2. Place the onion and garlic, and sauté for five minutes.
3. Put in the broccoli, carrot, and celery, and sauté for a couple of minutes.
4. Mix in the broth, salt, lemon juice, and lemon zest, and flavor with pepper. Heat to a simmer, and cook for minimum ten minutes. Serve instantly.

Nutritional Info: Calories: 80 , Total Fat: 4g , Saturated Fat: 2g , Cholesterol: 0mg , Carbohydrates: 10g , Fiber: 3g , Protein: 2g

ZUCCHINI AND CHICKEN BROTH

Time To Prepare: twenty minutes

Time to Cook: twenty minutes

Yield: Servings 2

Ingredients:
- ¾ cup coconut milk
- 1 big zucchini, thinly cut
- 1 pound (454 g) boneless, skinless chicken breasts, cut into little pieces
- 1 tablespoon fresh parsley or fresh cilantro, finely chopped
- 2 cups water
- 2 garlic cloves, minced
- 2 tablespoons olive oil, divided
- 2 white onions, finely chopped
- 3 tablespoons green curry paste
- Salt and ground black pepper, to taste

Directions:
1. Sprinkle 1 tablespoon of olive oil in a deep cooking pan and warm on moderate heat.
2. Reduce the heat and cook the onions and garlic in the deep cooking pan using low heat for three to four minutes until translucent.
3. Then put the curry paste, coconut milk, parsley and water into the deep cooking pan. Bring them to a simmer for about three minutes.
4. Put in the chicken pieces and simmer for another six minutes until the chicken is thoroughly cooked.
5. In the meantime, warm the rest of the olive oil in a nonstick frying pan, then sauté the zucchini in the frying pan for about three minutes. Drizzle with salt and ground black pepper and sauté for another two minutes until tender.
6. Put in the cooked zucchini into the chicken broth and serve warm.

Nutritional Info: calories: 790 , total fat: 54g , net carbs: 18g , fiber: 5g , protein: 54g

ALMOND BUTTER BALLS VEGAN

Time To Prepare: 10 Minutes

Time to Cook: 0 0 Minute

Yield: Servings 4

Ingredients:
- 12 dates, pitted and diced
- 2 and a ½ tablespoon of almond butter

- 1/3 cup of unsweetened shredded coconut

Directions:
1. Take a container and put in dates, almond butter, and coconut. Mix thoroughly
2. Use the mixture to make small balls
3. Store them in the refrigerator and chill them
4. Enjoy!

Nutritional Info: , Calories: 62 Cal , Fat: 3 g , Carbohydrates:8 g , Protein:1 g

ALMOND COOKIES

Time To Prepare: fifteen min

Time to Cook: fifteen min

Yield: Servings 12

Ingredients:
- ½ tsp honey
- ½ tsp vanilla
- 1.7oz / 50g coconut butter
- 14oz / 400g non-wheat flour
- 1tsp baking powder
- 1tsp baking soda
- 3.5oz / 100g tahini
- Salt

Directions:
1. Combine the flour, soda, salt, baking powder together.
2. Mix tahini and coconut butter together and put in 2 tbsp. water in the same container.
3. Put in honey, vanilla to the tahini mixture and blend it well with a mixer.
4. Preheat the oven (180C/356F) and place a baking sheet on it.
5. Put in 24 tablespoons of the mixture onto the baking sheet and allow it to bake in your oven for 11-fifteen minutes.
6. Allow it to get cold a little bit before you serve.

Nutritional Info: , Calories: 112 , Carbohydrates:18 g , Protein: 3.2 g , Fat: 1.6 g , Sugar: 23.1 g , Fiber: 7.4 g , Sodium: 28 mg

ANTI-INFLAMMATORY APRICOT SQUARES

Time To Prepare: twenty minutes

Time to Cook: 0 minute

Yield: Servings 8

Ingredients:

- 1 cup apricot, chopped
- 1 cup apricot, dried
- 1 cup macadamia nuts, chopped
- 1 cup shredded coconut, dried
- 1 teaspoon vanilla extract
- 1/3 cup turmeric powder

Directions:
1. Put all ingredients in a food processor
2. Pulse until the desired smoothness is achieved
3. Put the mixture into a square pan and press uniformly

Best enjoyed chilled.

Nutritional Info: , Calories: 201 , Fat: 15g , Carbohydrates: 17g , Protein: 3g

APPLE FRITTERS

Time To Prepare: fifteen minutes

Time to Cook: ten minutes

Yield: Servings 4

Ingredients:
- ½ cup cashew milk
- 1 apple, cored, peeled, and chopped
- 1 cup all-purpose flour
- 1 egg
- 1½ teaspoons of baking powder
- 2 tablespoons of stevia sugar

Directions:
1. Preheat the air fryer to 175 degrees C or 350 degrees F.
2. Place parchment paper at the bottom of your fryer.

Line with cooking spray.
3. Mix together ¼ cup sugar, flour, baking powder, egg, milk, and salt in a container.
4. Mix well by stirring.
5. Drizzle 2 tablespoons of sugar on the apples. Coat well.
6. Mix the apples into your flour mixture.
7. Use a cookie scoop and drop the fritters with it to the air fryer basket's bottom.
8. Now air fry for five minutes.
9. Flip the fritters once and fry for another three minutes. They must be golden.

Nutritional Info: Calories 307 , Carbohydrates: 65g , Cholesterol: 48mg , Total Fat: 3g , Protein: 5g , Sugar: 39g , Fiber: 2g , Sodium: 248mg

AVOCADO BROWNIES

Time To Prepare: 10 Minutes

Time to Cook: 25 Minutes

Yield: Servings 16

Ingredients:
- ¼ tsp. Sea Salt
- ½ cup Applesauce, unsweetened
- ½ cup Cocoa Powder, Dutch-processed & unsweetened
- ½ cup Coconut Flour
- ½ cup Maple Syrup
- 1 Avocado, big
- 1 tap. Vanilla Extract
- 1 tsp. Baking Soda
- 3 Eggs, large

Directions:
1. First, preheat your oven to 350 ° F.
2. Next, place avocado, vanilla, applesauce, and maple syrup in a high-speed blender and blend for a couple of minutes or until the desired smoothness is achieved.
3. After this, move the smooth mixture to a big mixing container.
4. To this, mix in the eggs and mix until whisked well.
5. Next, spoon in the coconut flour, sea salt, and cocoa powder to the mixture.
6. Give a good stir until everything comes together.
7. Now, pour the mixture to a greased baking dish and bake for 23 to twenty-five minutes or until cooked.
8. Finally, take off from the oven and let it cool for fifteen to twenty minutes before you serve.

Nutritional Info: , Calories: 91Kcal , Protein: 1.9g , Carbohydrates: 12.1g , Fat: 4.3g

AVOCADO CHIA PARFAIT

Time To Prepare: five minutes

Time to Cook: twenty minutes

Yield: Servings 2

Ingredients:
- ⅛ teaspoon nutmeg powder
- ½ teaspoon cinnamon powder
- ¾ teaspoon cinnamon powder
- 1 banana, mashed
- 1 tablespoon cashew nuts, chopped
- 1¼ cups almond milk
- 2 avocados, diced

- 2 tablespoons chia seeds
- 2 tablespoons pumpkin seeds
- For the Avocado Jam
- For the Parfait Base
- Pinch of sea salt

Directions:
1. In a container, mix almond milk, banana, nutmeg powder, cinnamon powder, and pumpkin seeds. Mix until well blended. Chill in your refrigerator.
2. In the meantime, put the deep cooking pan on moderate heat. Mix avocados, nutmeg powder, cinnamon powder, and salt. Bring to its boiling point. Allow simmering for about twenty minutes.
3. Remove the heat. Mash half of the jam using a wooden spoon. Allow to cool. Set aside.
4. Ladle 2 tablespoons of parfait base and apple jam into parfait glasses. Decorate using cashew nuts and serve.

Nutritional Info: , Calories: 671 kcal , Protein: 13.13 g , Fat: 54.86 g , Carbohydrates: 43.76 g

AVOCADO CHOCO CAKE

Time To Prepare: ten minutes

Time to Cook: twenty-five minutes

Yield: Servings 8

Ingredients:
- ¼-tsp sea salt
- ½-cup applesauce, unsweetened
- ½-cup cocoa powder, unsweetened and Dutch-processed
- ½-cup coconut flour
- ½-cup maple syrup
- 1-pc big avocado
- 1-tsp baking soda
- 1-tsp vanilla extract
- 3-pcs big eggs

Directions:
1. Preheat the oven to 350°F. Grease a baking pan with coconut oil.
2. Mix the avocado, vanilla, syrup, and applesauce in a food processor. Blend until meticulously blended.
3. Move the mixture to a big mixing container. Whisk in the eggs. Put in the baking soda, cocoa powder, coconut flour, and sea salt. Mix thoroughly until meticulously blended.
4. Put in the batter in the baking pan. Place the pan in your oven. Bake for about twenty-five minutes.
5. Allow cooling for about twenty minutes before cutting the cake into 16 squares.

Nutritional Info: , Calories: 253 , Fat: 8.4g , Protein: 12.6g , Sodium: 245mg , Total Carbohydrates: 43.9g , Fiber: 12.3g , Net Carbohydrates: 31.6g

AVOCADO CHOCOLATE MOUSSE

Time To Prepare: ten minutes

Time to Cook: 0 minute

Yield: Servings 9

Ingredients:
- ¼ cup espresso beans, ground
- ¼ cup of cocoa powder
- ½ teaspoon salt
- 1 bar dark chocolate
- 1 teaspoon vanilla extract
- 1/8 cup almond milk, unsweetened
- 2 tablespoons raw honey
- 3 ripe avocado, pitted and flesh scooped out
- 6 ounces plain Greek yogurt

Directions:
1. Put all ingredients in a food processor
2. Pulse until the desired smoothness is achieved

Best enjoyed chilled.

Nutritional Info: , Calories: 208 , Fat: 4g , Carbohydrates: 17g , Protein: 5g

BANANA & AVOCADO MOUSSE

Time To Prepare: ten minutes

Time to Cook: 0 minutes

Yield: Servings 4

Ingredients:
- ½ cup of fresh lemon juice
- ½ cup of fresh lime juice
- 1 teaspoon of fresh lemon zest, grated finely
- 1 teaspoon of fresh lime zest, grated finely
- 1/3 cup of raw honey
- 2 cups of bananas (peeled and chopped)
- 2 ripe avocados (peeled, pitted, and chopped)

Directions:
1. Combine all ingredients in a blender and pulse to puree.
2. Move the mousse to four serving glasses.
3. Place in your fridge for around three hours before eating.

Nutritional Info: , Calories: 368 , Fat: 20.1g , Carbohydrates: 50.2g , Sugar: 33.6g , Protein: 3.1g , Sodium: 14mg

BANANA BARS

Time To Prepare: ten minutes

Time to Cook: 60 minutes

Yield: Servings 4

Ingredients:
- ½ Cup Coconut Milk
- ½ Cup Melted Butter
- 1 Cup Chocolate Chips
- 1 Tsp. Baking Soda
- 1 Tsp. Pure Vanilla Extract
- 1/4 Tbsp. Cinnamon
- 2 Cup Brown Sugar
- 2 Cup Whole Wheat Flour
- 2 Eggs
- 5 Cup Ripe Mashed Banana
- Salt

Direction:
1. Preheat your oven to 170C.
2. Mix all together the ingredients to make the batter.
3. Put the batter in a wide tray and bake for about twenty minutes at 170C.
4. Serve with liquid chocolate or fruits.

Nutritional Info: , Calories: 330 kcal , Carbohydrates: 8.80 g , Fat: 13.0 g , Protein: 12.4 g.

BANANA CINNAMON

Time To Prepare: two minutes

Time to Cook: 8 minutes

Yield: Servings 2-4

Ingredients:
- 1 big banana, chopped into ½ inch
- 1 tsp. cinnamon
- 2 tsp. honey

Directions:
1. In a small container, put the honey and cinnamon and mix well.
2. Heat the olive oil in a pan. Cook banana slices for a couple of minutes or until browned all over.
3. Pour honey and cinnamon mixture over the bananas and serve.

Nutritional Info: , Calories: 33 kcal , Protein: 1.64 g , Fat: 1.52 g , Carbohydrates: 3.43 g

BANANA CINNAMON COOKIES

Time To Prepare: five minutes

Time to Cook: ten minutes

Yield: Servings 2

Ingredients:
- 2 ripe bananas, peeled
- ¼ cup almond milk, unsweetened
- 4 pitted dates
- 1 tablespoon cinnamon
- 1 teaspoon vanilla
- 1 ½ teaspoon lemon juice
- 3 tablespoons dried and chopped cranberries
- 1 teaspoon baking powder
- 2 tablespoons dried and chopped raisins
- 2/3 cup applesauce, unsweetened
- 2/3 cup coconut flour

Directions:
1. Preheat your oven to 350 degrees F.
2. Use a food processor to mix almond milk, applesauce, dates, and bananas. Blend until you achieve a smooth consistency.
3. Put in in coconut flour, baking powder, cinnamon, vanilla, and lemon juice. Blend for a minute. Fold in cranberries and raisins.
4. Pour a baking sheet with the cookie dough. Put inside the oven for about twenty minutes.
5. Let sit for five minutes and allow it to harden and serve.

Nutritional Info: , Calories: 53 kcal **,** Protein: 9.28 g **,** Fat: 7.58 g **,** Carbohydrates: 65.87 g

BEET PANCAKES

Time To Prepare: ten minutes

Time to Cook: twelve minutes

Yield: Servings 3

Ingredients:
- ½ Cup Heavy Milk
- ½ Cup Melted Butter
- 1 Cup Flour
- 1 Large Egg
- 1 Tbsp. Baking Powder
- 1 Tsp. Vanilla Extract
- 1/3 Cup Plain Greek Yoghurt
- 1/4 Tsp Baking Soda

- 3 Cup Whole Wheat Flour
- 4 Cups Roasted Beet, Puree
- 6 Tsp. Brown Sugar
- Salt

Directions:
1. Combine the dry ingredients in a container.
2. In another container, combine the wet ingredients.
3. Mix both mixtures until the desired smoothness is achieved.
4. Fry the batter on a pan to make pancakes.
5. Serve with whip cream.

Nutritional Info: , Calories: 359 kcal , Carbohydrates: 60 g , Fat: 3.0 g , Protein: 18.4 g.

BERRY ICE POPS

Time To Prepare: 3 Hours 5 Minutes

Time to Cook: 0 minutes

Yield: Servings 4

Ingredients:
- ¼ Cup Water
- 1 Cup Blueberries, Fresh or Frozen
- 1 Cup Strawberries, Fresh or Frozen
- 1 Teaspoon Lemon Juice, Fresh
- 2 Cups Whole Milk Yogurt, Plain
- 2 Tablespoons Honey, Raw

Directions:
1. Put all together the ingredients in a blender, and blend until the desired smoothness is achieved.
2. Pour into your molds, and freeze for minimum three hours before you serve.

Nutritional Info: , Calories: 140 , Protein: 5 Grams , Fat: 4 Grams , Carbohydrates: 23 Grams

BERRY PARFAIT

Time To Prepare: 10 min

Time to Cook: 10 min

Yield: Servings 5

Ingredients:
- 14oz / 400g mixed berries
- 2 tsp honey
- 3.5oz / 100g Greek yogurt
- 7oz / 200g almond butter
- 7oz / 200g mixed nuts

Directions:
1. Combine the Greek yogurt, butter, and honey until its smooth.
2. Put in a layer of berries and a layer of the mixture in a glass until it's full.
3. Serve instantly with sprinkled nuts.

Nutritional Info: , Calories: 250 , Carbohydrates: 17 g , Protein: 7.2 g , Fat: 19.4 g , Sugar: 42.3 g , Fiber: 6.6 g , Sodium: 21 mg

BERRY-BANANA YOGURT

Time To Prepare: ten minutes

Time to Cook: 0 minute

Yield: Servings 1

Ingredients:
- ¼ cup collard greens, chopped
- ¼ cup quick-cooking oats
- ½ banana, frozen fresh
- ½ cup blueberries, fresh and frozen
- 1 container 5.3ounes Greek yogurt, non-fat
- 1 cup almond milk
- 5-6 ice cubes

Directions:
1. Take microwave-safe cup and put in 1 cup almond milk and ¼ cup oats
2. Put the cups into your microwave on high for 2.5 minutes
3. When oats are cooked and 2 ice cubes to cool
4. Combine them well
5. Put in all ingredients in your blender

Blend until smooth and creamy

Best enjoyed chilled.

Nutritional Info: , Calories: 379 , Fat: 10g , Carbohydrates: 63g , Protein: 13g

BLACK TEA CAKE

Time To Prepare: ten minutes

Time to Cook: thirty-five minutes

Yield: Servings 10

Ingredients:
- ½ cup coconut butter
- ½ cup coconut oil
- 1 teaspoon baking soda
- 2 cups coconut milk

- 2 teaspoons vanilla extract
- 3 ½ cups almond flour
- 3 teaspoons baking powder
- 4 eggs
- 6 tablespoons black tea powder
- Chicory root powder to the taste

Directions:
1. Place the coconut milk in a pot and warm it up on moderate heat. Put in tea, stir thoroughly, take off the heat and cool down, In a container, mix the coconut butter with the chicory powder, eggs, vanilla, coconut oil, almond flour, baking soda, baking powder, and tea mix. Stir thoroughly, pour into a lined cake pan, and bake in your oven at 350 degrees F for half an hour Slice, split between plates, before you serve.
2. Enjoy!

Nutritional Info: , Calories: 170 , Fat: 4 , Fiber: 5 , Carbohydrates: 6 , Protein: 2

BLUEBERRY CRISP

Time To Prepare: five minutes

Time to Cook: thirty minutes

Yield: Servings 4

Ingredients:
- ¼ cups pecans, chopped
- ¼ teaspoon nutmeg
- ½ teaspoon ginger
- 1 cup buckwheat
- 1 lb. blueberries
- 1 teaspoon of cinnamon
- 1 teaspoon of honey
- 2 tablespoons olive oil

Directions:
1. Preheat the oven to 350 degrees F.
2. Grease a baking dish.
3. Mix together the pecans, wheat, oil, spices, and honey in a container.
4. Put in the berries to your pan. Layer the topping on your berries.
5. Bake for thirty minutes at 350 F.

Nutritional Info: Calories 327 , Carbohydrates: 35g , Fat: 19g , Protein: 4g , Sugar: 14g , Fiber: 5g , Sodium: 2mg , Potassium: 197mg

BLUEBERRY ENERGY BITES

Time To Prepare: ten minutes

Time to Cook: 0 minutes

Yield: Servings 6

Ingredients:
- ¼ teaspoon of cinnamon
- ½ cup of gluten-free oat flour
- ½ cup of unsweetened almond milk
- ½ teaspoon of sea salt
- 2 tablespoons of dried blueberries
- 2 tablespoons of organic peanut butter
- 2 tablespoons of pure maple syrup

Directions:
1. Put the dry ingredients into a mixing container, including the peanut butter, and stir until blended.
2. Put in the almond milk and maple syrup, and stir.
3. Form into an inch balls, and place in your fridge to firm up before you serve.

Nutritional Info: , Total Carbohydrates: 13g , Fiber: 1g , Net Carbohydrates: , Protein: 3g , Total Fat: 1g , Calories: 93

BLUEBERRY SOUR CREAM CAKE

Time To Prepare: twenty minutes

Time to Cook: 70 minutes

Yield: Servings 4

Ingredients:
- 1 Cup Blueberry
- 1 Cup Of Melted Butter
- 1 Cup Sour Cream
- 1 Tsp Vanilla Extract
- 1 Tsp. Baking Powder
- 1 Tsp. Cinnamon Powder
- 2 Cups Of Brown Sugar
- 2 Large Eggs
- 2 Tbsp. All-Purpose Flour
- Salt

Direction:
1. Preheat oven on 175C.
2. Mix together the butter and sugar till light and fluffy.
3. Put sour cream, vanilla extract, and eggs into the mixture.
4. In another container, put all together the dry ingredients then mix.
5. Place the dry mixture into the butter mixture, putting in blueberries, then mix well.
6. Put the batter into a greased pan then bake for about fifty minutes at 170C.

7. Serve with sour cream and blueberries.

Nutritional Info: , Calories: 234 kcal , Carbohydrates: 43 g , Fat: 21 g , Protein: 14.4 g.

BLUEBERRY TARTS

Time To Prepare: 10 Minutes

Time to Cook: 30 Minutes

Yield: Servings 5

Ingredients:

To make the crust:
- ½ cup Raisins
- ½ tsp. Himalayan Salt
- 1 cup Cashews
- 1 cup Dates
- 1 cup Walnuts

To make the filling:
- 1 tbsp. Maple syrup
- 1/8 tsp. Cinnamon
- 4 cups Blueberries

Directions:
1. To make this yummy dessert fare, keep all the nuts in a food processor and process the nuts until it becomes coarse flour.
2. After this, spoon in the dates, salt, and raisin to the nuts mixture and process them once more.
3. Next, spread this mixture onto a greased parchment paper-lined baking sheet and place it in your fridge until set.
4. To make the filling, mix all the ingredients needed in a moderate-sized container and mix them well.
5. To finish, spoon in the filling on to the crust and spread across uniformly on all sides.
6. Top with blueberries if you wish.

Nutritional Info: , Calories: 544 Kcal , Protein: 12.4g , Carbohydrates: 69.2g , Fat:28.1g

CAFÉ-STYLE FUDGE

Time To Prepare: ten minutes + chilling time

Time to Cook: 0 minutes

Yield: Servings 6

Ingredients:
- ½ teaspoon vanilla extract
- 1 stick butter
- 1 tablespoon instant coffee granules

- 4 tablespoons cocoa powder
- 4 tablespoons confectioners' Swerve

Directions:
1. Beat the butter and Swerve at low speed.
2. Put in in the cocoa powder, instant coffee granules, and vanilla and continue to stir until well blended.
3. Ladle the batter into a foil-lined baking sheet. Place in your fridge for two to three hours. Enjoy!

Nutritional Info: 144 Calories 15.5g , Fat: 2.1g , Carbs: 0.8g , Protein: 1.1g Fiber

CARAMELIZED PEARS

Time To Prepare: twenty minutes

Time to Cook: five minutes

Yield: Servings 5

Ingredients:
- ¼ Cup Toasted Pecans, Chopped
- 1 Tablespoon Coconut Oil
- 1 Teaspoon Cinnamon
- 1/8 Teaspoon Sea Salt
- 2 Cups Yogurt, Plain
- 2 Tablespoon Honey, Raw
- 4 Pears, Peeled, Cored & Quartered

Directions:
1. Get out a big frying pan, and then heat the oil on moderate to high heat.
2. Put in in your honey, cinnamon, pears, and salt. Cover, and let it cook for four to five minutes. Stir once in a while, and your fruit must be soft.
3. Uncover it, and let the sauce simmer until it becomes thick. This will take a few minutes.
4. Soon your yogurt into four dessert bowls. Top with pears and pecans before you serve.

Nutritional Info: , Calories: 290 , Protein: 12 Grams , Fat: 11 Grams , Carbohydrates: 41 Grams

CHOCO CHIA CHERRY CREAM

Time To Prepare: 4 hours and five minutes

Time to Cook: 0 minutes

Yield: Servings 4

Ingredients:
- ¼-cup chia seeds, powdered
- ½-cup cherries, pitted and cut + extra for plating
- 1½-cups almond milk
- 2-Tbsps pure maple syrup or honey

- 3-Tbsps raw cacao, powdered
- Additional toppings: extra raw cacao nibs, cherries, and 70% or higher dark chocolate shavings

Directions:

1. Mix in all the ingredients, excluding the cherries in a mason jar. Mix thoroughly until meticulously blended. Place in your fridge overnight or for 4 hours.
2. Before you serve, split the pudding equally among four serving plates. Top each plate with the cherries. Decorate using the additional toppings.

Nutritional Info: , Calories: 502 , Fat: 16.7g , Protein: 25.1g , Sodium: 68mg , Total Carbohydrates: 86.3g , Fiber: 23.6g , Net Carbohydrates: 62.7g

CHOCOLATE BANANAS

Time To Prepare: 5 Minutes

Time to Cook: fifteen Minutes

Yield: Servings 4

Ingredients:

- 1 tbsp. Coconut Oil
- 12 oz. Dark Chocolate
- 3 Bananas, big & cut into thirds

Directions:

1. Melt the chocolate and coconut oil in a twofold boiler for three to four minutes, till you get a smooth and shiny mixture.
2. After this, keep the popsicles into the end of each of the banana by inserting it.
3. Next, immerse the chocolate into the warm chocolate mixture.
4. Shake off the surplus chocolate and put them on parchment paper.
5. Drizzle with the topping of your choice.
6. To finish, place them in the freezer for a few hours or until set.

Nutritional Info: , Calories: 427Kcal , Protein:5.9g , Carbohydrates: 80g , Fat: 15.6g

CHOCOLATE CHERRY CHIA PUDDING

Time To Prepare: 4 hours and five minutes

Time to Cook: 0 minutes

Yield: Servings 4

Ingredients:

- ¼ cup Chia seeds You can also use chia seed powder.
- ½ cup Sliced pitted cherries
- 1 ½ cup Any non-dairy milk like coconut or almond milk

- 3 tbsp. Maple syrup or honey
- 3 tbsp. Raw cacao powder

Additional toppings:
- Dark chocolate shavings (Preferably 70% dark chocolate or more)
- Extra cherries
- Raw cacao nibs

Directions:
1. Use a mason jar or a container. If you're using a container, just pour in the milk, maple syrup, chia seeds or powder, and raw cacao. Stir meticulously and place in your fridge for 4 hours or more.
2. If you decide to use a mason jar, just pour in the same ingredients, screw the lid on and shake vigorously!
3. Serve in separate dishes and top with any or all of the toppings I listed above.
4. Enjoy!

Nutritional Info: , Calories: 811 kcal , Protein: 2.38 g , Fat: 83.36 g , Carbohydrates: 16.88 g

CHOCOLATE CHIP COOKIES

Time To Prepare: 10 Minutes

Time to Cook: 20 Minutes

Yield: Servings 16

Ingredients:
- ½ cup Almond Butter
- ½ cup Dark Chocolate Chips, sugar-free
- ½ cup Maple Syrup
- 2 cups Almond Flour, finely sifted

Directions:
1. Preheat your oven to 350 ° F.
2. After this, mix the almond flour, almond butter, and maple syrup in a moderate-sized mixing container until combined well.
3. To this, mix in the chocolate chips and mix once more.
4. With the help of an ice cream scooper, scoop out the mixture to a greased baking sheet. Flatten the top slightly with your hand.
5. To finish, bake them for ten to twelve minutes or until they are going to get browned.

Nutritional Info: , Calories: 176Kcal , Protein: 5g , Carbohydrates: 16g , Fat: 11g

CHOCOLATE CHIP QUINOA GRANOLA BARS

Time To Prepare: five minutes

Time to Cook: ten minutes

Yield: Servings 16

Ingredients:
- ¼ teaspoon salt
- ½ cup flax seed
- ½ cup of chia seeds
- ½ cup of chocolate chips
- ½ cup of honey
- ½ cup walnuts, chopped
- 1 cup buckwheat
- 1 cup uncooked quinoa
- 1 teaspoon of cinnamon
- 1 teaspoon of vanilla
- 2/3 cup dairy-free margarine

Directions:
1. Preheat the oven to 350 degrees F.
2. Spread the walnuts, quinoa, wheat, flax, and chia on your baking sheet.
3. Bake for about ten minutes.
4. Coat a baking dish using plastic wrap. Line with cooking spray. Keep aside.
5. Melt the margarine and honey in a saucepot.
6. Mix together the vanilla, salt, and cinnamon into the margarine mix.
7. Keep the wheat mix and quinoa in a container. Pour the margarine sauce into it.
8. Mix the mixture. Coat well. Let it cool. Mix in the chocolate chips.
9. Spread your mixture into the baking dish. Push tightly into the pan.
10. Plastic wrap. Place in your fridge overnight.
11. Cut into bars and serve.

Nutritional Info: Calories 408 , Carbohydrates: 31g , Fat: 28g , Protein: 8g , Sugar: 14g , Fiber: 6g , Sodium: 87mg

CHOCOLATE COVERED STRAWBERRIES

Time To Prepare: fifteen Minutes

Time to Cook: 0 Minute

Yield: Servings 24

Ingredients:
- 16 ounces milk chocolate chips
- 1-pound fresh strawberries with leaves
- 2 tablespoons shortening

Directions:

1. In a bain-marie, melt chocolate and shorter, once in a while stirring until the desired smoothness is achieved. Hold them by the toothpicks and immerse the strawberries in the chocolate mixture.
2. Put toothpicks in the top of the strawberries.
3. Turn the strawberries and put the toothpick in the Styrofoam so that the chocolate cools.

Nutritional Info: , Calories: 115 Cal , Fat: 12.5 g , Carbohydrates: 3.2 g , Protein: 6g

CHOCOLATE FUDGE BITES

Time To Prepare: ten minutes

Time to Cook: three minutes

Yield: Servings 10

Ingredients:
- ½ cup of coconut milk powder
- ½ cup of cold water
- ½ cup of raw cocoa powder
- 1 and a ¼ cup of boiling water
- 1 cup of coconut oil
- 1/3 cup of pure maple syrup
- 3 tablespoons of grass-fed gelatin

Directions:
1. Mix one and a quarter cup of boiling water with the gelatin, and boil for about three minutes. Next, put the gelatin mixture into a blender with the cold water and rest of the ingredients. Blend for about 2 minutes to help the gelatin solidify.
2. Put the mixture into the bottom of a greased baking dish, then place in your fridge until firm.
3. Cut into little serving squares.

Nutritional Info: , Total Carbohydrates: 30g , Fiber: 3g , Net Carbohydrates: , Protein: 2g , Total Fat: 24g , Calories: 317

CHOCOLATE MOUSSE

Time To Prepare: 10 Minutes

Time to Cook: 0 Minute

Yield: Servings 4

Ingredients:
- 1 teaspoon of vanilla extract
- 3 tablespoons of Agave Nectar
- 4 tablespoons of cocoa
- Coconut cream scraped from the upper side of 2 pieces of 13.5-ounce chilled cans of full-fat coconut milk

Directions:

1. Take a big container and scoop out the thick coconut cream from the can to the container
2. Put in nectar, vanilla extract and cocoa to the container
3. Beat it well using an electric mixer, beginning from low and going to moderate until a foamy texture appears
4. Split the mix uniformly amongst ramekins and chill to your desired level of cold
5. Enjoy!

Nutritional Info: , Calories: 134 Cal **,** Fat: 3.8 g **,** Carbohydrates: 16 g **,** Protein: 3.8 g

CINNAMON APPLE CHIPS

Time To Prepare: 10 Minutes

Time to Cook: 2 Hours

Yield: Servings 3

Ingredients:
- ¾ tsp. Cinnamon, grounded
- 3 Honey crisp Apple, big & sweet

Directions:
1. For making this dessert fare, preheat your oven to 200 ° F.
2. Next, keep a parchment paper-lined baking sheet in the center and lower rack.
3. With the help of an apple corer, core the apples and then slice the apples into 1/8-inch-thick rounds.
4. Next, position the apples in the preheated baking sheet in a single layer.
5. After this, drizzle the cinnamon over the apples.
6. Once sprinkled, bake them for an hour.
7. Take away the baking sheet and then switch their position.
8. Bake them for another one to 1 ½ hour or until the chips are crunchy.
9. To finish, once they are crisp in accordance with your liking, remove the apple chips from the oven.
10. Let the chips cool for one hour before you serve.

Nutritional Info: , Calories: 96Kcal **,** Protein: 0g **,** Carbohydrates: 25.5g **,** Fat: 0g

CITRUS CAULIFLOWER CAKE

Time To Prepare: 5 hours and thirty minutes

Time to Cook: 0 minutes

Yield: Servings 10

Ingredients:

For the Crust:
- 1-cup dates, pitted
- 2½-cups pecan nuts
- 2-Tbsps maple syrup or agave

For the Filling:
- ½-tsp lemon extract
- ½-tsp pure vanilla extract
- ¾-cup maple syrup or agave
- 1½-cups pineapple, crushed
- 1½-cups plain coconut yogurt
- 1-pc lemon, zest, and juice
- 1-tsp pure vanilla extract
- 3-cups cauliflower, riced
- 3-pcs avocados, halved and pitted
- 3-Tbsps maple syrup or agave
- A pinch of cinnamon
- For the Topping:

Directions:

For the Crust:
1. Coat a baking tray using parchment paper. Set the outer ring of a 9-inch springform pan onto the baking tray.
2. Pulse the pecans in a food processor to a thoroughly ground texture. Put in the remaining crust ingredients, and pulse further until the mixture holds together.
3. Move and press the mixture to a uniform layer in the baking tray.

For the Filling:
1. Wipe the container of your food processor, and put in in the avocado, cauliflower, pineapple, syrup, and lemon zest and juice. Process the mixture to a smooth consistency.
2. Put in the cinnamon and the lemon and vanilla extracts. Pulse until meticulously blended. Pour the mixture over the crust. Put the tray in your freezer overnight, or for around five hours.
3. Take the cake out from your freezer, and allow it to sit at room temperature for about twenty minutes. Take away the outer ring.
4. For the Topping:
5. Mix in all the topping ingredients in a mixing container. Pour the mixture over the cake and spread uniformly.

Nutritional Info: , Calories: 667 , Fat: 22.2g , Protein: 33.3g , Sodium: 237mg , Total Carbohydrates: 88.1g , Fiber: 4.8g , Net Carbohydrates: 83.3g

CITRUS STRAWBERRY GRANITA

Time To Prepare: fifteen minutes

Time to Cook: 0 minutes

Yield: Servings 4

Ingredients:
- ¼ cup of raw honey
- ¼ lemon

- 1 grapefruit (peeled, seeded, and sectioned)
- 12 ounces of fresh strawberries, hulled
- 2 oranges (peeled, seeded and sectioned)

Directions:

1. Put strawberries, grapefruit, oranges, and lemon in a juicer and extract juice according to the manufacturer's instructions.
2. Put 1½ cups of the veggie juice and honey to a pan and cook on moderate heat for five minutes while stirring constantly.
3. Remove it from heat and put in it to the rest of the juice.
4. Set aside for roughly thirty minutes.
5. Move the juice mixture into an 8x8-inch glass baking dish.
6. Freeze for 4 hours while scraping after every thirty minutes.

Nutritional Info: , Calories: 145 , Fat: 0.4g , Carbohydrates: 37.5g , Sugar: 32.4g , Protein: 1.7g , Sodium: 2mg

COCONUT AND CHOCOLATE CREAM

Time To Prepare: 2 hours

Time to Cook: 0 minutes

Yield: Servings 4

Ingredients:

- ½ teaspoon cinnamon powder
- 1 cup dark chocolate, chopped and melted
- 1 teaspoon vanilla extract
- 2 cups coconut milk
- 2 tablespoons ginger, grated
- 2 tablespoons honey

Directions:

Throw all the ingredients into a blender and blend. Split into bowls and store in the refrigerator for about two hours before you serve.

Nutritional Info: , Calories: 200 , Fat: 3 , Fiber:5 , Carbohydrates: 12 , Protein: 7

COCONUT BUTTER FUDGE

Time To Prepare: ten minutes

Time to Cook: 0 minutes

Yield: Servings 6

Ingredients:

- ¼ teaspoon of salt
- 1 cup of coconut butter

- 1 teaspoon of pure vanilla extract
- 2 tablespoons of raw honey

Directions:
1. Start by lining an 8 x 8 inch baking dish using parchment paper.
2. Melt the coconut butter, honey, and vanilla using low heat.
3. Place the mixture into the baking pan, and place in your fridge for about two hours before you serve.

Nutritional Info: , Total Carbohydrates: 6g , Fiber: 0g , Net Carbohydrates: , Protein: 0g , Total Fat: 36g , Calories: 334

COCONUT MUFFINS

Time To Prepare: 5 Minutes

Time to Cook: 25 Minutes

Yield: Servings 8

Ingredients:
- ¼ cup of cocoa powder
- ¼ teaspoon vanilla extract
- ½ cup ghee, melted
- 1 cup coconut, unsweetened and shredded
- 1 teaspoon baking powder
- 3 tablespoons swerve
- eggs, whisked

Directions:
1. In a container, mix the ghee with the swerve, coconut, and the other ingredients, stir thoroughly and split it into a lined muffin pan.
2. Bake at 370 degrees F for about twenty-five minutes, cool down before you serve.

Nutritional Info: , Calories: 324 , Fat: 31g , Carbohydrates: 8.3g , Protein: 4g , Sugar: 11g

COFFEE CREAM

Time To Prepare: ten minutes

Time to Cook: fifteen minutes

Yield: Servings 4

Ingredients:
- ¼ cup brewed coffee
- 1 teaspoon vanilla extract
- 2 cups heavy cream
- 2 eggs
- 2 tablespoons ghee, melted
- 2 tablespoons swerve

Directions:
1. In a container, mix the coffee with the cream and the other ingredients, whisk well and split it into 4 ramekins and whisk well.
2. Introduce the ramekins in your oven at 350 degrees F and bake for fifteen minutes.
3. Serve warm.

Nutritional Info: Calories 300 , Fat: 11g , Carbohydrates: 3g , Protein: 4g , Sugar: 12g

COMFORTING BAKED RICE PUDDING

Time To Prepare: ten minutes

Time to Cook: twenty minutes

Yield: Servings 8

Ingredients:
- ¼ cup of almond flakes
- ¼ cup of raw honey
- ½ tsp. of ground cardamom
- ½ tsp. of ground ginger
- 1 peeled and cut banana
- 1 tsp. fresh lemon zest, finely grated
- 1 tsp. of ground cinnamon
- 2 big organic eggs
- 2 cups of cooked brown rice
- 2 cups of unsweetened almond milk

Directions:
1. Set the oven to 390 F, then grease a baking dish.
2. Spread cooked rice at the bottom of the readied baking dish uniformly.
3. In a big container, put together the coconut milk, eggs, honey, lemon zest, spices, and beat until well blended.
4. Put the egg mixture over the rice uniformly.
5. Position banana slices over egg mixture uniformly and drizzle with almonds.
6. Bake for approximately twenty minutes.
7. Serve warm.

Nutritional Info: , Calories: 264 , Fat: 4.9g , Carbohydrates: 50g , Protein: 6.2g , Fiber: 2.9g

COOKIE DOUGH BITES

Time To Prepare: 10 Minutes

Time to Cook: 5 Minutes

Yield: Servings 2

Ingredients:
- ¼ cup Almond Flour

- ¼ cup Chocolate Chips, dairy-free & sugar-free
- ½ cup Almond Butter or any nut butter
- ½ tsp. Salt
- 1 ½ cups Chickpeas, cooked
- 1 tsp. Vanilla Extract
- 2 tbsp. Maple Syrup

Directions:
1. First, place all the ingredients excluding the chocolate chips in a high-speed blender for about three minutes or until you get a thick, smooth mixture.
2. After this, move the mixture to a moderate-sized container.
3. Next, fold in the chocolate chips into the batter.
4. Check for sweetness and put in more maple syrup if required.
5. Serve and enjoy.

Nutritional Info: , Calories: 373 Kcal , Protein: 12.6g , Carbohydrates: 59.1g , Fat:10g

CREAMY & CHILLY BLUEBERRY BITES

Time To Prepare: 2 hours and five minutes

Time to Cook: 0 minutes

Yield: Servings 2

Ingredients:
- 1-pint blueberries
- 2-tsp lemon juice
- 8-oz. vanilla yogurt

Directions:
1. Coat the blueberries with the lemon juice and yogurt in a mixing container. Toss cautiously without squishing the berries.
2. Scoop out each of the coated berries and arrange them on a baking sheet coated with parchment paper. Place the sheet in your freezer for a couple of hours before you serve.

Nutritional Info: , Calories: 394 , Fat: 13.1g , Protein: 19.7g , Sodium: 164mg , Total Carbohydrates: 58.9g , Fiber: 9.7g , Net Carbohydrates: 49.2g

CREAMY FROZEN YOGURT

Time To Prepare: ten minutes + 2-three hours freezing

Time to Cook:

Yield: Servings 3

Ingredients:
- ½ cup of coconut yogurt

- ½ cup of unsweetened almond milk
- 1 tbsp. of raw honey
- 1 tsp. of fresh mint leaves
- 1 tsp. of organic vanilla extract
- 2 peeled, pitted and chopped medium avocados
- 2 tbsp. of fresh lemon juice

Directions:
1. Throw all the ingredients into a blender apart from mint leaves and pulse till creamy and smooth.
2. Put into an airtight container then freeze for minimum 2-three hours.
3. Take off from the freezer and keep aside for about fifteen minutes.
4. With a spoon stir thoroughly.
5. Top with fresh mint leaves before you serve.

Nutritional Info: , Calories: 105 , Fat: 1.3g , Carbohydrates: 20.3g , Protein: 2.8g , Fiber: 1.4g

DARK CHOCOLATE GRANOLA BARS

Time To Prepare: ten minutes

Time to Cook: twenty-five minutes

Yield: Servings 12

Ingredients:
- ¼ cup dark cocoa powder
- ¼ cup of flaxseed
- ½ cup dark chocolate chips
- 1 cup of walnuts
- 1 cup tart cherries, dried
- 1 teaspoon of salt
- 1 teaspoon of vanilla
- 2 cups buckwheat
- 2 eggs
- 2/3 cup honey

Directions:
1. Preheat the oven to 350 degrees F.
2. Line with cooking spray your baking pan.
3. Pulse together the walnuts, wheat, tart cherries, salt, and flaxseed in a food processor. Everything must be chopped fine.
4. Mix together the honey, eggs, vanilla, and cocoa powder in a container.
5. Put in the wheat mix to your container. Stir to blend well.
6. Include the chocolate chips. Stir once more.
7. Now pour this mixture into a baking dish.
8. Drizzle some chocolate chips and tart cherries.
9. Bake for about twenty-five minutes. Allow to cool before you serve.

Nutritional Info: Calories 364 , Carbohydrates: 37g , Cholesterol: 60mg , Fat: 20g , Protein: 6g , Sugar: 22g , Fiber: 4g , Sodium: 214mg

DATE DOUGH & WALNUT WAFER

Time To Prepare: fifteen minutes

Time to Cook: eighteen minutes

Yield: Servings 8

Ingredients:
- ¼-cup coconut oil
- ¼-tsp sea salt
- ½-cup coconut, unsweetened
- ½-cup walnuts
- ½-tsp baking soda
- ½-tsp sea salt
- 1½-cup oats (divided)
- 18-pcs Medjool dates, pitted
- 1-pc egg
- 1-tsp lemon juice
- 2-Tbsps ground flaxseed
- 6-pcs Medjool dates, pitted and cut into four equivalent portions
- For the Date Layer:

Directions:
1. Preheat the oven to 325ºF. Coat a baking pan using parchment paper.
2. Pulse a cup of oats in a food processor until making a flour consistency.
3. Put in in the dates, coconut, baking soda, and sea salt. Pulse again until the dates completely break up.
4. Put in the remaining oats and walnuts, and pulse until the nuts break, but still a bit lumpy. Put in the flaxseed, egg, and oil. Pulse the mixture further until meticulously blended.
5. Set aside ½-cup of the date mixture to use as a topping later. Push down the rest of the mix to a uniform layer in the pan.
6. Wash your food processor, and put in all the date layer ingredients. Pulse the mixture until the dates completely break up and take on a light caramel color.
7. With wet hands, press the mixture down, smoothing it on the date mixture. Crumble and drizzle the reserved date mixture over the top.
8. Place the pan in your oven. Bake for eighteen minutes. Allow the wafer to cool to room temperature before cutting into 16 pieces.

Nutritional Info: , Calories: 203 , Fat: 6.7g , Protein: 10.1g , Sodium: 76mg , Total Carbohydrates: 28.3g , Fiber: 3g , Net Carbohydrates: 25.3g

EASY PEACH COBBLER

Time To Prepare: five minutes

Time to Cook: twenty minutes

Yield: Servings 6

Ingredients:
- ¼ brown rice flour
- ¼ cup coconut palm sugar, divided
- ¼ cup extra virgin olive oil
- ¼ cup ground flaxseeds
- ½ cup gluten-free oats
- ½ teaspoon cinnamon
- ¾ cup chopped pecans
- 5 organic peaches, pitted and chopped

Directions:
1. Preheat your oven to 3500F.
2. Grease the bottom of 6 ramekins.
3. In a container, combine the peaches, ½ of the coconut sugar, cinnamon, and pecans.
4. Distribute the peach mixture into the ramekins.
5. In the same container, combine the oats, flaxseed, rice flour, and oil. Put in in the rest of the coconut sugar. Mix until a crumbly texture is formed.
6. Top the mixture over the peaches.
7. Put for about twenty minutes.

Nutritional Info: Calories 26 , Fat: 11g , Carbohydrates: 28g , Protein: 10g , Sugar: 12g , Fiber: 6g

FALL-TIME CUSTARD

Time To Prepare: fifteen minutes

Time to Cook: 60 minutes

Yield: Servings 6

Ingredients:
- ¼ tsp. of ground ginger
- 1 cup of canned pumpkin
- 1 cup of coconut milk
- 1 tsp. of ground cinnamon
- 1 tsp. of organic vanilla extract
- 2 organic eggs
- 2 pinches of freshly grated nutmeg
- 8-10 drops of liquid stevia
- Pinch of salt

Directions:
1. Preheat your oven to 350 degrees F.
2. In a big container, put together pumpkin and spices then mix.

3. In another container, put in the eggs and beat thoroughly.
4. Put in the rest of the ingredients then whisk till well blended.
5. Put in egg mixture into pumpkin mixture and mix till well blended.
6. Move the mixture toto 6 ramekins.
7. Position the ramekins in a baking dish,
8. Put in sufficient water in the baking dish about two-inch high around the ramekins.
9. Bake for approximately 1 hour or till a toothpick inserted in the middle comes out clean.

Nutritional Info: , Calories: 131 , Fat: 11.1g , Carbohydrates: 6.1g , Protein: 3.3g , Fiber: 2.3g

FENNEL AND ALMOND BITES

Time To Prepare: ten minutes + three hours freezing time

Time to Cook: twenty-five minutes

Yield: Servings 10

Ingredients:
- ¼ cup almond milk
- ¼ cup of cocoa powder
- ½ cup almond oil
- 1 teaspoon fennel seeds
- 1 teaspoon vanilla extract
- A pinch of sunflower seeds

Directions:
1. Take a container and mix the almond oil and almond milk
2. Beat until the desired smoothness is achieved and shiny by using an electric beater

Stir in the remaining ingredients
3. Take a piping bag and pour into a parchment paper-lined baking sheet
4. Freeze for around three hours and stored in your refrigerator

Nutritional Info: , Total Carbohydrates: 1g , Fiber: 1g , Protein: 1g , Fat: 20g

FLOURLESS SWEET POTATO BROWNIES

Time To Prepare: ten minutes

Time to Cook: thirty minutes

Yield: Servings 9

Ingredients:
- ¼ cup Unsweetened Cocoa powder
- ½ cup Almond butter
- ½ cup Cooked sweet potato
- ½ tsp. Baking soda

- 1 big Whole egg
- 2 tsp. Vanilla extract
- 3 tbsp. Dairy-free chocolate chips, optional.
- 6 tbsp. Honey

Directions:
1. Prep the oven by preheating to 350°F.
2. Coat a baking pan using parchment paper leaving a few extra inches on the sides to make it easier to discard or remove
3. Blend all the ingredients, excluding the chocolate chips until you get a super smooth and tender batter.
4. Move the creamy batter to your readied baking pan and use a spatula to spread it around, so it looks almost even.
5. Slide it in your oven, then bake for thirty minutes or until a knife inserted into the pan comes out clean.
6. Remove from the oven and leave to cool in the pan for fifteen minutes before putting it up on a wire rack.
7. If you decide to use the chocolate chip topping, put the chips in a microwave-safe dish and heat until it completely melts. Remove from the microwave and sprinkle over the brownies.
8. Serve or store!

Nutritional Info: , Calories: 171 kcal , Protein: 5.17 g , Fat: 9.28 g , Carbohydrates: 20.01 g

www.ingramcontent.com/pod-product-compliance
Lightning Source LLC
Chambersburg PA
CBHW080221100925
32379CB00011B/544